Modern American Drama

Williams, Miller, Albee, and Shepard

The best of modern American drama is represented in the seventeen essays of this collection. They explore the works of four of the most celebrated playwrights of the twentieth century: Tennessee Williams, Arthur Miller, Edward Albee, and Sam Shepard.

Among the rich variety of modern American playwrights these four stand above the rest. All four have created works that have received great critical acclaim and produced intense critical controversy. Very different in temperament and style, they bring strikingly different perspectives to their work; and yet all share a fascination with social and family structures, and all demonstrate extraordinary gifts with language.

Each playwright is discussed in four or five essays, each essay in turn deals with one or two aspects of one play. Together these essays, originally published in the journal *Modern Drama*, provide a penetrating study of recent American theatre through the work of four of its very best dramatists.

DOROTHY PARKER is a professor of English at Victoria College, University of Toronto.

EDITED BY DOROTHY PARKER

ESSAYS ON
Modern American Drama

Williams, Miller, Albee,
and Shepard

Published in association with *Modern Drama* and
the Graduate Centre for the Study of Drama, University of Toronto, by
UNIVERSITY OF TORONTO PRESS
Toronto Buffalo London

© University of Toronto Press 1987
Toronto Buffalo London
Printed in Canada
ISBN 0-8020-3433-0 (cloth)
ISBN 0-8020-3434-9 (paper)

Canadian Cataloguing in Publication Data

Main entry under title:

Essays on modern American drama

ISBN 0-8020-3433-0 (bound) ISBN 0-8020-3434-9 (pbk)

I. American drama – 20th century – History and
criticism. I. Parker, Dorothy, 1928–
II. University of Toronto. Graduate Centre for
Study of Drama. III. Title: Modern drama.

PS350.E88 1986   812'.54'09   c86-095099-9

For R.B.P.

Contents

Contents

Contents

Introduction

In May 1959 when the first number of *Modern Drama* appeared, the founding editor, A.C. Edwards of the University of Kansas, wrote that its purpose was to stimulate interest in research and in the teaching of drama since Ibsen. And now, twenty-seven years and 108 numbers later, it seems appropriate that some of the major articles on the most distinguished modern dramatists should begin to be anthologized, and that one of the first areas to be collected should be American drama.

Out of the ferment of American playwrights who followed Eugene O'Neill, two dramatists rose almost simultaneously to the top in the third and fourth decades of the century: Tennessee Williams and Arthur Miller. Coming to manhood in the 30s, a period overshadowed by the spectre of the Great Depression, they began writing as the gloom of that Depression was gradually dissipated by the tremendous upsurge of employment and mobilization called into being by America's entry into World War II. The forties, when their first plays appeared, was a time of excitement, cultural ferment, and rapid social change.

Although very different in temperament and style, Williams and Miller shared many common concerns – the discrediting of the "American Dream," the isolation of the individual, even within the family, and his solitary search for values in a chaotic world. Both writers continued, with variations, the Ibsen/Chekhov tradition followed by the mainstream of American playwrights, with Williams leaning toward Chekhov in the veiling of prosaic things with a theatrical vision of beauty and sadness, and Miller tending more towards Ibsen's social concerns, didactic realism and well-crafted plots.

Then at the end of the 1950s, when Williams, overwhelmed by personal problems, was steadily declining in power, and Miller appeared for a time to have lost interest in the theatre, Edward Albee produced *The Zoo Story*, a play which not only combined the "didactic" structure of Miller and linguistic richness of Williams, but also showed promise of the young writer's ability to go beyond his predecessors. The works that followed – including *Who's Afraid of Virginia Woolf, Tiny Alice* and *All Over* – revealed a formal inventiveness, social acuity, emotional depth, and grace and wit with language, that make Albee perhaps America's outstanding dramatic voice. Miller's left-wing social theories became in Albee metaphysical concerns, and the family relationships that structured the plays of both writers were less socially oriented in Albee than symptomatic of spiritual questioning.

Shepard, the youngest of this group, is again related to the earlier three. His plays came out of the Off-off Broadway counterculture of the sixties, and from the first revealed his astonishing ear for language. In such a later play as *The Tooth of Crime* the virtuosity of language was dazzling, and came closer to being pure music (in this case Rock 'n' Roll) than the most poetic writing of either Williams or Albee. After his musical pieces, Shepard moved gradually closer to the Ibsen type of plot in *True West* and *Buried Child*, but in these later "family" plays he set off conventional structure against bizarre events and grotesque characters. The plots reiterated the family relationships of the earlier playwrights – father and sons, rival brothers, husbands and wives – and revealed the pathos of their sense of existential isolation. Where these things appeared in Albee as philosophical, however, in Shepard they became mythological and wildly, often grimly funny. These two younger dramatists merged traditional realism and absurdist theories of drama to create a new kind of realism in which reality was depicted as subjective, internal, and anarchic.

Among the rich variety of modern American playwrights these four – Williams, Miller, Albee, and Shepard – stand out above the rest. There was no difficulty in choosing them as representative of the main stream of American dramatic tradition. Each produced work that has received the highest critical acclaim as well as works which have provoked the kind of controversy that is generated only by those whose achievements have been widely recognized and praised.

Another reason for selecting this four is that all were born in the twentieth century and began writing after the characteristics peculiar to it were well established. Each represents a different geographical district of the United States, moreover: the South, the Midwest and New Jersey, the Eastern Seaboard, and the West. The problem in this book, therefore, was not in choosing the writers, but in having to limit the collection to four essays about each. This difficulty was compounded by another one: since the periodical format limits essays to between eight and twelve pages in length (the best essays in *Modern Drama* have tended to be those which deal with one or two aspects of a single play rather than broad articles of comparison or influence studies), it was necessary to select essays dealing with particular plays, rather than articles on the playwrights' ideas and work in general. Four articles meant only four plays by each writer, although Williams and Shepard both have written more than forty plays and Miller nearly twenty. It seemed best, therefore, to correlate the best articles with the major plays (though there is always some disagreement about which are the most significant works in any writer's canon) and the only obvious omission is perhaps Miller's *Death of a Salesman*.

In making this choice I have been aided by Nancy Copeland who did a very thorough preliminary reading of all the essays published on American topics in *Modern Drama* and by Professor Jill Levenson and Professor Brian Parker who helped at later stages with advice.

Part One

Tennessee Williams
1911–1983

Myth as a Basis of Dramatic Structure in *Orpheus Descending*

NANCY BAKER TRAUBITZ

Tennessee Williams' first professionally produced play, *Battle of Angels* (1940), failed during its Boston tryouts. However, the play did not die. Williams continued to rewrite, to add, to modify and in March, 1957, with the great successes of *Glass Menagerie* (1945), *Streetcar Named Desire* (1947), and *Cat on a Hot Tin Roof* (1955) behind him, he committed *Battle of Angels,* now titled *Orpheus Descending,* to another Broadway production. "I honestly believe," Williams wrote, "that it is finally finished. About 75 percent of it is new writing, but what is much more important, I believe that I have now finally managed to say in it what I wanted to say ... "[1] Few plays have been so long meditated and so staunchly believed in by their creators, yet after seventeen years of perpetual revising by America's most successful playwright and one of the most influential figures in the international theater, *Orpheus Descending* played only sixty-eight performances.

The purpose of this essay is to suggest through an analysis of the myths creating the dramatic structure that *Orpheus Descending* is a better play than its dismal performance record suggests, a play which has yet to fulfill its potential in production but which even in the printed text represents a significant attempt to re-create myths in the context of our own time.

Although I will consider only those myths with obvious referents in the text to the exclusion of whatever subconscious archetypes we might posit, Williams' autobiographical impulses are important, as he superimposed and strengthened the Orpheus myth upon the myth of the battle between light and dark, the good and evil angels who war in heaven. Williams does not suppress this battle-in-heaven myth, as Hugh Dickenson clearly demonstrates in his comparison of the two published versions of the play.[2] Rather, Williams comes to emphasize the responsibility which love places upon the poet/singer Orpheus and the pull toward life and fruitfulness that the Orpheus figure creates in those dead souls he meets in the hades of the Torrance Mercantile Store. Williams himself always considered *Orpheus Descending* autobiographical. "Well," he wrote, "nothing is more precious to anybody than the emotional record of his youth, and you will find the trail of my sleeve-worn heart in this completed play ... " (vi). The hero/savior Orpheus or Val, as Williams calls his hero, embodies the playwright as he chooses to see himself, heart on sleeve, "a wild spirited boy who wanders into a conventional community of the south and creates the commotion of a fox in a chicken coop" (vi).

In the play itself we are able to distinguish five separate myth patterns: the loss of Eden, the battle of angels, Christ, Orpheus, and Adonis. The setting of the play is the Torrance Mercantile Store, from late winter in Act I through the dark night before Easter dawn at the end of Act III. Throughout the play we are aware of rain, occasionally in torrents and at points accompanied by thunder and lightning, perceived through a giant "dusty" window looking out on "disturbing emptiness." Dogs, the hounds of hell, bark with varying degrees of menace. The store interior is almost entirely bare, but does contain "the black skeleton of a dressmaker's dummy" and "a sinister-looking artifical palm in a greenish-brown jardiniere." A much smaller bedroom alcove contrasts with the larger set. Across the alcove hangs an oriental drapery picturing two major myth motifs of the play, "fantastic birds" and a golden tree with scarlet fruit, a tree of life. Before the action of the play begins, the conflict is clearly anounced in this set: life, fruitfulness, freedom against sinister artificiality, barrenness and death. The conflict will be played out within the mercantile hell where there are only the ones who are bought, the buyers and those few who have never been branded (41).

The setting is completed by a prologue "treated frankly as exposition" (6), in which two of the local inhabitants act a Chorus filling in background and emphasizing the myths. The play is set in Two River County, at once introducing the Eden motif. We learn the power in the play, Jabe Torrance, embodies sterile impotence – he and his wife have money instead of children and do not sleep together – and is dying of a spreading cancer. Jabe "bought" his wife, Lady, and brought her into his hades from a different country and race. She is a "Dago"; her father, Papa Romano, was a "Wop from the old country" who built a garden of wine, music, and love. Lady had known love "like a fire" in her father's "wine garden," but the garden and with it Lady's father were burned by the local vigilantes, the Mystic Crew, led by Jabe Torrance, when Papa Romano violated their commandment and "sold liquor to niggers." Lady now plans to recreate her father's wine garden by opening a confectionary adjacent to the store on the Saturday before Easter. The Chorus introduces their husbands, two slouching, red-faced henchmen of death, Dog and Pee-Wee, and the Temple sisters, two old maid vestal virgins who prowl about the store. In both the store and the living quarters above it, they tell us "everything is so dingy and dark ... " (5). Surrounded by all this death, Beulah discovers the olives set out for the funeral-like reception for the dying Jabe are not stuffed but have seeds in them.

The action of the play begins with the entrance of Carol Cutrere, the outcast member of the oldest and most distinguished family in the county. In the earlier version of the play her name was Cassandra and she retains her function as a prophetess. At her behest the Negro Conjure Man gives the magic Choctaw cry and Valentine Xavior materializes in his snakeskin jacket and carrying his guitar. Almost immediately behind him is Vee, short for Veronica, wife of Sheriff Talbott. Her entrance fixes Val in the Christ role, for like Saint Veronica, who gave Christ her veil to wipe his forehead on his journey up Calvary, Vee dispenses mercy. She has sheltered Val and hopes Lady will accept him as a clerk in the store. Like Val, she is a creator, a primitive painter, capable of visions. She comes bearing gifts, pineapple sherbert for Jabe. Symbolically, her effort to bring together the pines of sterility and the apples of fruitfulness is "reduced to juice" (18).

As the play progresses, Vee clearly identifies Val as a savior, painting him as Christ in her long contemplated picture of the last Supper. Val understands her visions, which seek to metamorphose the horror and corruption of life among the living and dead into something of beauty. In their final confrontation, Val kneels to her as she sits in the shoe-fitting chair, symbolically re-enacting the ritual washing of the feet of the disciples. She recognizes him as the figure of Christ in her vision, a vision of such brilliance it has nearly destroyed her physical sight by an influx of spiritual insight.

– I heard this clap of thunder! Sky! – Split open! – And there in the split-open sky, I saw, I tell you, I *saw* the TWO HUGE BLAZING EYES OF JESUS CHRIST RISEN! – Not crucified but Risen! I mean Crucified and *then* RISEN! – The blazing eyes of Christ Risen! (92)

Like Saint Veronica, who received her veil back from Christ with the lasting impression of His face upon it, Vee – who "was born with a caul! a sort of thing like a veil" (66) and who on the Saturday afternoon before Easter meditated on the "mysteries of Easter, veils!" (91) – recognizes Val Xavior as the Christ of her vision, Christ harrowing the hell of Jabe Torrance's store in Two River County. "*She collapses, forward, falls to her knees, her arms thrown about Val. He seizes her to lift her*" (92–3). Vee's recognition of Val as Savior ensures his destruction; from this moment in the play he is turned over to the forces of corruption, the devils, to be tormented by Sheriff Talbott, Dog, Pee-Wee and then by Jabe before he is hung upon the tree and lynched by blowtorch, tying together both sacrifice and purification.

However, the legend of Christ and Saint Veronica as embodied by Val and

Vee is fraught with ambiguities. Vee paints her Church of the Resurrection with an all too blatant red phallic steeple. Although Val kisses her "soft woman hands" that paint "as if God touched your fingers" (68), in her vision Val/Christ touches her bosom. Their whole relationship is one of highly charged, barely repressed physical desire.

Structurally, the Val/Vee confrontations appear in the second scene of each act and always during the daylight hours. Vee is intensely aware of the light, "a blaze of light" outside the store, while Lady complains of darkness inside the store in an early speech. "We always had a problem with light in this store" (24). Vee and Val agree that "a world of light and shadow is what we live in, and – it's – confusing ... " (92). While Vee is associated with daylight, Lady belongs to the dark night in hell.

Val's function as Orpheus is less ambiguous than his function as Christ. In their first meeting, Lady, unaware of Val's presence, mutters, "I wish I was dead, dead, dead ... " to which Val responds quietly, "No, you don't, Lady" (32). Lady cannot sleep. She is obsessed with the fire which destroyed her father and his wine garden, and with her desire to re-create it in the confectionary. She is also "cold." Val immediately gives Lady the snakeskin jacket, symbolic of regeneration, to wear and introduces the guitar, a phallic life-giver. He also tells her he is a light-bringer. "I do electric repairs" (37). His supernatural qualities are quickly established. His temperature is always "a couple of degrees above normal and he is above such human needs as sleep, breathing, and elimination. "I can sleep on a concrete floor or go without sleeping, without even feeling sleepy, for forty-eight hours. And I can hold my breath three minutes without blacking out. ... And I can go a whole day without passing water" (40). And, ominously, Val can "burn down ... any two-footed woman." Against Lady's wish for death, Val juxtaposes the vision of the transparent birds with no legs who soar in the high blue sky near the sun and sleep on the wind, touching earth only in death (41–2). In the Orpheus myth, Orpheus is reincarnated as a swan, thus the transparent birds associated with both the dove of the Holy Spirit and the Orphic swan help to fix Val in the roles of Christ and Orpheus. Lady accepts the vision of life Val offers and although at first she is not interested in anything but a "working relation" with Val, she would "give this mercantile store and every bit of stock in it to be that tiny bird the color of the sky" (42).

Val and Lady establish the sexual liaison which creates life in the depths of hades when Lady/Eurydice realizes Val/Orpheus offers life. "I NEED YOU!!!" she cries, "TO LIVE ... TO GO ON LIVING!!!"

He looks up gravely at her from his guitar. She closes the curtain behind her. Its bizarre design, a gold tree with white birds and scarlet fruit in it, is softly translucent with the bulb lighted behind it. The guitar continues softly for a few moments; stops; the stage darkens till only the curtain of the alcove is clearly visible. (81)

With his music and his vision of earthly life and love, Val is almost able to bring Lady out of hades. But Lady refuses to leave until Jabe is destroyed and the wine garden recreated. She tells Val, "I guess my heart knew that somebody must be coming to take me out of this hell! ... – but DEATH has got to die before we go ... " (109). But Death survives. Lady/Eurydice will not escape hades nor will she bear life within it. Her suspected pregnancy confirmed by Jabe's nurse, Lady dismisses Val – "You've given me life, you can go!" (113) – and, in a lovely image, compares herself to the barren fig tree in her father's wine garden:

Time went by it, spring after useless spring, and it almost started to – die .... Then one day I discovered a small green fig on the tree they said wouldn't bear! ... I ran through the wine garden shouting, "Oh, Father, it's going to bear, the fig tree is going to bear!" – It seemed such a wonderful thing, after those ten barren springs, for the little fig tree to bear, it called for a celebration – I ran to a closet, I opened a box that we kept Christmas ornaments in! – I took them out ... I decorated the fig tree with glass bells and glass birds and stars and tinsel and snow! ... I've won. Mr. Death, I'm going to bear! (114)

The fig tree brings together the pagan and Christian myths. The difficulty of fertilizing fig trees led to symbolic marriages between human representatives of male and female fig trees and human sacrifice among the ancient Greeks.[3] Adam and Eve used fig leaves to cover their nakedness after eating the fruit of the Forbidden Tree (Genesis 3:7) and Christ cursed the barren fig tree (Matthew 2:19). The shape of the fig has lent itself to symbolic associations with both the testicles and the womb. By hanging Christmas decorations on the fig tree Lady celebrates not only her fertility, but foreshadows resurrection and eternal life. Among her decorations are the transparent "glass birds" but also "icicles and snow" of death. In her triumph Lady has stopped to look back at Jabe and Val has stopped to look back at Lady. The strangely rejuvenated Jabe shoots Lady and sets the waiting vigilantes on Val. What happens to Val is never completely clear. The vigilantes take rope and a blowtorch from the store and they repeatedly expostulate " – Christ!" However, we also hear dogs and remember that Vee and Val have seen chain-gang dogs tear fugitives to pieces, and Val and Lady actually hear a convict torn as the Maenads tore Orpheus (67, 79).

The ambiguities in the Val/Orpheus – Lady/Eurydice myth are not entirely the result of an overlap with the Val/Christ – Vee/Saint Veronica or the wine garden/Eden myths. Val is an extremely handsome young man appearing for the first time on his birthday (22). His attraction to the older Lady seems less strong than her's to him. He becomes almost a prisoner unable to escape Lady's need for him. We are reminded here of Adonis, so handsome at birth he is loved by Aphrodite. Aphrodite entrusts her mortal lover to Persephone, but Persephone, Queen of Hades, loves him too, and refuses to give him up until Zeus intervenes, giving him half the year to Love and half the year to Death.

Surrounded by hunting dogs, he is eventually gored to death by a maddened boar.

A simple diagram will perhaps clarify the position of the major myths in the structure of the play.

Act I			Act II			Act III		
Prologue	i	ii	i	ii	iii & iv	i	ii	iii
Eden	Jesus/ Veronica	Orpheus	Eden	Jesus/ Veronica	Orpheus (sexual) (liaison) Adonis	Eden	Jesus/ Veronica	Orpheus
A	B	C	A	B	C	·A	C	C

Figure 1

Several points now become clear. In each of the three acts an intense Lady/Val scene immediately follows the Vee/Val scene and concludes the act, thus emphasizing the descent into darkness, the pull of human physical love and the primacy of the Orpheus legend over the Christ analogue. The A block in each act is always a scene of exposition turning on the wine garden of the past. In Act I, Dolly and Beulah tell the story of the garden's destruction. In Act II, Lady confronts her former lover with, "that summer they burned my father in his wine garden. ... I carried your child in my body the summer you quit me" she tells him, "but I had it cut out of my body and they cut my heart out with it!" (61) Now she has grasped the vision of ascent, the transparent birds of the upper air. "I just wanted to tell you my life ain't over" (63). In Act III Jabe turns off the light in the confectionary, Lady's re-creation of the wine garden, and announces he was part of the Mystic Crew who destroyed her father. As we have seen, block B of each act carries the Christ/Veronica legend. In block C Val/Orpheus tries to rescue his Lady/Eurydice. The prophetess, Carol Cutrere, appears in block A of Acts I and II to warn Val of danger. In the final block of the play she causes Val to materialize, as she had upon his entrance into the -Torrance Mercantile Store, through the magic of the Conjurer Man's Choctaw cry. Her prophecy and her offer of help unheeded, she appears with the Conjurer at the final curtain to carry away Val's snakeskin jacket. Hades has no hold over her and she exits laughing to Sheriff Talbott's furious shouts of "Stay here! ... Stop! Stop!" (118).

Several additional points are clarified by a second diagram (cf. figure 2). Such a diagram has, of course, its fanciful elements, but we cannot escape the suggestive patterns which emerge. Each block repeats the four step narrative on both a literal and a mythic level. On both levels a hero or heroine offering love and life in some sense violates a supreme interdiction and thus brings upon him/her self loss of the beloved and, in all cases except Aphrodite (who suffers greatly), death. Also, we note that Val parallels Papa Romano in his struggle with Jabe, and we are reminded of the tradition which sees Jesus as the second Adam. Both Romano and Val are outsiders, superior to the local population of Twin River County; and both have descended into a hell in Twin River County through the traditional pattern. They have crossed water to reach Twin River County; they confront there the spirits of the dead. Both do battle with the monstrous tyrannical figure of Death, Jabe Torrance, and a host of demi-monsters, the Mystic Crew, the Sheriff, Pee-Wee and Dog. Both are associated with the beautiful Lady and each loses her to the monster as she, through her unborn child, is about to triumph over death and sterility. Val, whose descent is more fully chronicled, receives aid from the traditional helper with more than human powers, Carol Cutrere.

Unlike the cyclical heroes, Campbell's hero with a thousand faces, neither Romano nor Val rises from his descent. Death prevents their crossing the second river and Carol Cutrere's sky-blue Cadillac waits for Val in vain. The play ends in the dark night before Easter dawn. While Williams does not complete the expected pattern in his hero's quest, he does transfer the symbol of re-emergence and regeneration to Carol Cutrere, the embodiment of the transparent bird symbol, who knows love and life are "unbearably painful" and "dangerous." Carol also knows dead people chatter like birds, "but all they say is one word and that one word is 'live ...'" (28). Her exit from the hell of the store is perhaps as close as Williams can come to assent and affirmation. "Wild things leave skins behind them, they leave clean skins and teeth and white bones behind them, and these are tokens passed from one to another, so that the fugitive kind can always follow their kind ..." (117).

Occasionally, the relationship between the myth and its referent within the naturalistic context of the literal action becomes tenuous. For example, we can accept Val as Jesus or Orpheus but can we also accept him as Adonis without completely reassessing Lady's character? Jesus, Orpheus, and Adonis never physically consummate their love. Can we accept physical love as analogous to divine love? Jesus, Orpheus, Adonis, and Adam all have divine progenitors, Val is a drifter with hazy origins, something of a reprobate, who, although he refuses Carol's offered ride back across the water to safety, still poses a problem as to how willingly and deliberately he sacrifices his life. While Val's jacket associates him with the ancient's snakeskin symbol of regeneration, it also carries overtones of both the serpent's bite which sent Eurydice to hades, and the snake disguise assumed by Satan in the Garden of Eden. Val thus becomes a fallen angel, but his function in the Orpheus and Eden myths becomes ambiguous. Jabe is so viciously a god of death that even the most

A		B				C			
Literal	**Mythic**	**Literal**	**Mythic**	**Literal**	**Mythic**	**Literal**	**Mythic**	**Literal**	**Mythic**
Papa Romano = Val	= Angels or Adam	Val	= Jesus	Vee	= Veronica	Val	= Orpheus (Lady = Eurydice)	Lady	= Aphrodite
in wine garden / in alcove garden	in heaven / in Eden	—spiritual	nourishment—	shelter	scarf	—life—		—love—	
sells Liquor / loves Lady	rebel / eats fruit	offends	power structure			—ignores prophecy—	"looks back"	commits adultery	loves mortal
—burned—	burned / cast into desert	hung on tree	crucified	finishes picture	receives impression on scarf	—loses love— torn to pieces		—loses love—	
								dies	suffers

Figure 2

This diagram should be studied in conjunction with figure I on page 8. The structure of the myths becomes clear by reading both top to bottom and left to right. It should also be noted that the literal level of the Val-as-Adam myth takes place in Block C. It is placed in Block A to emphasize his parallel to Papa Romano and the fallen angels and lost Eden myths.

Romantic reading of Genesis cannot easily relate him to the God of fiery justice in the myths of Eden and the fallen angels myths. Despite such ambiguities, the myths of *Orpheus Descending* are integral to the dramatic structure, never imposed on the naturalist action or introduced self-consciously. The emphasis and shading of a direction and cast have overcome far more serious ambiguities in far less worthy plays. Even if we approach the play as text rather than production, Williams has managed, to a remarkable degree, to integrate five major myths into a dramatic structure.

NOTES

1 Tennessee Williams, "The Past, the Present and the Perhaps," in *Battle of Angels* (Norfolk, Connecticut, 1958), p. x. All quotations from *Orpheus Descending* are from this edition and will be indicated in the text by page number.

2 Hugh Dickenson, "Tennessee Williams: Orpheus as Savior," in *Myth on the Modern Stage* (Chicago, 1969), pp. 278–309. Dickenson's implication that Williams' myths show his religious conflict should be read in conjunction with Williams' own pronouncement on his religious commitment in "Playboy Interview: Tennessee Williams – Candid Conversation," *Playboy*, 20 (April, 1973), 84.

3 G. Frazer, *The Scapegoat*, Vol. IV of *The Golden Bough: A Study in Magic and Religion*, 3rd ed. (London, 1913), pp. 257–258.

4 Dr. Jackson Barry, who was kind enough to discuss the New York rehersals of *Orpheus Descending* with me, suggested the emphasis of the Orpheus myths does produce an integrated structure in production. He pointed out that the production, like many others, lost its interior cohesion while on its out-of-town tryouts. It is interesting, though not necessarily significant, that while out of town Cliff Robertson replaced Robert Logia as Val. Perhaps more significant is the fact that Williams wrote *Orpheus Descending* with Anna Magnani and Marlon Brando in mind.

The Composition of *The Glass Menagerie*: An Argument for Complexity

BRIAN PARKER

I

Though Mrs. Edwina Williams has pointed out the many differences between the Williams family and the Wingfields,[1] *The Glass Menagerie* is nonetheless Tennessee Williams's most autobiographical play, accurate to the imaginative reality of his experience even when it departs from fact in detail. The essentials of that experience – the mismatched parents; the shock of the family's move from early years in his grandfather's Mississippi rectory to a series of shabby flats in downtown St. Louis; Williams's breakdown after working as a clerk in a warehouse, trying to write at night; his close companionship with his sister, Rose, disrupted by her withdrawal into schizophrenia; and the disastrous mistake of submitting her to a frontal lobotomy – are too well known to bear expansion. The recent publication of Williams's *Memoirs*,[2] however, with their startling frankness about his sex life, helps fill in some further details. In particular, Williams is explicit about his feeling of personal guilt because new companions and interests, the excitements of university life, and perhaps especially his gradual discovery of his own homosexual preferences led him to neglect and even to be unkind to his sister at her period of greatest need. "It's not very pleasant to look back on that year [1937]," he writes, "and to know that Rose knew she was going mad and to know, also, that I was not too kind to my sister" (p. 121). He tells of her tattling on a wild party he gave at the house during their parents' absence, in resentment of which he hissed at her on the stairs, "I hate the sight of your ugly old face!", leaving her stricken and wordless, crouched against the wall. "This is the cruelest thing I have done in my life, I suspect," he comments, "and one for which I can never properly atone" (p. 122). Later that year Rose was put in an institution; and the following summer, while Williams was in Illinois with some of his new friends, his parents gave their permission for the operation that rendered Rose harmless but childish for the rest of her life.

This tragedy was one of the most traumatic experiences of Williams's life, from which he has never freed himself. It lies at the root of his feeling that love leads inevitably to loss and betrayal, as reflected in such poems as "Cortege" and "The Comforter and the Betrayer."[3] The pattern is extraordinarily clear in *Suddenly Last Summer*, written in the late fifties after psychoanalysis, in which the heroine is threatened with lobotomy for revealing the sado-masochistic homosexuality of her cousin, Sebastian, and an ambiguous brother-sister relationship recurs throughout Williams's work[4]; fittingly, the last pages of *Memoirs* express his concern to release his sister from her mental institution to live in a house he has bought for her near his own in Florida.

Not surprisingly, these events and tortured relationships are reflected in much more of Williams's early writing than just *The Glass Menagerie*: in short stories such as "Portrait of a Girl in Glass" and "The Resemblance between a Violin Case and a Coffin"; poems like "Cortege" and part 3 of "Recuerdo"; and one-act plays such as *The Long Goodbye, Auto-da-fé, The Last of My Solid Gold Watches*, and perhaps *The Purification*[5]; and the produced but unpublished full-length play, *Stairs to the Roof*. But exactly how obsessive and intractable, how emotionally complex and contradictory the memories were, can be grasped only when one looks at the mound of rewriting which lay before *The Glass Menagerie* itself. To set the final play against these earlier efforts reveals nuances that are easily overlooked.

Before examining this material, however, a word should be said about Williams's habit of constantly revising and reworking his creations. Typically, a Williams play starts life as a poem or short story, is revised to a one-act, then a full-length play; the play itself is changed during performance and again between performance and publication; if the production has not been as successful as was hoped, the play is likely to be completely redrafted, or it may be drastically reworked as a script for a film or television or even a novel. Nor is it always the case that the revision moves from shorter versions to longer ones: the published version of the short story "Portrait of a Girl in Glass," for example, is much briefer than the draft versions at Texas which already contain many of the details, such as Laura's lameness and unicorn or Amanda's reminiscences of Blue Mountain, that later appear in *The Glass Menagerie*, where they must therefore be considered reversions, not new insights or additions. Such instability is apt to offend literary critics, but it is wholly typical of Williams's attitude to life and work, in which no position or creation is to be considered complete till the author decides to finish with it. It is well to bear this in mind not only when one comes to evaluate the radical alterations Williams has always been ready to accommodate for purposes of immediate production or filming, but also when one considers the differences among the short story

"Portrait," the various drafts of *The Gentleman Caller* from which both "Portrait" and *Menagerie* emerge, the manuscript version of *The Glass Menagerie,* its acting version (as published by the Dramatists Play Service), the reading version authorized by Williams for publication by Random House and New Directions, and the alterations he agreed to, however reluctantly, for the movie and, more recently, for television. Though Williams's idol D.H. Lawrence may advise us to trust the tale and not the teller, in Tennessee Williams's case one is always faced with creation in process, and this turns one back inevitably towards the man.

II

Lester Beaurline's lucid appraisal of the Williams manuscripts in the Barrett Library of the University of Virginia pioneered the analysis of *Menagerie*'s development[6]; but since his article appeared, a great deal of extra material has been deposited at the Humanities Research Center of the University of Texas which shows that the genesis of the play was even more complex than he supposed. This new material is largely undated, however, and thus far has been sorted out only by text; so until an accurate time sequence can be worked out among the many drafts (and the Texas material collated with the archives in Virginia and Harvard), nothing like a definitive analysis will be possible. Nevertheless, certain details are already clear which can affect interpretation of the finished play.

For example, it is usually assumed that *Menagerie* developed directly from the screen-play called *The Gentleman Caller,* but a glance at the screen-play itself shows that this assumption can only have been true in part. Texas has two undated copies of Williams's general *Description of the Gentleman Caller,* each five pages long, plus a more elaborate seventeen-page "Provisional Story Treatment" dated 31 May 1943 (plus six extra pages of draft, dated 28 June 1943); also a more carefully typed but undated copy of the latter in a Liebling-Wood folder which turned up during the sorting of the David Selznick papers.[7] The *Description* has no narrator but opens with a lengthy account of Amanda's life at Blue Mountain, her gentleman callers, Wingfield's wooing, and his misadventure with an illicit still which forced the family to leave town. The "play" proper then begins on Christmas Eve with Laura, who is "morbidly shy" but not in this version lame, decorating a tree while her brother "Larry" reads poetry aloud; they attempt to attract passing carolers with a candle at the window; and Amanda gives them unsuitable Christmas presents, a six-month business course for Laura and books on salesmanship and "executive personality" for Larry. Laura fails at business college largely because she is bullied by a "hawklike spinster" instructor. Larry's restlessness is explained by the fact that "The Wingfields ... were pioneers, Indian fighters, trailblazers in the American wilderness," and there is "an amusing incidental scene" in which one of his wanderlust poems wins a $10.00 prize from the Ladies' Wednesday Club. Laura likes the gentleman caller Jim because his freckles remind her of the hero of her favourite Gene Stratton Porter novel (as in "Portrait"), not because she knew him in high school. The lights do not go off, there is no Paradise Dance Hall, little is made of the glass collection, and there is no unicorn to be broken. As in *Stairs to the Roof,* Larry loses his job for smoking on the roof, not for writing poems on cartons; and on the morning after his departure, Laura tries to comfort her mother by volunteering to telephone for magazine subscriptions, but does so too early – at 6:30 a.m. – which makes them both laugh and restores Amanda's morale.

The "Provisional Story Treatment" is even further from *Menagerie.* It is divided into three parts linked by Tom as narrator. Part I dramatizes events at Blue Mountain, with scenes of gentlemen callers visiting Amanda, her first meeting with Wingfield, his proposal at a picnic and fight with another of her admirers, and her snubbing of his next visit but sudden decision to elope with him. The narration then bridges to a hotel in Memphis where Amanda watches boats go down the river and tells Wingfield of her first pregnancy. Wingfield enlists for World War I and Amanda, pregnant with his second child, returns to Blue Mountain. Wingfield comes home a shell-shocked hero but begins bootlegging, and an elaborate sequence follows in which his still blows up, killing a Negro, and bloodhounds track him to his father-in-law's church. The dogs attack Laura on the church steps, and Wingfield, rescuing her, is arrested and taken to prison. Part II tells of the family's life in St. Louis, with the embittered father working in a shirt factory. Laura has been so traumatized by the bloodhounds that she cannot talk until her father delights her into speech by bringing home a Victrola on which he plays *Dardanella.* Amanda objects to the expense of this, and Wingfield leaves for good. The narrator then tells of the children growing up over shots of Tom (in this version) reading magazines instead of selling them and brooding despairingly in a warehouse, Amanda selling subscriptions over the telephone, and Laura having nightmares about dogs, failing to recite at school, playing *Dardanella,* polishing her glass collection, and endlessly rereading *Freckles.*

Part III covers the same sequence as the *Description,* beginning with the Christmas Eve scene. Once more Laura is bullied by her typing instructor, but now the machine clatter is described as sounding like "hounds baying." There is no poetry prize scene, but again Laura likes Jim solely because of his freckles and again there is no unicorn. Tom's speech on leaving home is now made to echo his father's earlier recriminations; and after the scene in which Laura makes her comically early telephone call, three alternative endings are suggested: either Amanda and Laura return to Blue Mountain, where Laura insists her mother is "just as beautiful as she was – in the beginning"; or Laura is shown welcoming hosts of gentlemen callers at Blue Mountain, like her mother earlier; or one or other of the Tom Wingfields returns: "At any rate – Amanda has finally found security and rest. What she searched for in the faces of Gentlemen Callers." This "Story Treatment's" note that Part III "covers the part of the story contained in the stage play 'The Gentleman Caller' ('The Glass Menagerie')"[8] is proof that the play already existed independently of the film treatment, but the fact that the Selznick version, which is a careful but rather mechanical copy of the Texas draft, must have been made soon after the end of June 1943 – well before the play was produced – shows how misapprehension about their order could easily arise. Moreover, both play and film treatment drew on earlier material.

The discrepancies relate back, in fact, to a more elaborate stage play of *The Gentleman Caller,* which survives in many partial versions but no complete one. The Texas archive contains multiple overlapping drafts, including a twenty-two page fragment with the title "The Gentleman Caller, or Portrait of a girl in glass (A lyric play)," twenty-nine disorderly pages called "The Gentleman Caller (original and only copy of a rather tiresome play)" and subtitled "(the ruins of a play)," another twenty-page fragment entitled "The Gentleman Caller (A Gentle Comedy)," and a composite typescript of 156 pages, plus forty pages of pencil draft in a notebook and some 254 further draft pages in typescript. Names and details change bewilderingly throughout these drafts: Laura is sometimes called Rose or Rosemary (and once Miriam) and varies between eighteen, twenty, and twenty-three in age; Tom is often called Larry; Jim has several Irish surnames and hails variously from Oregon, Nebraska, or Wyoming; and the St. Louis apartment is located on Maple Street, Enright, or, most often, Côte Brilliante Avenue.

The confusion reflects the trouble Williams had controlling his material. "It's the hardest thing I have ever tried to say!", Tom assures the audience in the "ruins of a play":

I've written this over ten times and torn it up, I've sweated over it, raged over it, wept over it! I think I have it and then it gets all misty and fades away. .... I must confine myself to a smaller ambition, not all but a little of it.[9]

Similarly, in the notebook pencil draft Tom says:

The original play filled several hundred pages. The top-heavy structure collapsed. And I lay under the ruins like a caterpillar. After a while I picked myself up again. I looked about me. Here and there I picked up a sound particle, a piece that survived. I put these fragments together. Out of the ruins of a monument salvaged this tablet, these remnants of a play, *The Gentleman Caller.*

This shortened version of *The Gentleman Caller* corresponds closely, but again not exactly, to the *Description* of the film-script,[10] and the sequence is complicated further by Williams's trying out sections of the material also as one-acters. *The Pretty Trap (A Comedy in One Act)*, for instance, has the title-page note: "This play is derived from a longer work in progress, *The Gentleman Caller*. It corresponds to the last act of that play, roughly, but has a lighter treatment and a different end." Jim's visit here takes place on Sadie Hawkins day (when girls may propose to men), and Laura is shy but not lame; the lights, however, do go out, much more is made of the glass animals than in the film-script, and the unicorn appears but is not broken. After Jim's kiss he mentions no fiancée but asks if he may take Laura for a walk; and when they have left, Amanda ends the play exulting to Tom: "Girls are a pretty trap! That's what they've always been, and always will *be*, even when *dreams* plus *action* – take over the world: Now – now, dreamy type – Let's finish the dishes!" A similar ending occurs in the full-length *The Gentleman Caller (A Gentle Comedy)*, with the addition that Amanda tells Tom to take out the suitcase he has hidden under his bed and leave now with her blessing: "Then come home and I'll be waiting for you – no matter how long!"

Other one-acters which seem to have preceded either version of *The Gentleman Caller* are *Carolers, our Candle*[11] (dated April 1943), which covers the Christmas Eve sequence, and the fragmentary "A Daughter of the Revolution (A Comedy)," dated March 1943 and inscribed to "Miss Lilian and Miss Dorothy Gish for either of whom the part of Amanda Wingfield was hopefully intended by the author," which presents Amanda's comic telephone subscriptions. Another early one-acter, *If You Breathe, It Breaks! or Portrait of a Girl in Glass*, takes place at Blue Mountain, where Mrs. Wingfield is represented as the widow of an episcopal clergyman, supporting her family by running a boarding-house; Rosemary, her shy, plain daughter, is teased by malicious boarders and treated badly by a younger brother Ronald, but is taken off to the White Star Pharmacy for a soda by a middle-aged widower, Mr. Wallard, to whom she gives her prized glass unicorn. Another, more farcical Blue Mountain one-acter, *With Grace and Dignity or The Memorial Service*, included among *The Gentleman Caller* drafts, depicts Rosemary's inability to carry a white taper during Mrs. Wingfield's celebration of her election as regent of the local chapter of the D.A.R. and the substitution for her of the Negro cook with a candle stub from the kitchen.

What one needs to understand from this welter of alternatives therefore is the difficulty Williams had in coming to terms with his material and the complexity of his responses to it, because clearly there was no steady progression in one direction – details come and go bewilderingly – and though in *Menagerie* he found a form which brilliantly controls the material, some of the rejected alternatives are still faintly there like an imaginative penumbra.

For instance, in drafts of the longer version of the stage *Gentleman Caller*, one can trace Williams's efforts to "place" the story. One recurring experiment is to try to set it within a "pioneer" framework, recounting the Williams family history in Sandburg-like verse at the beginning (against a large map of America) and returning to it at the end to explain the necessity of Tom's choice and to reassure the audience of the women's ability to survive "because we're daughters of the Revolution." The same element comes up more obliquely in a version where Williams introduces a young vagrant, Tom Lee, whom Amanda invites to breakfast when she finds him stealing milk bottles, then dismisses to the fire-escape again for "bolshevik" opinions, only to find that Tom prefers to join him there; and in another draft one of Williams's "fugitive kind," a street-musician named Tony, who calls Amanda disrespectfully "Mother Wing" and is dismissed by her as an "artistic bum," persuades Tom to join the merchant marine and leave the stolid Jim to take his room and place in the family.[12] A related experiment has the play remembered by Tom himself sleeping in a doss-house and deciding to return home when he hears carolers outside. Shades of this left-wing comment and romantic bohemianism remain in the Tom of *Menagerie,* but in a more qualified, ironic tone that is linked to another of Williams's experiments in *The Gentleman Caller* – the theatricalism of a framework in which Tom criticizes the lighting man and at several points argues directly with the audience in justification of the play. The combative, slightly aggressive relation to the audience in these last experiments is worth remembering.

A different kind of framework tries to set the children within a context of their parents, showing Amanda's relationship with Wingfield at the beginning and, in at least two versions, having the husband return to resolve the situation at the end; and this reflects a different kind of light that the drafts can shed on *Glass Menagerie*. Critics react so sympathetically to the Wingfields that they are apt to miss shades of characterization, but familiarity with the earlier attempts alerts us to Williams's own ambivalences, particularly his unexpected siding with his father. Amanda can be very sympathetic, as Williams surely meant her to be, but she is also grotesquely comic, and the drafts often emphasize this – by the story of the exploding still, for instance, which in some versions Tom uses to deflate her reminiscences of Blue Mountain, or the description of her waiting up for him in a dingy flannel wrapper, "smelling of Vicks Vap-o-rub – a portrait of Motherhood that would make Whistler turn in his grave." There is also a certain flexibility in the presentation of Laura. Besides varying her age and only occasionally making her lame, Williams presents her with very different degrees of neurasthenia, ranging from completely fey fantasies that she and Tom will escape to Freckles's "Limber-lost" in a blue coupé and live together in an old, abandoned house, to a moral strength that enables her both to assure Tom that she will not be harmed by the disappointment of Jim or by Tom's departure and to take over when her mother finally breaks down. And in the curious version with the street-musician Tony, she is transformed to a high-strung member of the local Little Theatre who wants be be "Duse! Bernhardt! Duncan! Pavlova! Garbo! Joan of Arc!," with a sharp, sarcastic tongue that is more than a match for her mother's, whereas Tom is the withdrawn and quiet one. This interesting transfer of identities was anticipated in the one-act *The Long Goodbye,* where the promiscuous sister is forced from home and the poetic brother finds it difficult to leave, and it also prefigures characterization in the revised version of *The Two-Character Play* more recently.

Most important of all, however, is the draft versions' evidence that Williams was uncertain how to end the story and constantly tempted to use optimistic conclusions, ranging from loud assertions of American independence, through happy returns of Wingfield Senior, Tom, or Jim, to attempts to show the women prospering in some way on their own. With hindsight, we can see that Williams was right to discard these experiments, but it is important to bear them in mind when, for instance, we consider the sentimental conclusion of the 1950 film, in which Laura, cured by her encounter with Jim, has her pick of gentlemen callers, "And the one she chose was named Richard."[13] It is usual to blame this travesty on Hollywood, noting that the script is credited to Williams and a rewrite man named Peter Berneis. But we have seen Williams experimenting with such conclusions in his drafts,[14] and Texas has a film-script of *The Glass Menagerie* by Williams alone in which Laura, cutting business school, makes friends with a little girl sketching in the botanical gardens and eventually falls happily in love with the child's sympathetic art teacher. To do Williams justice, he has scrawled across the cover of this script, "A Horrible Thing! Certified by Tennessee Williams."

A similar caution must be exercised with changes introduced into the original production and subsequently enshrined in the Dramatists Play Service acting edition. The director, Eddie Dowling (who also played Tom), influenced by George Jean Nathan, thought the play was not funny enough and introduced Tom's drunken return in scene 4. According to Williams (*Memoirs,* p. 82), Dowling wanted Tom to sing "My Melancholy Baby" and swig from a red, white, and blue flask,[15] but though Williams agreed to include the scene, he wrote it in his own way, weaving it into the pattern of the play by its motifs of rainbow scarf, magician, coffin, and escape. Actually the play is full of humour, but it is of Williams's own oblique and mordant kind. He credits Laurette Taylor with a special gift for this sort of wild, black comedy, and it was because she could balance it so carefully against Amanda's sympathetic qualities that he allowed her many small revisions of lines that, without the counterbalance she provided, can combine to make Amanda overly sympathetic.[16] Much the same reason may have influenced him in permitting the projection of titles to be cut. To my knowledge, the play has only once been produced as originally intended, and that quite recently and in German[17]; nonetheless, Williams insisted that the Random House–New Directions reading edition largely return to his original script. He has been criticized for doing this,[18] but when we remember his laborious experiments through draft after draft of *The Gentleman Caller,* searching for the proper framework, it seems probable that he was as right to do so as he was later in printing the original end to *Cat on a Hot Tin Roof* that Elia Kazan had sentimentalized in production. To insist, as most critics still do,[19] that the projection device is jejune or pretentious is to do Williams and his play a grave injustice.

III

The reasons for the original neglect of the projection device are not far to seek. In the early 1940's American audiences were familiar with realism and theatricalism separately but not with the simultaneity and tension between them on which Williams depends in *Menagerie*; the first production was so phenomenally successful that it is hardly surprising that critics should assume the projections must have been unnecessary; and Williams's own justifications for the device in his Production Notes to the play were rather misleading. Reflecting the influence of Erwin Piscator, with whom he had studied during the period of his Rockefeller fellowship in New York, the first two reasons Williams gives are that, in an "episodic" drama, captions serve to clarify the central values of each scene and to emphasize the structural relationships between them – arguments that the critics had no difficulty refuting by pointing out that scenic focus and structural sequence were perfectly clear without such aids. Williams goes on to suggest a third function, however, which was largely ignored, perhaps because its phrasing was so vague: " ... I think the screen will have a definite emotional appeal, less definable but just as important."[20] It is here that the importance of the projections lies. *The Glass Menagerie* is explicitly "sentimental," a play whose "first condition" is "nostalgia," and its besetting danger, therefore, is the sentimentality of which it has often been accused (ironically, sometimes by the same critics who dismiss the projections). It was by the complexity of its presentational effect that the original version guarded against this.

Just as the wording of Tom's framework speeches in the New Directions reading edition is much more ironically qualified than in the acting edition,[21] so too theatrical devices – Tom using an imaginary knife and fork (p. 24), or playing the first scene "*as though reading from a script*" (p. 26), with projections such as the "sailing vessel with the Jolly Roger" (p. 51) which accompanies his dreams of adventure (and links them to Jim's high-school performance in *The Pirates of Penzance*) – all serve to maintain an ironic distance between the early Tom-within-the-play and the later

Tom-remembering, through whose presentation the audience must, willy-nilly, experience the play.

Moreover, this device not only slakes sentimentality, but also reflects aspects of Tom's character. Its slightly jaunty, occasionally jarring irony is typical of Williams's black comedy, the not-quite-funny humour (that in *Out Cry* he calls the "jokes of the condemned")[22] by which his characters try to protect themselves against painful feeling. The exaggeration of projections such as "Annunciation" (p. 56) or "The Sky Falls" (p. 111), for example, like the obtrusive playing of the Ave Maria off-stage, both mocks Amanda's self-dramatizing and reflects Tom's attempt to control his pain at recognizing the hope and despair beneath his mother's absurdity.

The theatricalism has a further effect besides. It creates a gap between Tom-remembering and the audience (which is really why the projections are resented); there is a slight, Albee-like abrasiveness involved that recalls the element of antagonism in those early drafts where Tom was made to argue with the spectators directly. This appears most disturbingly in relation to Laura, who is a wholly sympathetic character without the absurdity that is clear in Amanda, Jim, and the early Tom himself. She is given such a dimension of absurdity, however, by projections like "Not Jim!" (p. 72), "Terror," "Ah!" (p. 83, followed soon by "Ha!" [p. 86]), or "Gentleman caller waving goodbye – gaily" (p. 109), which seem to run directly counter to the audience's response.

The significance of this effect is subtle, and can perhaps best be arrived at by noticing Williams's surprising lack of personal enthusiasm for this, his most popular play. In an early interview with *Time* he warned that in *The Glass Menagerie* " ... I said all the nice things I have to say about people. The future things will be harsher,"[23] and in letters to Donald Windham during the summer of 1943 he complained, " 'The Gentleman Caller' remains my chief work, but it goes slowly, I feel no overwhelming interest in it. It lacks the violence that excites me, so I piddle around with it," and "It is the *last* play I will try to write for the *now* existing theatre."[24] What *The Glass Menagerie* seems to lack, in fact, are Williams's characteristic ingredients of sex and violence. Yet it is clear from the drafts and alternative treatments that there were elements of both in his full response to the situation; and adumbrations of them can still be traced in the complexity of tone produced by the original theatricalism and by a certain exaggeration in the style of Tom's framework speeches, especially towards the end.

The play is usually talked of as Tom's exorcism of memory, but it can just as accurately be seen as repetition. After all, he does not really escape the family trap. The memory which forces him constantly to relive events that give so much pain and regret can be compared to Yeats's *Purgatory* or, even more closely, to Sartre's *Huis clos* – for which Williams has expressed great admiration (*Memoirs*, p. 149). And when the play is seen in this way, one must recognize that, besides it gentle sadness and remorse, there is also ruthlessness in Tom's final command, "Blow out your candles, Laura – and so goodbye ... " (p. 115). Like Othello's "Put out the light," this is a kind of loving murder, a repetition of the original violation. For Williams, in fact, love and betrayal are always two sides of the same emotion, as in his poem "The Comforter and the Betrayer"; his "brutal and gentle characters do more than co-exist, they inter-exist, one creates the other in a vicious circle of disaster."[25]

More interesting still, Laura is bidden to put out her own light. The image is of enforced self-killing, of ruthlessness turned in upon itself, because in rejecting Laura, Tom is also denying part of himself. This is more complex than the idea that "To leave home and Amanda is to insure self-preservation, but at the same time to kill something vital within the self."[26] It goes beyond the emotions of remorse and escape to touch the sado-masochism that is central to Williams's sensibility, according to which idealized love must be violated precisely because it is ideal, and in hurting others one also punishes onself.

The element of bravado in Tom's attitude, the uneasiness in his insistence on the need to break away in spite of the damage that will be caused (seen most flagrantly in the rodomontade of the pioneer America drafts), is reflected in *The Glass Menagerie* by a slightly false, posturing, overelaborate quality in his poetic self-justifications, a forcing of tone which has often been remarked but is usually condemned. And Williams's comment in the *Memoirs* (p. 84) that he too has never felt Tom's narrations were up to the rest of the play interestingly bears out an observation by Peggy Prenshaw on Williams's use of art as therapy:

viewing art as an extension of the artist, either for what he is or what he needs, leads solipsistically back to the mortal and flawed being that the artist seeks to transcend. ... Tom Wingfield casts a magical web over experience, transforming the ordinary and ugly, and even painful, into a thing of beauty. But undermining ... [his] transformations of life into art is [his] ... (and[his] ... creator's) lurking doubt that the vision is wholly truthful. ...[27]

Williams may not have intended this uneasiness consciously, of course, but it adds immensely to the richness of the play (besides avoiding the trap of sentimentality) and also relates *The Glass Menagerie* more closely to the rest of Williams's canon. In various displaced, oblique ways the mixture of guilt and identification which Williams feels for Rose has been a recurrent theme throughout his work.[28] In *Memoirs* he says: "My sister and I had a close relationship, quite unsullied by any carnal knowledge. ... And yet our love was, and is, the deepest in our lives and was, perhaps, very pertinent to our withdrawal from extrafamilial attachments" (pp. 119–120). He sees in Rose's retreat from life to imagination and in her final dreadful fate an equivalent of his own inescapable self-consciousness as an artist and of the confinement he talks of as his greatest fear (*Memoirs*, p. 223); and in no work is this to be seen more clearly than in the play called variously *Out Cry* (1973) and *The Two-Character Play* (1967, 1975), which has been described as "in some respects like a sequel to *Glass Menagerie*. ..."[29]

Though there are considerable revisions between the versions (particularly to make the relationship of the framework characters more antagonistic), the basic Pirandellian situation of *The Two-Character Play* remains unchanged. Two actors, a brother and sister androgynously named Felice and Clare Devoto, on tour in the capital of an unnamed northern country, find themselves abandoned by their company as "insane." They are alone on a stage dominated by a gigantic statue – representing, we are told, "things anguished and perverse" (p. 7); but since "if we're not artists, we're nothing" (p. 22), they put on a play that the brother is still in process of writing, ad-libbing as seems necessary. In this play within the play they represent a brother and sister, also called Felice and Clare, who are incapable of leaving the family house, where their father killed their mother, then himself. It is hinted that their love for each other has a sexual element (with sadistic overtones in the final revision), and as it becomes evident that Felice is shaping his play towards a repetition of the parents' killing-suicide, the actress Clare abruptly brings the performance to a halt – only to discover that their audience has left and they are now alone, locked in the darkening, icy theatre. To escape the cold, their one expedient is to go back into the southern past of the brother's play, where the killing-suicide can provide a solution to both levels of imprisonment. When it comes to the point, however, neither can kill the other, and the play ends with their embrace in what Williams has described as a "Liebestod," as the stage blackens out to represent death theatrically.[30] As epigraph Williams quotes the *Song of Solomon*: "A garden enclosed is my sister."

Such a summary does no justice to the subtlety of this play, of course, which Williams calls "the big one," "close to the marrow of my being" (*Memoirs*, pp. 129, 228), but it is sufficient perhaps to show its relevance to the reciprocal fantasies in *Menagerie* – Laura's retreat to a private world of glass reflected in Tom's theatrical obsession with the past, and his conscious cruelty of abandonment mirrored in the guilt she returns to him – as two aspects of the "Comforter-Betrayer" syndrome. Like Felice and Clare, though less schematically, Tom and Laura can be seen as related aspects of the "fugitive" sensibility,[31] and only if this complementarity is accepted, can the full complexity of Williams's brilliant final balancing of tones between love, pity, regret, guilt, self-lacerating ruthlessness, posing, and bravado be imaginatively realized, and the superiority of his original theatricalized version of the play become quite clear. Perhaps like Felice's *Two-Character Play* itself, this may be "a little too personal, too special for most audiences" (p. 62), in which case the acting edition will continue to be preferable for performance, as Beaurline reports Williams's agent as indicating.[32] But until the theatricalism has been shown to fail, there is certainly no a priori case for this; and Williams has ensured that in reading we pay attention to his original version, which reflects more truthfully the complexity of response that can be traced throughout his many drafts and rewritings of the play.[33]

NOTES

1 Edwina Williams and Lucy Freeman, *Remember Me to Tom* (New York, 1963).

2 Tennessee Williams, *Memoirs* (Garden City, N.Y., 1975). Subsequent references will appear in the text.

3 Tennessee Williams, *In the Winter of Cities* (Norfolk, Conn., 1964), pp. 53, 44.

4 See John Strother Clayton, "The Sister Figure in the Works of Tennessee Williams," *Carolina Quarterly*, 12 (Summer 1960), 47–60. A more extreme position is argued by Daniel A. Dervin, "The Spook in the Rain Forest: The Incestuous Structure of Tennessee Williams' Plays," *Psychocultural Review*, 3 (1979), 153–183.

5 All are in *27 Wagons Full of Cotton and Other One-Act Plays* (Norfolk, Conn., 1945).

6 Lester A. Beaurline, "*The Glass Menagerie*: From Story to Play," *Modern Drama*, 8 (1965), 143–149.

7 I am grateful to Gilbert Debusscher for helping me work out these relationships more accurately than in my original article in *Modern Drama*.

8 In an interview with Eileen Creelman for the *New York World-Telegram* on 9 September 1950, Williams remarked "perhaps the original title would have been better. I first called it 'The Gentleman Caller,' but 'The Glass Menagerie' seemed to me so effective a symbol that I changed it before typing it up."

9 My ellipsis; the speech is a very long one.

10 Cf. Williams's "scenic out-line of the play-script" in an undated letter to Audrey Wood, reproduced in Richard F. Leavitt, ed., *The World of Tennessee Williams* (New York, 1978), pp. 52–53.

11 This may be the earliest element in *The Gentleman Caller*. The Texas archive has a note scribbled on two loose sheets in what looks like a very early, juvenile hand, recording a brother's musing about what his sister can be thinking as she decorates a Christmas tree.

12 Jim is characterized in much the same way in *Stairs to the Roof*.

13 *Screen Hits Annual*, No. 5 (1950), p. 50.

14 As he also did with happy endings for *Streetcar*; cf. Vivienne Dickson, "*A Streetcar Named Desire*: Its Development through the Manuscripts," in *Tennessee Williams: A Tribute*, ed. Jac Tharpe (Jackson, Miss., 1977), p. 157.

15 Mrs. Williams remembers the song as the bawdiest verse of the "St. Louis Blues" (E. Williams, p. 145).

16 See James L. Rowland, "Tennessee's Two Amandas," *Research Studies (Washington State University)*, 35 (1967), 331–340, though Professor Rowland prefers the revised, sympathetic version.

17 Cf. pictures and discussion of a 1966 production at Ulm in Christian Jauslin, *Tennessee Williams* (Munich, 1976), pp. 129, 123–125. I am indebted to Professor Gilbert Debusscher for this reference.

18 See, for instance, Lester A. Beaurline, "The Director, the Script, and the Author's Revisions: A Critical Problem," in *Papers in Dramatic Theory and Criticism*, ed. David M. Knauf (Iowa City, 1969), p. 89.

19 E.g., Beaurline, "The Director"; S. Alan Chesler, "Tennessee Williams: Reassessment and Assessment," in Tharpe, p. 853; Mary Ann Corrigan, "Beyond Verisimilitude: Echoes of Expressionism in Williams' Plays," ibid., p. 392. A notable early argument against this attitude can be found in George Brandt, "Cinematic Structure in the Work of Tennessee Williams," in *American Theatre*, ed. John Russell Brown and Bernard Harris (London, 1967), pp. 184–185.

20 Tennessee Williams, Production Notes, *The Glass Menagerie* (New York, 1966), p. 8. Subsequent references to *The Glass Menagerie* are to this edition and will appear in the text.

The Texas archive has the typescript draft of what appears to have been intended as an open letter, entitled "A Reply to Mr. Nathan" and dated 9 April 1945, which throws further light on Williams's concept of the projections:

> It is true that in the original script I suggested – not insisted upon – the use of magic lantern slides to serve at intervals, carefully chosen, as a sometimes satirical and sometimes poetic counterpoint to the dialogue, and to sustain the narrative point of view even when he was not present on stage, *for these slides were the narrator's own commentary on what was taking place* (my italics).

Williams goes on to say that he did not object to the removal of the device in the first production and does not regret its loss because "the extraordinary power of Miss Taylor's performance, which I and nobody else had quite anticipated, made this play a play where that performance should be set as a pure jewel in the simplest of all possible settings." The letter seems never to have been published.

21 Cf. Thomas L. King, "Irony and Distance in *The Glass Menagerie*," *Educational Theatre Journal*, 25 (1973), 207–214.

22 Cf. Williams's unpublished Author's Notes for director and actors as quoted in Thomas P. Adler, "The Dialogue of Incompletion: Language in Tennessee Williams's Later Plays," *Quarterly Journal of Speech*, 61 (1975), 56. Subsequent references to *Out Cry* in my article refer to the New Directions edition (New York, 1973) and will appear in the text.

23 "The Theater: The Winner," *Time,* 23 April 1945, p. 88.

24 Tennessee Williams, Letters of 28 June 1943 and [18 or 25] August 1944, Letters 48 and 74, *Tennessee Williams' Letters to Donald Windham, 1940–1965,* ed. Donald Windham (New York, 1977), pp. 94, 148. Cf. Williams's statement, "I had never been able to avoid the undeniable fascination with violence until I wrote *The Glass Menagerie,*" quoted in E. Williams, p. 253, and Williams's admission that this violence is the obverse of constant fear (ibid.).

25 John Buell, "The Evil Imagery of Tennessee Williams," *Thought,* 38 (1963), 185.

26 Nancy M. Tischler, "The Distorted Mirror: Tennessee Williams' Self-Portraits," *Mississippi Quarterly,* 25 (Fall 1972), 389–403; rpt. in *Tennessee Williams: A Collection of Critical Essays,* ed. Stephen Stanton (Englewood Cliffs, N.J., 1977), p. 160.

27 Peggy W. Prenshaw, "The Paradoxical Southern World of Tennessee Williams," in Tharpe, p. 24.

28 Cf. Clayton; Victor A. Kramer remarks on the same obsession: "to write of his sister is to write of a complexity which can be observed but not understood; but it is also to find 'release' ..." "Memoirs of Self-Indictment: The Solitude of Tennessee Williams," in Tharpe, p. 673.

29 Prenshaw, p. 17.

30. Cf. Williams, Author's Notes, in Adler, 57, n. 27.

31. Esther M. Jackson goes further and suggests that Amanda and the father are also "masks" of Tom: *The Broken World of Tennessee Williams* (Madison, Wis., 1966), p. 86.

32 Beaurline, "The Director," p. 89.

33 Quotations from the Texas archive are by permission of Tennessee Williams and the Humanities Research Center, The University of Texas at Austin.

Realism and Theatricalism in
A Streetcar Named Desire

MARY ANN CORRIGAN

On the morning after the premiere of *A Streetcar Named Desire* in 1947, Joseph Wood Krutch commented: "This may be the great American play." From the perspective of more than a quarter of a century later *A Streetcar Named Desire* appears to be *one* of the great American plays. Its greatness lies in Tennessee Williams' matching of form to content. In order to gain sympathy for a character who is in the process of an emotional breakdown, Williams depicts the character from without and within; both the objectivity and the subjectivity of Blanche are present to the audience. In *A Streetcar Named Desire* Williams synthesizes depth characterization, typical of drama that strives to be an illusion of reality, with symbolic theatrics, which imply an acceptance of the stage as artifice. In short, realism and theatricalism, often viewed as stage rivals, complement each other in this play. Throughout the 1940s Williams attempted to combine elements of theatricalist staging with verisimilitudinous plots and characters. His experiments either failed utterly, as in *Battle of Angels* in which neither literal nor symbolic action is convincing, or succeeded with modifications, for instance by the removal of the screen device in *The Glass Menagerie*. In *A Streetcar Named Desire* Williams is in control of his symbolic devices. They enable the audience not only to understand the emotional penumbra surrounding the events and characters, but also to view the world from the limited and distorted perspective of Blanche. The play's meaning is apparent only after Williams exposes through stage resources what transpires in the mind of Blanche.

When the audience meets Blanche, she is at the same stage as Laura of *The Glass Menagerie*: one more of life's frustrating disappointments is enough to insure final retreat from the world. Blanche does not retreat without a struggle; the progress of her struggle determines the forward movement of the play's action. To communicate Blanche's subjective state at each stage of the action,

Williams asks in his stage directions for aural and visual effects, some of which distort the surface verisimilitude of the play. Elia Kazan was careful to preserve these elements of stylization when he directed the original Broadway production. He explains: "One reason a 'style,' a stylized production is necessary is that a subjective factor – Blanche's memories, inner life, emotions, are a real factor. We cannot really understand her behavior unless we see the effect of her past on her present behavior."[1] The setting, lighting, props, costumes, sound effects and music, along with the play's dominant symbols, the bath and the light bulb, provide direct access to the private lives of the characters.

Williams' setting is emotionally charged and, as usual, described in great detail in the stage directions. Both the inside and the outside of the Kowalski house appear on stage. The house is in a slum in the old section of New Orleans. The backdrop designed by Jo Mielziner for the original production featured angled telephone poles, lurid neon lights and ornately decorated facades on crumbling structures. Despite its dilapidation, Williams insists that the section "has a raffish charm," especially in the blue light of the sky "which invests the scene with a kind of lyricism and gracefully attenuates the atmosphere of decay." Stanley is at home in this neighborhood and Stella has learned to like it, but its charm eludes Blanche, who says of it: "Only Poe! Only Mr. Edgar Allan Poe! – could do it justice!" Blanche finds the Kowalski environment cramped, foul and ugly, so unlike her childhood home, Belle Reve, "a great big place with white columns." In coming to New Orleans, Blanche is brought face to face with an ugly reality which contrasts with her "beautiful dream." To show the relation between the decadent New Orleans street life and the events inside the Kowalski flat Williams asks that the back wall of the apartment be made of gauze to permit, under proper lighting, a view of the city alley. This wall becomes transparent in the rape scene.

Williams uses costuming, props, and lighting to convey the emotional strength of his characters and to reinforce the dichotomy between Blanche and Stanley. The overwrought, emotionally drained Blanche always wears pastels in half-lights; Stanley, the "richly feathered male bird," appears in vivid primary colors under strong, garish light. Blanche's clothes establish her uniqueness even in her first appearance on stage. Williams writes in the stage directions:

> Her appearance is incongruous in this setting. She is daintily dressed in a white suit with a fluffy bodice, necklace, and earrings of pearl, white gloves and hat, looking as if she were arriving at a summer tea or cocktail party in the garden district. ... There is something about her uncertain manner, as well as her clothes, that suggests a moth. (Scene I)

Gerald Weales points out that Blanche's clothes are a characterizing device and a way of separating her from her surroundings: "Blanche is going to be destroyed by the end of the play and Williams wants her first appearance ... to imply that end. Costume here becomes a way of foreshadowing the events to come."[2] By the time Blanche appears the audience has already met the bellowing Stanley, dressed in work clothes, who hurled a blood-stained package of raw meat at his wife. Stella, despite her surprise, deftly caught the bundle; she has learned to function in this society.

The Poker Night scene also exploits the capacity of light and color to create mood. As he so often does, Williams cites an example from the visual arts as a model for the effect he wishes to create:

> There is a picture of Van Gogh's of a billiard-parlor at night. The kitchen now suggests that sort of lurid nocturnal brilliance, the raw colors of childhood's spectrum. Over the yellow linoleum of the kitchen table hangs an electric bulb with a vivid green glass shade. The poker players – Stanley, Steve, Mitch and Pablo – wear colored shirts, solid blues, a purple, a red-and-white check, a light green, and they are men at the peak of their physical manhood, as coarse and direct and powerful as the primary colors. There are vivid slices of watermelon on the table; whiskey bottles and glasses. (Scene III)

Williams' description seems to emphasize the vibrancy of this scene, but Van Gogh's *Night Café*, obviously his model, is harrowing in its luridness, its color contrasts and tilted perspective suggesting moral degeneracy. Surely Williams intends the poker players to be frightening in their physical strength. Primitive tastes and pleasures are the norm in the Kowalski set, and those who fail to conform to this norm have no chance of survival.

Music and other sounds also communicate a sense of the ineluctable primitive forces that operate in the Vieux Carré. From the Four Deuces, a nearby night spot, come the sounds that express New Orleans life: blues, jazz, honky-tonk. Elia Kazan comments on the function of the "blue piano" music which is in the background of much of the action:

> The Blues is an expression of the loneliness and rejection, the exclusion and isolation of the Negro and their longing for love and connection. Blanche, too, is looking for a home, abandoned and friendless. ... Thus the Blue piano catches the soul of Blanche, the miserable unusual human side of the girl which is beneath her frenetic duplicity, her trickery, lies, etc.[3]

The Blues plays as Blanche arrives in the Vieux Carré and is particularly dominant when she recounts the deaths at Belle Reve (Scene I) and when she

kisses the newsboy (Scene V). As Blanche is being led away to the asylum and
Stella cries uncontrollably, the music of the blue piano swells (Scene XI). At
one point this music catches the soul of Stanley too: when Stella leaves him, and
he sobs, "I want my baby," the " *'blue piano'* plays for a brief interval" (Scene
III). But normally, the uncomplicated obtrusive rhythms of the honky-tonk
express Stanley's personality. This music dominates the rape scene.

There is subjective as well as objective music in the play. Only Blanche and
the audience hear the Varsouviana polka, which was played as Blanche's
husband shot himself. The music, through its association in her memory with
impending death, becomes a symbol of imminent disaster. Blanche hears it, for
instance, when Stanley hands her a Greyhound bus ticket for a trip back to
Laurel (Scene VIII). The music of the Varsouviana weaves in and out of the
scene in which Mitch confronts Blanche with his knowledge of her background. Williams writes in the stage directions: *"The rapid, feverish polka
tune, the 'Varsouviana,' is heard. The music is in her mind; she is drinking to
escape it and the sense of disaster closing in on her, and she seems to whisper
the words of the song"* (Scene IX). In the same scene the polka tune fades in as
the Mexican street vendor, harbinger of death, arrives, chanting "Flores para
los muertos." Reality in all its harshness and ugliness is epitomized for Blanche
in these aural and visual reminders of death. She hears this music too in the last
scene, when Stanley and the asylum matron corner her. Williams uses the
symbolism attaching to Blanche's frequent bathing in order to further
lay bare her inner nature. As an aspect of the visiting in-law joke, Blanche's
"hogging" of the bathroom is amusing, and the earthy Stanley's references to
his bursting kidneys add to the humor. But the serious symbolism is
nevertheless obvious: "Blanche's obsessive bathing is a nominal gesture of
guilt and wished-for redemption."[4] Like her drinking, her bathing is an escape
mechanism. The ritual cleansing which takes place in the tub restores Blanche
to a state of former innocence. Once again she is young and pure in a beautiful
world.

The bath is a particularly functional symbol in Scene VII, in which it is used
to reveal the dual world of Blanche's existence and the tension between
Blanche and Stanley. Stella is setting the table for Blanche's birthday party, to
which Mitch, the one person who offers Blanche a genuine possibility for
redemption, has been invited. As the scene progresses, it becomes apparent that
this birthday will be anything but happy. The festive occasion that falls flat is a
staple of drama. Shakespeare, Chekhov, Pinter and Williams use it to intensify
the ironic discrepancy between appearance and reality. As Blanche bathes in
preparation for the party, Stanley reveals to Stella the particulars of her sister's
sordid life. The stage directions read: *"Blanche is singing in the bathroom a
saccharine popular ballad which is used contrapuntally with Stanley's
speech."* The louder Stanley gets in his insistence upon the undeniable facts

about Blanche, the louder Blanche sings in the bathroom. Her song asserts the capacity of the imagination to transform mere facts:

> Say, it's only a paper moon, Sailing over a cardboard sea –
> But it wouldn't be make-believe If you believed in me!
> ....
> It's a Barnum and Bailey world, Just as phony as it can be –
> But it wouldn't be make-believe If you believed in me!

When Stanley's recital reaches it climax with the most damning charge of Blanche's seduction of a student, "*in the bathroom the water goes on loud; little breathless cries and peals of laughter are heard as if a child were frolicking in the tub.*" Thus the two Blanches are counterpoised. In emerging from the bathroom, Blanche immediately senses the threat that Stanley's world of facts poses to her world of illusions. Her usual contented sigh after the bath gives way to uneasiness: "A hot bath and long, cold drink always give me a brand new outlook on life! ... Something has happened! – What is it?" Background music reflects her fear: "*The distant piano goes into a hectic breakdown.*"

Blanche is as obsessed with lights as she is with baths. Her first request when she comes to the Kowalski home is that the overhead light be turned off; subsequently she buys a paper lantern to cover it. On one level, of course, Blanche's dislike of bright lights is a matter of vanity: dimness hides the signs of aging. But it is clear that the light bulb has a further significance, perhaps unconscious, for Blanche, who says to Mitch: "I can't stand a naked light bulb, any more than I can a rude remark or a vulgar action" (Scene III). Just as the naked light must be toned down by an articial lantern, so every sordid reality must be cloaked in illusion. Stanley, on the other hand, likes as much light as possible; the clear cold light of day and the naked bulb reveal to him what is *real* and, therefore, what is *true*. And the *facts* of Blanche's former life, which Stanley assiduously "brings to light" for all to see are necessarily abhorrent to Blanche, who has different standards of truth. Mitch, having been "enlightened" by Stanley, tears the paper lantern from the bulb and demands to take a good look at Blanche.

> BLANCHE. Of course, you don't really mean to be insulting!
> MITCH. No, just realistic.
> BLANCHE. I don't want realism. I want magic! Yes, yes, magic! I try to give that to people. I misrepresent things to them. I don't tell the truth, I tell what *ought* to be truth. And if that is sinful, then let me be damned for it! – *Don't turn the light on!* (Scene IX)

Being forced to face the kind of reality that she refuses to recognize as significant is the cause of Blanche's breakdown. In the last scene, as Blanche is led away, Stanley tears the paper lantern off the light bulb – he has no use for it – and extends it to her: "*She cries out as if the lantern was herself.*" Blanche is as delicate and pathetic as a paper lantern; she cannot deflect the hard light of Stanley's vision of reality.

The scene in which Stanley imposes his vision of reality on Blanche, the rape scene, is comprehended and accepted by the audience largely because of the visual and aural details through which psychological intangibles are made objective. At the beginning of Scene X the audience is aware of Blanche's tenuous emotional state. Her appearance indicates that she is beginning to re-treat into her world of illusions:

> ...*she has decked herself out in a somewhat soiled and crumpled white satin evening gown and pair of scuffed silver slippers with brilliants set in their heels.*
> *Now she is placing the rhinestone tiara on her head before the mirror of the dressing-table and murmuring excitedly as if to a group of special admirers.*

Blanche, although revelling in her fantasies, is still capable of distinguishing them from actual events. In the middle of her feigned discussion with her admirers she catches sight of her face in a hand mirror, recognizes it as real, and breaks the mirror. At this point Stanley appears in his "*vivid green silk bowling shirt,*" to the tune of honky-tonk music, which continues to be heard throughout the scene. When Stanley confronts Blanche with his knowledge of her background, the abominable reality that Blanche detests begins to impinge upon her: "*Lurid reflections appear on the walls around Blanche. The shadows are of a grotesque and menacing form. She catches her breath, crosses to the phone and jiggles the hook.*" For Blanche the telephone is an avenue to a better world. When she sought what she called a "way out" for herself and Stella in Scene III, the telephone and telegraph were the means to effect her plan. Again she attempts to escape into a different world by calling her Texas millionaire. But when she can't give a number or an address, the operator cuts her off. Reality again! The stage directions indicate the result on Blanche of this thwarting of her plans: "*She sets the phone down and crosses warily into the kitchen. The night is filled with inhuman voices like cries in a jungle.*" Blanche has been sensitive to sound throughout the play. In the first act she jumped at the screech of a cat; later, when Stanley slammed a drawer closed, she winced in pain. Now "the cacophony that we hear is inside Blanche's head – imaginary sounds and real sounds turned grotesque and horrible by her fear."[5] To make Blanche's mounting fears tangible Williams uses the scrim:

> *Through the back wall of the rooms, which have become transparent, can be seen the sidewalk. A prostitute has rolled a drunkard. He pursues her along the walk, overtakes*

her and there is a struggle. A policeman's whistle breaks it up. The figures disappear. Some moments later the Negro woman appears around the corner with a sequined bag which the prostitute had dropped on the walk. She is rooting excitedly through it.

The New Orleans street figures are analogues of all that reality means to Blanche: violence, theft, immorality, bestiality. No wonder she tries to escape it. She returns to the telephone: "Western Union? Yes! I – want to – Take down this message! 'In desperate, desperate circumstances! Help me! Caught in a trap. Caught in –' Oh!" There is no escaping reality now, for its arch crusader, Stanley, is back:

The bathroom door is thrown open and Stanley comes out in the brilliant silk pajamas. He grins at her as he knots the tassled sash about his waist. ... The barely audible 'blue piano' begins to drum up louder. The sound of it turns into the roar of an approaching locomotive. ...

Blanche reads the meaning of the sounds perfectly: she will be forced to become part of this world of hot music and lust. Her tormentor teases her with the spectre of her fears:

You think I'll interfere with you? Ha-ha!
(The 'blue piano' goes softly. She turns confusedly and makes a faint gesture. The inhuman jungle voices rise up. He takes a step toward her, biting his tongue which protrudes between his lips.)

Blanche's gesture of threatening Stanley with a broken bottle is the last and the easiest of the challenges she poses for him. Springing like an animal at prey, he catches her wrist: "*The bottle top falls. She sinks to her knees. He picks up her inert figure and carries her to the bed. The hot trumpet and drums from the Four Deuces sound loudly.*" Blanche's involuntary journey to the depths of sordidness results in her losing contact completely with any kind of reality. The theatrical devices, aural and visual, which represent not objective occurrence, but inner action, enable the audience to understand Blanche's ordeal and her retreat into insanity.

Williams depicts the total defeat of a woman whose existence depends on her maintaining illusions about herself and the world. Blanche is both a representative and a victim of a tradition that taught her that attractiveness, virtue, and gentility led automatically to happiness. But reality proved intractable to the myth. Blanche's lot was Belle Reve, with its debts and deaths, and a homosexual husband who killed himself because, for once, her sensitivity failed her. Blanche's "amatory adventures ... are the unwholesome means she uses to maintain her connection with life, to fight the sense of death which her whole background has created in her."[6] Since "the tradition" allows no place for the physical and sensual, she rejects this aspect of her personality, calling it "brutal desire." Kazan writes: "She thinks she sins when she gives into it ... yet she does give into it, out of loneliness ... but by calling it 'brutal desire,' she is able to separate it from her 'real self,' her 'cultured,' refined self."[7]

If Blanche is the last remnant of a moribund culture, Stanley is in the vanguard of a vital and different society. Even Blanche recognizes his strength when she says, "He's just not the type that goes for jasmine perfume, but maybe he's what we need to mix with our blood now that we've lost Belle Reve" (Scene II). If Blanche's philosophy cannot make room for "brutal desire," Stanley's comprehends little else. Williams describes him:

Since earliest manhood the center of his life has been pleasure with women. ... He sizes women up at a glance, with sexual classifications, crude images flashing into his mind and determining the way he smiles at them. (Scene I)

It is only fitting that Stanley destroy Blanche with sex. As Benjamin Nelson writes, sex "has been her Achilles heel. It has always been his sword and shield."[8]

The conflict between Blanche and Stanley is an externalization of the conflict that goes on within Blanche between illusion and reality. The illusion sustaining her is her image of herself as a Southern belle, a fine, cultured, young lady. The reality is a lonely woman, desperately seeking human contact, indulging "brutal desire" as an affirmation of life. Blanche's "schizoid personality is a drama of man's irreconcilable split between animal reality and moral appearance."[9] This drama is played out not only in Blanche's mind, but between Stanley and Blanche as well. Stanley strips away Blanche's illusions and forces her to face animal reality. In doing so, he demonstrates that reality is as brutal as she feared. She has no choice but to retreat totally into illusion. Thus, the external events of the play, while actually occurring, serve as a metaphor for Blanche's internal conflict.

In pitting Blanche and Stanley against one another, Williams returns to his oft-told tale of the defeat of the weak by the strong. But, for a change, both figures represent complex and morally ambiguous positions. Blanche is far from perfect. She is a liar, an alcoholic, and she would break up the Kowalski marriage if she could. Despite his rough exterior, Stanley genuinely loves and needs his wife, and he cannot be blamed for protecting his marriage against the force that would destroy it. The ambiguity of Blanche and Stanley makes them more realistic than many of Williams' characters, who are often either demons (philistines with power, wealth and influence) or angels (helpless, sensitive, downtrodden artists or women). Although Williams depicts both positive and negative personality traits in Blanche and Stanley, his attitude toward the two charcters changes in the course of the play. In the beginning Williams clearly favors Stanley by emphasizing his wholesome natural traits, while dwelling on Blanche's artificiality. But such, we learn, are the deceptive appearances. The more Williams delves into Blanche's inner life and presents it on stage, the more sympathetic she becomes. Stanley's true nature also becomes apparent, in its negative effect upon her psyche, and, in the end, she is the undisputed moral victor.

Kazan's production deliberately emphasized Stanley's positive traits. In his notes on directing the play Kazan specifies that Blanche be presented as the "heavy" at the beginning of the play. Simultaneously, of course, Stanley is to evoke the audience's sympathy. Harold Clurman reports on this aspect of the original production: "Because the author does not preach about him but draws him without hate or ideological animus, the audience takes him at his face value. ... For almost more than two-thirds of the play, therefore, the audience identifies itself with Stanley Kowalski. His low jeering is seconded by the audience's laughter, which seems to mock the feeble and hysterical decorativeness of the girl's behavior"[10] Clurman, in going on to condemn the attempt to ingratiate Stanley with the audience, overlooks the dramatic value of making Stanley appealing initially. Stanley is, after all, not a monster. He bears remarkable resemblance to the kind of hero that Americans love, the hero of the westerns or the tough detective stories: the gruff masculine pragmatist who commands the adulation of women even as he scorns them for his male companions. That he is not as harmless, as "right" as he seems is precisely Williams' point. The play forces the members of the audience, as well as Blanche, to face "harsh reality," for they learn that what they instinctively admire and view as healthy is really a base egotistical force, destructive of what it cannot comprehend. The audience too moves from illusion to reality. The initial tendency is to resent Blanche and her airs, to applaud Stanley every time he "takes her down a peg." But slowly, as the veil of illusion lifts, both Stanley and Blanche are seen more clearly. Marlon Brando, who played Stanley in the Kazan production and in the movie, was an excellent choice for an appealing Stanley. Irwin Shaw commented on Brando's Broadway performance:

He is so appealing in a direct, almost childlike way in the beginning and we have been so conditioned by the modern doctrine that what is natural is good, that we admire him and sympathize with him. Then, bit by bit, with a full account of what his good points really are, we come dimly to see that he is ... brutish, destructive in his healthy egotism, dangerous, immoral, surviving.[11]

It is the rape scene that finally reveals the true horror of Stanley. As Blanche is made to face unpleasant reality in this scene, so is the audience.[12]

Williams remains as much as possible within the conventions of versimilitude in using theatrical devices to reveal Blanche's distorted vision of reality. The audience is, however, aware that baths and light bulbs have a meaning for Blanche apart from their functional existence. The further Blanche retreats from reality, the more Williams distorts the surface realism of the play. The purpose of the transparent wall in Scene I is not to reveal what is actually occurring in the alley, but to provide the necessary milieu for the defeat of illusion and to offer objective correlatives for Blanche's fears. Similarly, the subjective sounds enable the audience to share Blanche's past experiences and her present terrors.

In theme and technique *A Streetcar Named Desire* is, in the words of Henry Taylor, the play "toward which ... all Williams' work has been heading."[13] The characters of his early one-act plays, of *The Glass Menagerie* and of *A Streetcar Named Desire* who doggedly cling to an imaginative vision of what life ought to be, while resolutely ignoring what life is, are invested with a dignity denied those who accommodate themselves to imperfect existence. The theme of the necessity of illusions lends itself to theatricalist treatment, since the non-objective world, which is far more important to Williams' characters than the objective one, must somehow be made tangible on stage. Williams' use of theatrical devices to objectify thoughts and feelings is much more sophisticated in *A Streetcar Named Desire* than in his hitherto most successful play, *The Glass Menagerie*. In the earlier play Williams thought he needed a screen to depict exact and obvious equivalents for his characters' thoughts. In *A Streetcar Named Desire* he relies more upon the suggestive qualities of costuming and staging to communicate psychological tendencies more subliminal than thought. *The Glass Menagerie*'s musical themes, particularly the sentimental fiddling and the jolly roger tune, reflect not so much the characters' inner lives, as the author's ironic perspective on them. On the other hand, in *A Streetcar Named Desire,* the nightclub music and the Varsouviana convey the emotional states of the characters at each stage of the action.

The realism of *A Streetcar Named Desire* distinguishes it from *Summer and Smoke* (written before, but produced after *Streetcar*), with which it is superficially related. In *Summer and Smoke* the conflict is between two abstractions; in *A Streetcar Named Desire,* it is between two people. The angel, anatomy chart, and divided stage of Summer and Smoke simplify Alma and John so that they represent abstract qualities. John, who represents first Body and later soul, lacks the ambiguity that makes Stanley a good dramatic character and a worthy opponent for Blanche. Stanley is as much a bundle of contradictions as his antagonist. His strength, brutality, and virility are balanced by his vulnerability to Blanche's attacks, his awkward attempts at tenderness, and his need for his wife's approval. The unexpected character changes of *Summer and Smoke,* the "turnabouts" necessary to demonstrate the proposition that Body and Soul are irreconcilable, have no parallel in

A Streetcar Named Desire. The only event of any significance in *Summer and Smoke,* Alma's transformation, is not depicted on stage; it occurs between the acts. By contrast, Blanche's gradual emotional collapse is presented stage by stage. When Williams can no longer convey the disintegration of her mind by depicting only objective reality, he resorts to distortion of verisimilitude in order to present subjective reality. Blanche does not mechanically move from one extreme to the other; she suffers and undergoes – on stage. The difference between *A Streetcar Named Desire* and *Summer and Smoke* is not, as an occasional critic has suggested, between a melodramatic and a "subtle" presentation of the same action, but between a play that finds adequate expression for the conflicts between and within individuals and one that sidesteps such conflicts completely.

Williams achieves his most successful revelation of human nature in its totality in this play in which he distorts the realistic surface as little as possible and only when necessary. The audience accepts as believable the direct depiction of Blanche's fantasies because the necessary touchstone in recognizable reality is consistently maintained. John Gassner writes: "The solution of the esthetic crisis in the theatre depends on our knowing when and how to combine the resources of realistic and theatricalist artistry."[14] *A Streetcar Named Desire* reveals an unerring sense of when and how to combine realism and theatricalism.

NOTES

1 Elia Kazan, "Notebook for *A Streetcar Named Desire,"* in *Directors on Directing,* eds. by Toby Cole and Helen Chinoy (Indianapolis, 1963), p. 364.

2 Gerald Weales, *A Play and Its Parts* (New York, 1964), p. 118.

3 Kazan, p. 371.

4 Joseph N. Riddel, *"A Streetcar Named Desire*: Nietzsche Descending," *Modern Drama,* 5 (Spring, 1963), 426.

5 Weales, p. 106.

6 Harold Clurman, *The Divine Pastime* (New York, 1974), p. 12.

7 Kazan, p. 368.

8 Benjamin Nelson, *Tennessee Williams: The Man and His Work* (New York, 1961), p. 146.

9 Riddel, 425.

10 Clurman, p. 16

11 Irwin Shaw, "Masterpiece," *The New Republic,* 22 December 1947, 35.

12 The sympathetic bond between the audience and Stanley is not merely the result of Brando's interpretation of the character. Stanley has been played differently, notably by Anthony Quinn, who emphasized the brutality of the character. But even Eric Bentley, who preferred Quinn's performance to Brando's, remarks

on the inconsistency that occasionally arose between the text and the interpretation by Quinn (e.g., "When Anthony Quinn portrays Kowalski as an illiterate we are surprised at some of the big words he uses"). He also concedes: "In all fairness, I should admit that when I directed the play myself I could not stop the audience's laughing *with* Kowalski *against* Blanche." *In Search of Theater* (New York, 1947), p. 88.

13 Henry Taylor, "The Dilemma of Tennessee Williams," *Masses and Mainstream,* I (April, 1948), p. 54.

14. John Gassner, *Directions in Modern Theatre and Drama* (New York, 1956), p. 138.

The Grotesque Children of *The Rose Tattoo*

LELAND STARNES

That realism should be the convention fundamental to the work of Tennessee Williams is altogether logical. Until his late adolescence, Williams had little opportunity to see any form of theater other than the American cinema, and this form, of course, is firmly grounded in the realistic approach. Even the external shape of Williams's theater shows especially clear evidence of this cinematic influence:[1] a succession of episodes, "fade-outs" and "fade-ins," background music, gauze scrims, and expressive lights focussed to simulate "close-ups" – all devices immediately recognizable as film technique, itself a more poetic kind of realism.

Often clearly aspiring to the conditions of poetry, Williams creates for himself an advantage which is not always available to other dramatists who start from the realistic or naturalistic base: like Synge and O'Casey, he puts his words into the mouths of an essentially imaginative people who speak in the rhythms and colorful imagery of a region favorable to poetry. Even more to the point for our present subject, by staging his dramas in a realm just so much apart from "average" American life as the deep South and by having his characters speak in the distinctive language of that realm apart, Williams succeeds in distancing his plays from the purely realistic mode to a degree sufficient to justify and disguise a certain characteristic exaggeration and distortion of reality which permeates his entire canon. Under the speech of most of his characters there runs the faint but unmistakable thorough-bass of grotesque folk comedy. The tone provided by this suggestion of the comic folk tale varies according to Williams's intention, and, accordingly, the success of its effect depends upon the amount of distance he would have us put between the characters and ourselves.

Williams's opening scene in *Orpheus Descending,* for example, is an excellent study of his use of regional elements for these ends; we have only to examine the craftsmanship in this Prologue to an imperfect play to perceive how ingeniously (and how meticulously) this restless perfectionist has always gone about the business of constructing the artistic reality he thought indispensable to the coming to life of his vividly theatrical people.

> The set represents in non-realistic fashion a general dry-goods store and part of a connecting 'confectionery' in a small Southern town. ... Merchandise is represented very sparsely and it is not realistic. ... But the confectionery, which is seen partly through a wide arched door, is shadowy and poetic as some inner dimension of the play.[2]

Then immediately, before this nonrealistic background, we hear language of such color that we realize the realm in which our action will take place is indeed very much apart.

> DOLLY Pee Wee!
> BEULAH Dawg!
> DOLLY Cannonball is comin' into th' depot!
> BEULAH You all git down to th' depot an' meet that train! (p. 4)

Pee Wee and Dog, "heavy, red-faced men," verify the initial comic impression with a gag line as they "slouch through ... in clothes that are too tight for them ... and mud-stained boots."

> PEE WEE I fed that one-armed bandit a hunnerd nickels an' it coughed up five.
> DOG Must have hed indigestion. (p. 4)

As Pee Wee and Dog go out the door, Beulah begins the play's exposition:

> I wint to see Dr. Johnny about Dawg's condition. Dawg's got sugar in his urine again, an as I was leavin' I ast him what was the facks about Jabe Torrance's operation in Mimphis. (p. 4)

When a few lines later Beulah begins her monologue, which "should be treated frankly as exposition," Williams says, "spoken to audience ... she comes straight out to the proscenium, like a pitchman. This monologue should set the nonrealistic key for the whole production" (p. 6). The exposition is thus delivered in the idiom of folk comedy and takes advantage of the comedic possibilities in its theatricalist style. Beulah first describes with grim relish the circumstances of Papa Romano's death; as she expounds at some length upon her convictions concerning the faithlessness of most marriages, her manner is that of back-fence gossip. But as she thus prepares a mordantly ironic background for our first view of Lady and Jabe Torrance, the tone of the scene modulates from what at first appeared to be cracker-barrel comedy to the extreme grotesque.

BEULAH Then one of them – gits – *cincer* or has a – stroke or somethin'? – The other one –
DOLLY – Hauls in the loot? (p. 10)

The comic grotesquery of these women is obviously essential to Williams's initial exposition of both characters and situation. As a kind of comic chorus, they provide not only environmental context in terms of which we are to interpret events, but, in their comic hypocrisy, an objective view of both the appearance and the reality of the principal characters and their predicament as well. When Jabe Torrance, mortally ill with cancer, returns from the hospital they greet him with mendacity the ironic significance of which the audience immediately perceives.

BEULAH I don't think he's been sick. I think he's been to Miami. Look at that wonderful color in his face.
DOLLY I never seen him look better in my life!
BEULAH Who does he think he's foolin'? Ha ha ha! – not *me*! (p. 23)

There are two groups of women, and two women in each group. Williams even arranges their lines so as to verify the comic effect he intends us to see in this visual repetition by having them echo each other's words in almost music-hall style.

BEULAH Lady, I don't suppose you feel much like talking about it right now but Dog and me are so worried.
DOLLY Pee Wee and me are worried sick about it.
LADY – About what?
BEULAH Jabe's operation in Memphis. Was it successful?
DOLLY Wasn't it successful? ...
SISTER Was it too late for surgical interference?
EVA Wasn't it successful?
BEULAH Somebody told us it had gone past the knife.
DOLLY We do hope it ain't hopeless.
EVA We hope and pray it ain't hopeless. (*All their faces wear faint, unconscious smiles.*) (pp. 25-26)

We are reminded of T.S. Eliot's similar handling of verbal repetition in *The Cocktail Party* when Julia tells the story of Lady Klootz and her son who could hear the cry of bats. But Williams's use of the device here, of course, is probably intended as comic suggestion of repetition as it is usually heard in the classic chorus.

It is obvious that Williams is nowadays more concerned than ever with this matter of distance between his characters and his audience. The recent unfortunate production of *Slapstick Tragedy* and Williams's own remarks about his intentions in that work indicate that he is in the process of experimentation and is therefore, we should hopefully say, in transition. Some critics have gone so far as to argue that *Slapstick Tragedy* should not have been given professional production. The two short plays are indeed more clearly akin to thumbnail sketches than to finished canvasses, and each has been written with baffling incompatibilities of content and style. But whatever the aesthetic shortcomings of this latest effort, we are forced to observe in *Slapstick Tragedy* that Williams again instinctively seeks the freedom from the strictures of photographic realism that grotesque comedy allows him, and his natural antic gifts have always been such that we should be encouraged to believe that it is within the realms of such comedy that he may eventually find the new mode he seeks. *The Rose Tattoo,* which was first produced in 1951, endures as a model of Williams's stylistic integrity, and it is appropriate that such a play should have been chosen for successful revival in the 1966-67 season at New York's City Center. In this surprisingly profound play, Williams of course again resorted to the creation of his own realm and to the writing of the language of that world, both of which provided aesthetic distance for the characters inhabiting that realm and explained or justified their exaggerated behavior. His context was the South again – the Gulf Coast between New Orleans and Mobile – and it was, moreover, an Italian community within that area. We were thus twice removed from "normal" reality, and Williams worked with extraordinary effectiveness within the self-imposed limitations of that reality.

In production, it would be unwise if not impossible to attempt to minimize the distancing effect that the national or regional characteristics of Williams's central characters should have upon an audience. This ethnic identity is manifestly Williams's keystone for the structure of his characters, and in *The Rose Tattoo* he stresses it repeatedly and purposefully in every scene of the play:

JACK Mrs. Delle Rose, I guess that Sicilians are emotional people ...[3]
BESSIE I'm a-scared of these Wops. (p. 42)
THE STREGA ... They ain't civilized, these Sicilians. In the old country they live in caves in the hills and the country's run by bandits. (p. 24)

Williams wants us to see clearly that he is writing about a special people with a special set of given circumstances: "they ain't civilized"; they are "wild," "emotional," "childlike," and they do everything "with all the heart." So it is, then, that our introduction to Serafina Delle Rose takes place in "an interior that is as colorful as a booth at a carnival." Indeed, we cannot avoid noticing the extreme and vivid uses of color; such Van Gogh audacities are apropos for the broader statement that Williams wants to make. Moreover, the set in which Serafina sits is scarcely more colorful than the lady herself. As vivid as a circus poster, she

looks like a plump little Italian opera singer in the role of Madame Butterfly. Her black hair is done in a high pompadour that glitters like wet coal. A rose is held in place by glittering jet hairpins. Her voluptuous figure is sheathed in pale rose silk. On her feet are dainty slippers with glittering buckles and French heels. ... She sits very erect, ... her ankles daintily crossed and her plump little hands holding a yellow paper fan on which is painted a rose. Jewels gleam on her fingers, her wrists and her ears and about her throat. (p. 2)

This, it scarcely need be said, is exaggeration. It is enthusiastic – and not actually terribly extreme – intensification of an already intense person for the purposes of vivid theatrical examination of her being. Quite obviously, the actress entrusted with the performance of such a role should have at least a working knowledge of the bigger, more "operatic" styles of acting and should not, as was unfortunately the case with Maureen Stapleton in both New York productions, be circumscribed by an earthbound naturalism which allows few if any glimpses of the theatrical size ultimately attainable in this characterization. While the Serafina Williams describes has not actually left the realm of naturalism, those characteristics which mark her individuality are stressed to just such a degree that they verge upon or actually become both theatricalist and comically grotesque; and by this preliminary visual presentation of the character and the realm she inhabits, we are alerted to expect the comic incongruity which ensues in her subsequent actions.

And so it is that our introduction to Alvaro Mangiacavallo, Serafina's thematic antagonist, is accomplished in a scene which borders upon farce and which makes heavy use of national characteristic for comedic effect. Alvaro, sobbing in pain and frustration because he has been kicked in the groin during a fight with an irate salesman, flees into the house to hide his shame, and Serafina, weeping in sympathy, offers to repair his torn jacket. The scene is audacious in its comedy – comedy which is, moreover, ingenious as expositional device – as the two characters continue a conversation which would probably be unexceptional if it were not for the fact that each of them is shaking with sobs. "Stop crying so I can stop crying," Serafina says. "I am a sissy," says Alvaro. "Excuse me. I am ashame" (p. 81). At some point in our laughter, however, it might occur to us to ask if perhaps the exaggeration of national or folk characteristic had not been carried to too great an extreme and whether we might have passed altogether into the realm of the stage Italian and from thence into mindless farce. The question, surely, is not as primly academic as might at first appear, as upon its answer depend our interpretation of this play and our evaluation of the spiritual worth of these persons. Critical reaction to the play at its first appearance in 1951 was such as to provide reason to conclude – at that time, at any rate – that Williams's work here was at least uneven or uncertain. For example, Margaret Marshall, reviewing the play in *The Nation,* said that "in the second act the serious mood quickly evaporates; and the proceedings descend into cheap farce which must be seen to be believed. The absurd and the vulgar contend for place. ..."[4] Kenneth Tynan, always a great admirer of Williams, found "the play's complex structure – short scenes linked by evocative snatches of music – too poetic for its theme,"[5] and George Jean Nathan simply said that the play was "sensational sex melodrama, pasted up with comedy relief. ..."[6] Such critics at that time, then, asked whether Williams had not indeed drawn his ironies and exaggerations with too bold a stroke in this play. They apparently assumed that to push the protagonist so far into comic or grotesque incongruity as to make this incongruity his or her dominant dramatic value was to risk making the character so childlike or of such an inferior level of sensibility as to become a target for the destructive laughter of superiority. A playwright of Williams's genre is limited by his protagonist's perception, they believed, and so, then, is the force of his play. *The Rose Tattoo* was thought by many at that time to be a less significant play – "just a comedy" – because Williams had resorted to farcical exaggeration which all but destroyed any serious thematic intent. Some writers went so far as to deny the probability of any really new or valuable insights into the condition of human suffering in the "vulgar farce" of "child-minded Sicilians," and others questioned the likelihood that "the psychological aberrations of the universe can be quickly settled on one big bed."[7] We can enjoy Serafina, they implied, and we can even sympathize with her on occasion, but we cannot see her as representative of anything significant in reality after having laughed at her shenanigans for three acts.

It is interesting and even a little amusing to compare such reactions with those of the writers who received the play with surprised enthusiasm when it was revived at City Center last season. Laughter which had in 1951 been deplored as destructive or emblematic of cheap farce was now seen to be either a mark of the play's timelessness or the work of a skillful director who had managed through perceptive reinterpretation to bring the play up to date. Walter Kerr decided that the play had "outwitted time. Outwitted 16 years, anyway, and likely to improve the score further."[8] Henry Hewes, writing for the *Saturday Review,* perhaps best exemplified this new vision of the play when he said that it "probably was not Mr. Williams's intention to write *The Rose*

Tattoo as a grotesque comedy, but that is what this new presentation seems, and that is why it appears not the least bit dated." Hewes said, moreover, that to emphasize the grotesquery, the director, Milton Katselas, concentrated on creating the "wild and irrational" surroundings for Williams's fable, and, as a result, "everything that happens is ironic – so that we laugh at the ridiculousness of the events at the same time that we recognize the characters' agonizedly sincere involvement in them."[9] And yet, in 1951, as Williams waited for his play to open at the Martin Beck Theatre, he had said, "I always thought of [*The Rose Tattoo*] as funny in a grotesque sort of way";[10] and in his famed Preface to the play[11] he had specified grotesquery or "a certain foolery" as the probable stylistic solution for the playwright who would satisfy the peculiar conditions laid down for him by his modern, skeptical audiences.

What Hewes and a surprising number of critics both in 1951 and in 1966 have failed to realize is that comedy is and always has been an essential part of the typical Williams drama. A certain amount of laughter may, or indeed *must*, be at the expense of the Williams protagonist, as it is clear that Williams has always meant us to see that even the noblest human being is often guilty of ridiculous incongruity and is thereby laughable. Most of the modern writers – certainly those of the so-called Absurdist genre – find that they have to reduce the protagonist (when there is one) to imperception in order to make the point they want to make. The concomitant feeling of superiority toward the protagonist in such case is, we recognize, a necessary part of Absurdist technique: we must be kept aloof and at a distance from the characters, because their actions and not the characters themselves are the important things, and our involvement with them as people would serve to establish the existence of values or of a coherence that the play was written to deny. But Williams does not typically concern himself with the faceless protagonist of Absurdist or surrealist farce.[12] In *The Rose Tattoo,* he clearly wanted to acknowledge and accept the limitations imposed upon him by characters of "instinctive" – rather than rational – sensibility, and to see this condition as altogether fundamental to his design. "Our purpose," he said, "is to show these gaudy, childlike mysteries with sentiment and humor in equal measure ..." (p. xiv). In any but the most superficial reading of *The Rose Tattoo,* one cannot help but be struck with the frequency of references concerning the childlike qualities of these characters, and most particularly of Serafina and Alvaro. "Their fumbling communication," Williams says, "has a curious intimacy and sweetness, like the meeting of two lonely children for the first time" (p. 88). Serafina, having climbed upon a chair to reach a bottle of wine, "finds it impossible to descend ... Clasping the bottle to her breast, she crouches there, helplessly whimpering like a child" (p. 83). The acceptance of the childlike characterstics of Williams's characters is not only fundamental to their proper interpretation and performance, but leads as well – almost syllogistically – to comprehension of the symbolism of the play, and from thence, as in any poetic work of integrity, back again to even deeper understanding of the characters. Having once conceded that most of Williams's Romantic symbolism is appropriately akin to association psychology one finds the logic of this statement somewhat nearer to hand.

Thus, by way of penetrating Williams's almost Wordsworthian concept of the importance of the childlike element in Serafina and Alvaro, it is, strangely enough, most pertinent to consider first the significance that he would have us see in the Strega's black goat. Normally an easy "symbol" of sexual desire, the goat makes a significant appearance to objectify Serafina's emotional situation at several pivotal points in the action – once, for example, when Rosario's mistress, Estelle Hohengarten, appears to order the silk shirt; again after Alvaro and Serafina have discovered their attraction for each other in Act II; and as an offstage bleat when Serafina makes her desperate assignation with Alvaro in Act III. The device as staged is grotesquely comic, and each time the goat escapes to run wild in Serafina's backyard the incident begins in farcical pandemonium and evolves finally into a ludicrous parody of a Bacchic procession, with a "little boy ... clapping together a pair of tin pan lids ... wild cries of children ... the goat's bleating ... and farther back follows the Strega ... her grey hair hanging into her face and her black skirts caught up in one hand, revealing bare feet and hairy legs" (pp. 98–99).

Having once established an aural connection between the goat and the "wild cries of children," Williams goes on to introduce these child sounds almost as choric amplification at subsequent points when something happens to stir Serafina's wild passion for Rosario. Alvaro unwraps the rose silk shirt, and the cries are heard again; Serafina suffers the desperate urge to smash the urn containing her husband's ashes as a little boy's cries parallel her excitement outside the window. And at the end of Act II when Serafina lifts her eyes to the sky and begs the dead Rosario's forgiveness for believing the "lie" about his infidelity, "a little boy races into the yard holding triumphantly aloft a great golden bunch of bananas. A little girl pursues him with shrill cries. He eludes her. ... The curtain falls" (p. 101).

Obviously then, the connection between children and goat is more than merely aural. For Williams, their significance is reciprocal and complementary; they are altogether thematic, and as lyrical devices they symbolize or objectify in tangible form both "lyric and Bacchantic impulses" which Williams sees embodied in their purest crystalline state in his Sicilians. *The Rose Tattoo*, he said,

is the Dionysian element in human life, its mystery, its beauty, its significance. ... Although the goat is one of its most immemorial symbols, it must not be confused with mere sexuality. The element is higher and more distilled than that. Its purest form is probably manifested by children and birds in their rhapsodic moments of light and play

... it is the limitless world of the dream. It is the fruit of the vine that takes earth, sun, and air and distills them into juices that deprive men not of reason but of a different thing called prudence.[13]

Serafina and Alvaro are Italian, and, for Williams, "the Italians [reveal] a different side of human nature than any I [have] ever known. I think Italians are like our Southerners without their inhibitions. They're poetic, but they don't have any Protestant repressions. Or if they do have any, their vitality is so strong, it crashes through them. They live from the heat."[14]

It follows, then, that Williams's portraits of these Sicilians – and particularly that of Serafina – will reveal them as vivid embodiments of these impulses. These are Serafina's special set of given circumstances; she is at the outset, like Williams's Southerner, a more intense person than most, a creature from a realm apart. And, again like Williams's Southerner, being thus unique, she excites Williams with motivation and material for the creation of another intensely theatrical person. As almost pure distillation of those elements of human character most meaningful to Williams she will necessitate from him a bolder stroke of the brush, a more daring use of color, a stronger contrast of light and shade – or, to vary J.L. Styan's metaphor, a wider swing of the pendulum of dramatic balance on both sides of the neutral reality.[15] And as crystallization of those grotesque human characteristics more typically instinctive than rational, more visceral than cerebral, and more childlike than mature, she will inevitably commit certain of the comic incongruities usually attributed to children and will be "criticized" accordingly by the corrective laughter of her "civilized" audiences. Our laughter at Serafina, then, is as Williams would have it: in our very act of laughing we are to verify her freedom from "prudence," "empiric evidence," and "civilization." In the first few pages of the play, this Dionysian freedom is acknowledged immediately as we sense her gusty vitality and her intensely sexual devotion to her husband; we perceive that she is aware of life, that she reaffirms life and rejoices in it, and in so doing she prepares us for laughter that is free and full. Then, as we, the audience, realize that we see a reality above and beyond her limited or childish conception of it, we naturally react to her at first in much the same way that we respond to persons we recognize as being of inferior sensibility; as we realize that she in effect inhabits a world that is out of step or incongruous with "the everyday man's" reality, we criticize her with the laughter of superiority and consider her as by definition comic. Henri Bergson would probably have described her behavior as "mechanical" as she ignores or is unable to recognize fact as it appears before her but rather chooses to continue to act upon the conventions and maxims peculiar to her world, even as they are disproved or denied:

JACK It is a hard thing to say. But I am – also a – virgin. ...

SERAFINA *What? No.* I do not believe it.
JACK Well, it's true though. ...
SERAFINA You? A sailor? (p. 57)

SERAFINA What are you? Catholic?
JACK Me? Yes, ma'am, Catholic.
SERAFINA You don't look Catholic to me! (pp. 58–59)

And, of course, Serafina's vehement condemnation of her daughter's passion for the young sailor is in ironic – and laughable – contrast to her own concern with sexuality. We soon realize, of course, that this comes about because of the fact that in her own world of intense sexuality she is led to see the same exaggeration in her daughter's world, and she in effect flails out at chimeras which are largely of her own making. Moreover, the incongruous contrast between the enormity of the effort she expends and the size of the problem with which she is dealing – what Freud would term the "quantitative contrast" – causes her to be seen as a grotesquely comic character. Thus, in her eyes, no sailor, regardless of how young, can be innocent; tight trousers must inevitably signify sexual license; a spring dance at a high school is manifestly given for purposes of sensual indulgence; and a school picnic chaperoned by teachers becomes a maenadic orgy: "The man-crazy old-maid teachers! – They all run wild on the island!" (p. 71). So Serafina forces the young man to pledge chastity while kneeling before the shrine to the Virgin – a shrine which she herself has dedicated to sexual love.

The scene at the beginning of Act III in which we see Serafina struggling frantically, "with much grunting," to get the girdle from around her knees before Alvaro arrives is almost pure vaudeville; by Joseph Wood Krutch's definition, our protagonist is here reduced to the status of a clown. Speaking of the typical farcical character, Krutch says that "the climax of our amusement coincides with the climax of his discomfort, or worse. The chief personages in farce usually are – or are put in a situation where they seem to be – clowns. And a clown is a butt, or victim. In high comedy we usually are laughing at ourselves; in farce, at somebody else."[16] But more to the point of our present discussion – in allowing us this glimpse of Serafina, Williams achieves another of his bold critical strokes whereby we are made to scrutinize the protagonist from the objective viewpoint that such grotesque comedy provides.

But to make endless catalogue of Serafina's comic incongruities would profit us but little; most of them could be analyzed, if analysis were needed, by reference to the "quantitative contrast" idea, or some version thereof, and to the Freudian "release of inhibitive energy." In any event, the resulting laughter is gratifying to Williams, as it is in all senses Dionysian. However, the essential fact concerning this laughter has yet to be said. It is simply that having criticized Serafina to such an extent and from such a superior vantage point, we end by retaining a clear image of her dignity and worth: she remains, when all is said and done, a person of some stature and significance. Of course, it must be said that it is altogether indicative of Williams's success in this play that we are able to say of Serafina, after having laughed long and loudly at her, that we recognize her genuine and sizable capacity for love, and that it is in very point of fact this same extraordinary characteristic which is the significant element in her downfall. It is, in a sense, her *hamartia*, her tragic flaw.

In recognizing Serafina's special stature in this respect, we perceive in her being a universal in which we all share, and we sympathize. Even as we are led to laughter by Serafina's extremities of behavior in her loss of control after Rosario's death –

[Rosa] crouches and covers her face in shame as Serafina heedlessly plunges out into the front yard in her shocking déshabille, making wild gestures. ... As Serafina paces about, she swings her hips in the exaggeratedly belligerent style of a parading matador. (pp. 28–29)

– we recognize an extremity which is as peculiar to tragedy as it is to comedy. Even as we are made to laugh by the incongruity of her actions – or, as by them we see our own standards of "normal," adult reality reaffirmed – we see the intensity of the grief which alone could cause such behavior; in our very act of laughing we seem almost heartlessly – but how effectively – to verify the extent of this visceral being's feeling. Hers is a love and a grief so great they threaten her destruction; by this fact alone she suggests a greatness, and in that tragic flaw is centered the principal tension of *The Rose Tattoo*.

With Rosario's death, Serafina's predictable reaction was to attempt to continue her worship in as close an approximation to its former pattern as possible. In so doing, of course, she chose to continue in blind devotion to her dead husband and became a prisoner of her own self-deception. Instead of association with living beings, she chose the motionless dummies of the dressmaker; instead of love bestowed on the living, she chose adoration before the ashes of the dead; and instead of actuality and engagement in the present, she chose memory and nostalgia for the past. It is interesting, then, to note that in speaking thus of Serafina, we find her to be another of Williams's variations of the "weak, beautiful people who give up with such grace," and around whom he structures his every play. In terms of Williams's typical character deployment, Serafina is actually a direct descendent of Laura Wingfield in *The Glass Menagerie* and of Alma Winemiller in *Summer and Smoke*. But, on the other hand, like Blanche DuBois, she is an active protagonist rather than a passive, and to her in turn will come thematic antagonists – like Alvaro – who will contest her view of herself and who will thereby provide the means for a gradual, cumulative view of her character.

In our admission that Serafina's remarkable capacity for love triumphs over her more comedic aspects – or, rather, by having us concede that those very childlike characteristics which make her comic also give Serafina stature – Williams succeeds in having us reaffirm for him that fact about human relationships which is woven somehow into most of the work of this avowed Romanticist and which, however, phrased, expresses what remains for him man's closest approximation to a dependable absolute: the human being transcends his own pathetic insignificance only when he puts himself aside to love another person. In loving another, Williams would have us see in *The Rose Tattoo,* man most nearly succeeds in conquering the ultimate enemy of all significance, time. Before Rosario's death, Serafina says of her life with him:

Time doesn't pass. ... My clock is my heart and my heart don't say tick-tock, it says love-love! (p. 8)

At the end of Act I, however, after Rosario has been killed, Serafina winds her daughter's watch before her shrine, and glaring fiercely at the watch she pounds her chest three times and says:

Tick-tick-tick! ... Speak to me Lady!
Oh, Lady give me a sign! (p. 64)

With love gone from her life, time's passing and the transience of all meaning are now all she can see.

Then, at the end of the play, when Serafina has re-entered life through the discovery of new love with Alvaro,

she holds the watch to her ear again. She shakes it a little, then utters a faint, startled laugh. (p. 140)

Time has been arrested for her again, and Williams, the supreme Romanticist, would have us see the stopping of her daughter's watch as significant of Serafina's spiritual rebirth.

Love is itself unmoving,
Only the cause and end of movement,
Timeless. ...[17]

NOTES

1 See Esther Merle Jackson's excellent study of Williams's form in *The Broken World of Tennessee Williams* (Madison, 1965), pp. 37–42.

2 *Orpheus Descending* (New York: New Directions, 1958), p. 3. Subsequent quotations from this play will refer to this edition, and pagination will be given in the text.

3 *The Rose Tattoo* (New York: New Directions, 1951), p. 60. Subsequent references to *The Rose Tattoo* will pertain to this edition, and pagination will be indicated in the text.

4 "Drama," *The Nation*, CLXII (February 17, 1951), 161–162.

5 *Curtains* (New York, 1961), p. 264.

6 *Theatre Book of the Year, 1950–51* (New York, 1951), p. 211.

7 Walter Kerr, "Theatre," *The Commonweal*, LIII (February 23, 1951), 493.

8 "A 'Rose' Flowers Anew," New York *Times*, November 20, 1966, Sec. 2, p. 31.

9 "Theater – Off the Leash," *Saturday Review* (November 26, 1966), 60.

10 Quoted in Vernon Rice, "Tennessee Williams Writes a Comedy," New York *Post* (February 1, 1951), 36.

11 "The Timeless World of a Play," pp. vi–xi, esp. p. x.

12 It is true, of course, that character was not uppermost in Williams's methodology in *Camino Real*, but even in this extraordinary play he depended upon it for some of his most startling scenes. In the "Gnädiges Fräulein" of *Slapstick Tragedy*, his title character vacillates confusingly between surrealism and naturalism and at last founders in ineffectuality for lack of definition; we have the frustrating impression, therefore, of a potentially exciting concept that might have worked but which was either carried too far or not far enough. The explanation in this case, I suggest again, lies in Williams's present and hopefully transient uncertainty concerning point of view and subject matter in his work.

13 "Tennessee Williams Explains His ... Comedy, 'The Rose Tattoo,'" *Vogue* (March 15, 1951), 96.

14 Williams, quoted in Rice.

15 *The Dark Comedy* (Cambridge, England, 1962), p. 85.

16 "The Fundamentals of Farce," *Theatre Arts*, XL (July 1956), 92.

17 T.S. Eliot, "Burnt Norton," *Collected Poems* (New York, 1936), p. 220.

Part Two

Arthur Miller
1915–

All My Sons and the Larger Context

BARRY GROSS

Arthur Miller has always maintained that his plays have not been immediately understood, that *After the Fall* was not about Marilyn Monroe and *Incident at Vichy* was not about anti-Semitism, that *A View from the Bridge* was not about longshoremen and *The Crucible* was not about McCarthyism, that *Death of a Salesman* was not about the business world and *All My Sons* was not about war-profiteering. What, then, twenty-five years later, is *All My Sons* about?

In 1947 the generation gap was not the cliché it has since become and *All My Sons* is certainly, on one level, about that. Joe Keller is almost twice his son Chris's age. He is an "uneducated man for whom there is still wonder in many commonly known things," for instance, that new books are published every week or that a man can earn "a living out of ... old dictionaries." He is the product of a vanished America, of a time when "either you were a lawyer, or a doctor, or you worked in a shop," a time of limited possibilities for someone "put ... out at ten" to "earn his keep," for someone who learned English in "one year of night-school" and still does not know what "roué" means or that it is French, still says "brooch" when he means "broach."

We can only guess at Joe Keller's history because the kind of play Miller had in mind would, of necessity, exclude it. *All My Sons* was to be a "jurisprudence," and, as Miller says in the introduction to *Collected Plays,*

when a criminal is arraigned ... it is the prosecutor's job to symbolize his behavior for the jury so that the man's entire life can be characterized in one way and not in another. The prosecutor does not mention the accused as a dog lover, a good husband and father, a sufferer from eczema, or a man with a habit of chewing tobacco on the left and not the right side of his mouth.[1]

Well and good: Miller is entitled to establish the design for his own work and to be judged according to the terms he proposes. But the jury is also entitled to hear the defense, indeed must hear it if it is to reach a fair verdict, and Joe Keller's unrevealed history *is* his defense. "Where do you live, where do you come from?" Chris asks him, "Don't you have a country? Don't you live in the world? What the hell are you?" The answers lie buried in Joe Keller's past.

Is he an immigrant? The son of an immigrant? If he had to learn English in night-school, does that mean he grew up speaking German? Yiddish? These are not irrelevant questions if Joe Keller's crime is to be understood in human, rather than aberrational, terms, and it is clearly an important part of Miller's design that Keller's crime be seen as a profoundly human one. There are logical answers to Chris' questions; that Chris cannot imagine them is both result and proof of the generation gap that inevitably separates father and son. The gap can be defined by their differing perceptions of and attitudes toward the idea and the reality of community. Joe Keller is guilty of an anti-social crime not out of intent but out of ignorance; his is a crime of omission, not of commission. For him there is no society, and there never has been one. It is not simply that Joe's "mind can see" only "as far as … the business" or that for Joe "the business" is "the world." Actually, he does not see as far as that and for him the world is smaller. Where does he live? He lives at home. Does he live in the world? No. Does he have a country? No. What the hell is he? Provider, bread-winner, husband and father. His world is bounded by the picket fence that encloses the suburban back yard in which the play takes place, his commitments and allegiances do not extend beyond its boundaries. He is an engaged man, but not to man or to men, only to his family, more precisely to his sons, not all the sons of the title but the two sons he has fathered.

"In my day," Joe Keller says wistfully, "when you had a son it was an honor." What else "did [he] work for"? That is not an excuse but it is an explanation. It is not that Joe Keller cannot distinguish between right and wrong, it is that his understanding of what is right and what is wrong has been ineluctably determined by the only reality he has ever known. When he advises Ann not to hate her father he begs her to "see it human," and if we fail to see Joe Keller human then we relegate him to that dark other-world where only monsters dwell, safely removed from the world in which we think we live so we do not have to identify with it or admit our own compliance in it. What is right in Joe Keller's ethos – and it *is* an ethos – is the familial obligation, the father's duty to create something for his son. He is not proud of being a self-made man or of his material success, he is proud that he has made something for his son. There is no zealot like a convert and there is probably no more devoted parent than a neglected or an abandoned child. We know that Willy Loman was abandoned by his father when he was an infant, and that goes far to explain his passionate involvement in his sons' lives. If Joe's father turned him out at age ten, it is not surprising that his first article of faith should be "a father is a father and a son is a son." Impossible as it may be for Chris to understand or appreciate the fact, Joe was keeping that faith when he shipped out the faulty plane parts: "I did it for you, it was a chance and I took it for you. I'm sixty-one years old, when would I have another chance to make something for you? ... For you, a business for you!" Misguided, yes; malevolent, no, no more so, in intent, than Willy Loman's suicide, Willy's refusal to die empty-handed, Willy's commitment to the paternal obligation as he understands it, Willy's need to express his love for his son in the only way he knows how. Joe "didn't want [the money] that way" any more than Willy wanted it the way he chose, but he had "a family" and for Joe "nothin' is bigger ... than the family": "There's nothin' he could do that I wouldn't forgive. Because he's my son. Because I'm his father and he's my son. ... Nothin's bigger than that. ... I'm his father and he's my son." There is literally no other frame of reference. It is not only that "a man can't be a Jesus in this world," it is that, to Joe, Jesus is irrelevant. Jesus was never a father.

As a change of heart and a change of mind the denouement is, thus, unconvincing. Joe promises to "put a bullet in [his] head ... if there's something bigger" than family, he reads Larry's letter, agrees that "they were ... all [his] sons," and shoots himself. Joe Keller has not overthrown sixty years of thinking and feeling in a minute. Like Willy Loman, he goes to his death deluded, dies in the name of his delusion, dies a believer. He knows only that his sons think there is something bigger than family, that he has shamed them, one to the point of suicide, that his sons for whom he has lived consider him an animal and do not want to live in the same world with him. Joe's suicide is less a moral judgment than an act of love. In effect, Joe kills himself so that Chris need not kill *him*self – Chris: "What must I do?" – and because Chris tells him to – Chris: "Now you tell me what you must do." Joe commits his second anti-social crime in the name of the same love that motivated the first.

For Joe Keller there is no conflict beyond the fact that time has passed and values have, at least according to his sons, changed. The conflict in the play is Chris Keller's, not so much between him and his father, or between his generation's and his father's but within his own generation, within himself. Chris's is the conflict between who and what he is and who and what he wants to be, or thinks he ought to be. He wants to be, or thinks he ought to be, different from his father. Watching his comrades die for each other and for him, he has become aware of "a kind of – responsibility, man to man." Upon returning from the war, he had thought "to bring that on to the earth again like some kind of a monument and everyone would feel it standing there, behind him, and it would make a differenc to him." He knows that if he is alive at all "to open the bank-book, to drive the new car, to see the new refrigerator," it is because of the love a man can have for man." Yet when Chris returns home he finds "no meaning in it here," finds that "nobody ... changed at all."

So Chris knows things his father cannot know, and yet he remains his father's son. He will spend his life in a business that "doesn't inspire" him for more than "an hour a day," he will "grub for money all day long," if it can be "beautiful" when he comes home in the evening. The only monument he can think to build is precisely the one his father has constructed: "I want a family. I want some kids, I want to build something I can give myself to. ... Oh, Annie, Annie, I'm going to make a fortune for you!" In this light, it is not fair for Chris to make other people feel guilty for their "compromises" or for their inability or unwillingness "to be better than it's possible to be." Chris makes no visible efforts to be better than it is possible to be, or even to be as good as it is possible to be. Sue's branding of Chris as hypocrite – "if Chris wants people to put on the hair-shirt let him take off his broadcloth" – is valid. His shame and guilt are meaningless because they do not lead to action. Society's case against Chris Keller is stronger than its case against Joe Keller because Chris knows better. His tendency is to embroider what he obviously thinks of as an unacceptable reality – Ann: "As soon as you get to know somebody you find a distinction for them" – rather than to attempt to transform that reality into something different, something better.

Chris's self-proclaimed love for his parents is also suspect. "You're the only one I know who loves his parents," Ann exclaims, to which he replies with some self-congratulation, "I know. It went out of style, didn't it?" He thinks his father is "a great guy," he promises his mother he will "protect" them against George's attacks – but Chris's devotion to his father is based on his assumption that "the man is innocent." He could not love a guilty father, not out of moral fastidiousness but out of self-love. If, as George says, Chris has lied to himself about his father's guilt, it is more to deny what he himself is than what his father is. When Biff Loman stumbles and weeps when he discovers at age seventeen that his father is not the god he thought him, we understand that an adolescent has made a painful but inevitable discovery. When Chris Keller, who has been "a killer" in the war, does the same thing at thirty-two, we must conclude that he is responding to some private drama unwinding inside him rather than to the revelation of his father's guilt. Even his mother is surprised that it is "such a shock" to him; she "always had a feeling that in the back of his head ... Chris almost knew." Jim insists that Chris could not have known because he "would never know how to live with a thing like that," but Jim idolizes Chris, though we never see why, and his testimony is not reliable. Chris has not allowed himself to admit what he knew *because* he would not know how to live with it. Chris will come back, Jim tells Kate, he will make the necessary compromise; he has gone off so he can "be alone to watch ... the star of [his] honesty ... go out." The star Chris has gone out to watch flicker and die is not the star of his honesty but the star of his image of himself as honest, not the fact of his innocence but the lie of his innocence which he has persisted in believing. It is not that he *will* compromise himself, it is that he *has* compromised himself, and now he can no longer deny it.

When Chris returns from his vigil he admits that he "suspected his father and ... did nothing about it," less in the name of love of father, we suspect, than of love of self. Like his brother Larry, Chris could not imagine himself such a man's son, he would not be able to "face anybody" or himself. Joe Keller's sin, it would seem, is not so much that he profited from the war or sold faulty plane parts to the government or indirectly caused the death of twenty-one men, but that, in revealing himself to be no better "than most men," he "broke his son's heart." For Chris "thought" he *was* "better," that distinction he must assign those he knows: "I never saw you as a man. I saw you as my father. I can't look at you this way. I can't look at myself!" An unwittingly illuminating admission: he cannot look at his father as no better than most *because* he cannot look at himself as no better than most, he has never seen his father as a man because he has not wanted to see himself as one. In Act One Sue makes a remark about how uncomfortable it is living next door to the Holy Family and now we know what she means: as long as Joe (Jehovah?) is The Father, Chris (Christ?) is surely the son, by definition. What Chris cannot forgive Joe for is that, by his crime, the father has robbed the son of his "distinction." Chris laments that he is "like everyone else now," meaning he is "practical now" like "the cats in the alley" and "the bums who ran away when we were fighting," meaning he is not "human any more." But the converse is true: he is now and finally human *because* he must admit he is like everybody else. If "only the dead ones weren't practical" Chris has always been practical but has never admitted it. Quentin reaches the same conclusion in *After the Fall*: no one who did not die in the concentration camps, he says, can ever be innocent again. As a survivor, Chris will have to learn to live with his "practicality," which is his loss of innocence, which is his humanity.

We do not see this happen. Chris is allowed to have Miller's final words and to point the moral of the play: "It's not enough ... to be sorry. ... You can be better! Once and for all you can know there's a universe of people outside and you're responsible to it." Fine words, but their validity is undercut by our knowledge that Chris no more lives in that world outside than his father does, and his father has, at least, always known where he has lived. Similarly, Chris' criticism of America – "This is the land of the great big dogs, you don't love a man here, you eat him. That's the principle; the only one we live by. ... This is a zoo, a zoo!" – is compromised by his own inability to put the great principle he presumably learned in the war into practice and his own inability to love. However narrowly his values are circumscribed by the family circle, Joe does love, Joe does live by another and better principle, one he is even willing to die for. The gunshot with which Joe ends his life casts Chris's fine words into a silent void because we know that, behind them, Chris is incapable of the commitment and love his father's suicide represents. Not only is Chris incapable of fulfilling his responsibility to the universe of people out there, he is even incapable of assuming his responsibility for the few people in here, in the enclosed back yard: his last words in the play are "Mother, I didn't mean to – ." But he did, and that, too, Chris will have to learn to live with.

The Arthur Miller who wrote *All My Sons,* Miller told Josh Greenfield in a 1972 interview for the *New York Times Sunday Magazine,* thought of "writing as legislating, as though the world was to be ordered by the implications in [his] work."[2] He thought then, he says in the introduction to *Collected Plays,* of each member of his audience as "carrying about with him what he thinks is an anxiety, or a hope, or a preoccupation which is his alone and isolates him from mankind," and of the play as the antidote to that condition, as "an experience which widens his awareness of connection," which reveals "him to himself so that he may touch others by virtue of the revelation of his mutuality with them."[3] He thought all serious plays had that function, but especially *All My Sons,* in which he meant to lay "siege" to the specific "fortress of unrelatedness," in which he meant to arraign a particularly heinous anti-social crime, Joe Keller's failure to acknowledge "any viable connection with his world, his universe, or his society."[4] His ultimate goal in the play was to suggest a new order, "the right way to live so that the world is a home and not a battleground or a fog in which disembodied spirits pass each other in an endless twilight."[5]

But it is precisely in Miller's own terms, it is precisely as legislation, that *All My Sons* fails, fails where, oddly enough, *Death of a Salesman,* a far less obviously "legislative" work, succeeds. The similarities between *All My Sons* and *Death of a Salesman* are sufficiently obvious to render their elucidation unnecessary, but something should be said about the basic difference between them. *Death of a Salesman,* Miller says in the *Collected Plays* introduction, grew from "simple" but specific "images":

From a little frame house on a street of little frame houses, which had once been loud with the noise of growing boys, and then was empty and silent and finally occupied by strangers. Strangers who could not know with what conquistadorial joy Willy and his boys once re-shingled the roof. Now it was quiet in the house, and the wrong people in the beds.

It grew from images of futility – the cavernous Sunday afternoons polishing the car. Where is that car now? And the chamois cloths carefully washed and put up to dry, where are the chamois cloths?

And the endless, convoluted discussions, wonderments, arguments, belittlements, encouragements, fiery resolutions, abdications, returns, partings, voyages out and voyages back, tremendous opportunities and small, squeaking denouements – and all in the kitchen now occupied by strangers who cannot hear what the walls are saying.

The image of aging and so many of your friends already gone and strangers in the seats of the mighty who do not know you or your triumphs or your incredible value.

The image of the son's hard, public eye upon you, no longer swept by your myth, no longer rousable from his separateness, no longer knowing you have lived for him and have wept for him.

The image of ferocity when love has turned to something else and yet is there, is somewhere in the room if one could only find it.

The image of people turning into strangers who only evaluate one another.

Above all, the image of a need greater than hunger or sex or thirst, a need to leave a thumbprint somewhere on the world.[6]

In short, *Death of a Salesman* is dominated and conditioned by the father's point of view, and *All My Sons* is one of those plays Miller derides in "The Shadow of the Gods" as being dominated by "the viewpoint of the adolescent," one of those predictable plays "in which a young person, usually male, usually sensitive, is driven either to self-destructive revolt or impotency by the insensitivity of his parents, usually the father."[7] As such, *All My Sons* bears less of a resemblance to *Death of a Salesman* than it does to *Cat on a Hot Tin Roof*, or, rather, to Miller's reading of Williams's play:

Essentially it is ... seen from the viewpoint of the son. He is a lonely young man sensitized to injustice. And his is a world whose human figures partake in various ways of grossness. ... In contrast, Brick conceives of his friendship with his dead friend as an idealistic, even gallant and valorous and somehow elevated one. ... He clings to this image as to a banner of purity to flaunt against the world.[8]

For Brick, read Chris; for Brick's dead friend, read Chris's dead comrades-in-arms. But Miller insists that *Cat on a Hot Tin Roof* ultimately fails, not because of the adolescent viewpoint, which "is precious because it is revolutionary and insists upon justice," but because Williams fails "to open up ultimate causes," because the father should have been "forced to the wall in justification of his world" and the son should have been "forced to his wall in justification of his condemning that world," because the father should not have been portrayed as "the source of injustice" but as "its deputy," not as "the final authority" but as "the shadow of the gods."[9] As he told the *Paris Review* interviewers, Williams, in emphasizing "the mendacity of human relations. ... bypasses the issue which the play seems ... to raise, namely the mendacity in social relations."[10] No play that ignores social relations, Miller argues in "The Family in Modern Drama," can achieve what he considers to be the goal and justification of drama, an "ultimate relevancy to the survival of the race," because, as he insists must be "obvious to any intelligence, ... the fate of mankind is social."[11]

It is useful to keep Miller's criticisms of *Cat on a Hot Tin Roof* in mind as we turn to a consideration of the failures of *All My Sons*. Most notable is what might be termed its failure in mode, a serious flaw in methodology: simply and baldly stated, the play is too insistently "realistic" – which is, of course, what Miller meant it to be – to accommodate Chris's fine speeches or to give any weight or resonance to their words. In the narrow and pedestrian setting of the Keller back yard they announce themselves as speeches, in this mundane place the words ring loud and hollow. Miller himself provides the best analysis of this conflict of modes in "The Family in Modern Drama," in which he argues that "the force or pressure that makes for Realism, that even requires it, is the magnetic force of the family relation within the play, and the pressure which evolves in a genuine, unforced way the unrealistic modes is the social relation within the play."[12] The realistic mode is adequate to *All My Sons* as long as the play is dominated by the family relation; it is not adequate to the social relation Miller requires the play to represent, nor does Miller attempt to express that social relation in another, less realistic mode. The problem is clearly illustrated in the case of appropriate stage speech:

When one is speaking to one's family one uses a certain level of speech, a certain plain diction perhaps, a tone of voice, an inflection, suited to the intimacy of the occasion. But when one faces an audience ... it seems right and proper for him to reach for the well-turned phrase, even the poetic word, the aphorism, the metaphor.[13]

Chris's speeches fall flat because they violate our sense of suitability, our sense of context. They are made at the wrong time in the wrong place to the wrong people.

What Miller might have done is suggested by his discussion of how other playwrights have handled similar problems. Ibsen solved them by bursting "out of the realistic frame" altogether when he came to write *Peer Gynt,* leaving behind not only "the living room" but "the family context" as well, to allow Peer Gynt to confront "non-familial, openly social relations and forces."[14] *All My Sons* does not burst out of the living room, or, more precisely, the back yard, and yet Miller insists that his characters confront non-familial, openly social relations and forces which exist only beyond it. The result is that same tension Miller feels in *The Cocktail Party,* that "sense of ... being drawn in two opposite directions."[15] In Eliot's play, Miller argues, the tension is created by the language, or, rather, by "the natural unwillingness of our minds to give to the husband-wife relation – a family relation – the prerogatives of the poetic mode," whereas no such problem existed in Eliot's more successful *Murder in the Cathedral* which "had the unquestioned right to the poetic" because its situation was "social, the conflict of a human being with the world."[16] It is, of course, Miller's thematic and philosophic intention to draw us in two opposite directions in *All My Sons,* to dramatize the polar conflict between the familial and the social. But he fails to counter the natural unwillingness of our minds to give to the social relation the prerogatives of the prosaic mode. We grant *All My Sons* the unquestioned right to the prosaic as long as its situation is familial, but if the situation is also to be social, then Miller must extend his play to the poetic, not just in language but also in concept, as, he argues, Thornton Wilder does in *Our Town*:

The preoccupation of the entire play is … the town, the society, and not primarily this particular family – and every stylistic means used is to the end that the family foreground be kept in its place, merely as a foreground for the larger context behind and around it. … This larger context … is the bridge to the poetic for this play. Cut out the town and you will cut out the poetry.[17]

Miller's preoccupation in *All My Sons* is no less social than Wilder's, but the society never becomes the larger context it is in *Our Town*. In Miller's play the foreground the Keller family occupies looms too large, so large as to obliterate any other context which might or should be behind or around it.

The absence of the larger context does not represent a failure in technique alone – it also represents, and more unaccountably, a failure in content. Miller says in the introduction to *Collected Plays* that *All My Sons* is usually criticized for lack of subtlety, for being too insistently "moral" and too aggressively "straightforward,"[18] but I want to argue that, for its stated intentions, the play is not straightforward enough. During an interesting interview with Philip Gelb, published under the title of "Morality and Modern Drama," Miller recalls "a book by Thomas Mann about Moses in which … he portrays Moses as being a man bedevilled by the barbaric backwardness of a stubborn people and trying to improve them and raise up their sights," the Ten Commandments being Moses's "way of putting into capsule form what probably the most sensitive parts of the society were wishing would be stated," Moses's attempt to "pinpoint … things that were otherwise amorphous and without form."[19] That is no less, Miller would certainly agree, the writer's presumption and his function. In *All My Sons* Miller is not guilty of presuming to teach, or even of presuming to preach, but of not doing it with sufficient force and directness, of not pinpointing with sufficient sharpness Chris's amorphous and formless sentiments. *That* the world should be reordered is not at issue; *how* it should is.

"Where the son stands," Miller says in "The Shadow of the Gods," "is where the world should begin,"[20] but this does not happen in *All My Sons* anymore than it does in the "adolescent" plays Miller criticizes. It is undeniably true that "the struggle for mastery – for the freedom of manhood … as opposed to the servility of childhood – is the struggle not only to overthrow authority but to reconstitute it anew,"[21] but by this token Chris has achieved neither mastery nor manhood by the play's end. It might be argued that it is only after the play ends that Chris is equipped to make the world begin, to reconstitute authority anew, that is, only after he learns that his brother killed himself and watches his father do the same thing. If so, that is a high price in human life – to Miller, perhaps because he is not Christian, the highest price imaginable – to rouse Chris Keller to action. And, judging from Chris's past record, one cannot be sure that these two deaths will have that effect. The deaths of his comrades presented him with that opportunity before the play began and he has done nothing to reconstitute authority in their name. If we are to take Chris's stated sentiments about the men who died so that he might live seriously, then he is in the position at the beginning of *All My Sons* that Miller (in the *Sunday Times Magazine* article "Our Guilt for the World's Evil") sees the Jewish psychiatrist in at the end of *Incident at Vichy*: his is "the guilt of surviving his benefactors" and whether he is "a 'good' man for accepting his life in this way, or a 'bad' one, will depend on what he makes of his guilt, of his having survived."[22] By that criterion, Chris Keller is a bad man when *All My Sons* begins and he is no better when the play ends.

Am I arraigning Miller unfairly? Am I asking more of his play than it need do or is supposed to do? Is not Miller entitled to exclude Chris Keller's vision of the future as well as Joe Keller's past in order to pinpoint the particular crime Joe is being prosecuted for? I think not. Our full awareness of that crime and our willingness to convict him of it is based on our belief that a better world is not only preferable but possible, that it not only should be made but could be made. Joe Keller's failure to find a connection with the world is a crime only if there is a world to connect with and only if there is a way to connect with it. Chris's case would be strengthened if, for instance, he expressed himself in the terms in which Miller defines the meaningful rebellions of the sixties generation in "The War Between Young and Old":

When a man has spent the best years of his life punishing himself with work he hates, telling himself that in his sacrifice lie honor and decency, it is infuriating to confront young people who think it is stupid to waste a life doing hateful work. It is maddening to hear that work ought to be a pleasure, a creative thing rather than a punishment, and that there is no virtue in submission to the waste of one's precious life.[23]

These are, essentially, the terms, if not the immediate causes, of Biff Loman's rebellion. But Chris Keller does not have or propound a theory of work different from his father's: he will waste his precious life doing hateful work as long as he can have it beautiful in the evening when he comes home to wife and kids. As Miller admits in the introduction to *Collected Plays*, Chris does not "propose to liquidiate the business built in part on soldiers' blood; he will run it himself, but cleanly."[24] Perhaps: the only line in the play that allows for even this modest hope is Joe's remark that Chris gets upset about a two-cent overcharge.

Chris should not be at such a loss to know how to reconstitute authority anew. If, as he complains, nothing changed at home, and if, as he says, it is a moral imperative for those who have survived to return home to change things, he should know what kind of changes should be made and how they might be accomplished. Chris is, after all, a contemporary of Miller's; he grew up in the depression thirties, he is a member of the generation Miller describes in "The Bored and the Violent," a generation "contemptuous of the given order" which translated its contempt into social action – "joining demonstrations of the unemployed, pouring onto campuses to scream of some injustice by college administrations, and adopting to one degree or another a Socialist ideology."[25] It might be argued that the post-war forties was a different time altogether, that the Socialist ideology was not as attractive as it had been in the thirties. But Miller is his own best argument against such contentions: he certainly did not hesitate to involve himself in causes and programs which promised to alleviate social injustice. As he told the House Committee on Un-American Activities, he was not "a dupe" or "a child" but "an adult ... looking for the world that would be perfect."[26] an honorable and, to Miller's way of thinking, necessary search. As a child of the thirties he knew where to look – to that "old illusion" Miller pays tribute to in *In Russia*

which the great October Revolution raised before the world — that a government of and by the insulted and injured had finally risen on the earth, a society which had somehow abolished the motivations for immorality, the incarnation at long last of the human community.[27]

Miller translated the Russian idea into American terms in his radio play *That They May Win,* a modest playlet which achieves in fifteen minutes the larger context two hours of *All My Sons* fails to approximate and which suggests the direction *All My Sons* might have – and should have – taken. A soldier returns from the war to find his wife and child living in a slum and prices out of control. Like Chris, he was a killer in the war, he is "proud" that he "killed twenty-eight of the lowest dogs in the world," but unlike Chris he has learned from his experience: he has learned the efficacy of united action, and he is appalled by his wife's apparent apathy toward and helplessness before unfair conditions:

What's the matter with you? They knock you down; they walk all over you; you get up, brush yourself off and say it's workin' out great. What do you pay taxes for; what do you vote for? ... What do you do, just go around and let them take the money out of your pocket? Doesn't anybody say anything? What're they all, dumb? ... Write to Congress ... stand on the street corner ... go to the Mayor ... talk!

True, we are still in the back yard, the living room, the kitchen. But Miller even tackles and even solves that problem in this play, a contrived borrowing from Pirandello, but a solution nevertheless: a member of the audience begins to argue with the actors, others argue with him, and finally one man emerges as spokesman and makes the speech that the actors concede would have ended the "play" had they been allowed to continue, a speech much more acceptable coming from him than if "husband" had made it to "wife":

You got to *keep* fighting. The people can work it out. ... You don't seem to realize the power we got. ... Enough people together can do anything! ... Don't it stand to reason in a democracy? The big guys have organized to lobby for laws *they* want in Washington. What about the people waking up and doing the same thing? ... We the people gotta go into politics. ... You have to go to those Senators and Congressmen you elected and say, "Listen here, Mister! We're your boss and you have to work for us!"

Idealistic, to be sure, maybe even an illusion. But an ideal and an illusion worthy of and necessary to anyone – Chris or Miller – who believes in the even older ideal, the even greater illusion, that the world can be saved and that the individual can do something about saving it.

NOTES

1   "Introduction," *Arthur Miller's Collected Plays,* New York, 1957, p. 6.
2   Josh Greenfield, "Writing Plays is Absolutely Senseless, Arthur Miller Says, 'But I Love It. I Just Love It,'" *New York Times Magazine,* February 13, 1972, p. 38.
3   *Collected Plays,* p. 11.
4   *Ibid.,* p. 19.
5   *Ibid.,* p. 32.
6   *Ibid.,* p. 29.
7   Arthur Miller, "The Shadow of the Gods," *American Playwrights on Drama,* ed. Horst Frenz, New York, 1965, p. 144.
8   *Ibid.,* p. 148.
9   *Ibid.,* p. 150.
10 *Writers at Work, Third Series,* ed. George Plimpton, New York, 1969, p. 207.
11 Arthur Miller, "The Family in Modern Drama," *Modern Drama: Essays in Criticism,* ed. Travis Bogard and William I. Oliver, New York, 1965, p. 230.
12 *Ibid.,* p. 221.
13 *Ibid.,* p. 225.
14 *Ibid.,* pp. 221–222.
15 *Ibid.,* p. 226.
16 *Ibid.,* p. 226.
17 *Ibid.,* pp. 227–228.

18 *Collected Plays*, p. 22.

19 Arthur Miller, as interviewed by Philip Gelb, "Morality and Modern Drama," *Educational Theatre Journal*, 10, October 1958, p. 191.

20 "The Shadow of the Gods," p. 151.

21 *Ibid.*, p. 151.

22 Arthur Miller, "Our Guilt for the World's Evil," *New York Times Magazine*, January 3, 1965, p. 11.

23 Arthur Miller, "The War between Young and Old," *McCalls*, July 1970, p. 32.

24 *Collected Plays*, p. 37.

25 Arthur Miller, "The Bored and the Violent," *Harpers*, November 1962, p. 52.

26 *Thirty Years of Treason*, ed. Eric Bentley, New York, 1971, p. 824.

27 Arthur Miller, "In Russia," *Harpers*, September 1969, p. 45.

The Fall And After –
Arthur Miller's Confession*

C.W.E. BIGSBY

After the Fall probes deeper than Miller has attempted before in an attempt to penetrate to the very nature of man. In *All My Sons* and *Death of a Salesman* he was concerned with a society which had inverted its values and placed the importance of success in economic and social spheres above the necessity to establish real contact between human beings. In *After the Fall* he sees a concern with success as being merely one aspect of man's egotism – an egotism which leads him on to cruelty and in the name of innocence and truth to a dissociation from fellow man which is itself a source of guilt. Its theme is an extension of Biff's statement in *Death of a Salesman,* "I'm just what I am that's all." This statement of amoral existence is expressed here in terms which tend to remind one of Steinbeck's naturalism, " ... is there no treason but only man, unblameable as trees or cats or clouds?"[1] The "truth" which the play's protagonist, Quentin, discovers is the need to accept the inconsistency and violence of man and yet to renew love constantly in the face of this knowledge. He learns in the course of the play to accept the world he inhabits as a world seen after the Fall. Happiness, in so far as it is not the natural happiness of non-involvement, derives, he discovers, purely from this knowledge. "Is the knowing all? To know, and even happily, that we meet unblessed; not in some garden of wax fruit and painted trees, that lie of Eden, but after, after the Fall, after many, many deaths. Is the knowing all?" (p. 127) In this knowledge, to Miller, is implicit the end of fear and the beginning of new life.

In *After the Fall* Miller is attempting to come to terms with the fact of violence. That he is doing this in what has been called "the age of violence" is but a further indication of his sensitivity to contemporary problems which in themselves offer an entrée into the more basic study of man and the survival of the race. This he claims must always be the true subject of the committed dramatist. It has been hailed as a play stemming so directly from his personal experience as to constitute an affront both to good taste and to the generalized validity which he clearly claims for his drama. While it is true that a critic in full knowledge of the personal parallels might find it difficult to view the play with the requisite objectivity, it is also true to say that the difficulty is no greater than that which awaits the critic of a Hemingway or even a Lawrence. If *After the Fall* fails, then its failure does not lie in the intrusion of the personal, any more than it did in Strindberg's *The Father,* but rather in Miller's failure to transmute the personal into art.

The form of the play constitutes a return to the technique of *Death of a Salesman* – a technique which Miller has identified as that of a confession. *After the Fall* represents not merely the confession of an individual anxious to resolve the paradox of his life but also man's attempt to catalogue the sins of a generation in a search for comprehension.

Quentin, who has been twice married, is now considering a third marriage but feels a compulsive need to understand himself and the reasons for his past marital failures. He stands in a position where, looking back over his life, he sees clearly the irrelevance of his success. "His success as an attorney has crumbled in his hands as he sees only his own egotism and no wider goal beyond himself."[2] He is appalled by the potential for violence, particularly in personal relationships, which is constantly realized. He is horrified by his ability to hurt others. The play consists of his recollection of various incidents which taken together reveal this violence between individuals which derives out of the essential egotism of humanity.

Adam fell in learning to look at things in the light of his own consciousness. The first act of liberated man was to cover himself. The birth of knowledge was thus the birth of self-awareness and the fruit of this was egotism. It is this egotism, then, which Quentin discovers as the unifying element in the spectrum of individual and corporate violence and cruelty with which he is surrounded and in which he participates. He relives moments of his life which serve to highlight both this violence and the alienation which he had thought had guaranteed his innocence. Now he comes to believe that innocence is a myth and that continued insistence on it carries with it its own kind of guilt. He is oppressed, therefore, by an innocence which he comes to recognize as culpability. To turn one's back is not to escape evil: it is merely to become guilty through refusal to accept responsibility. In urging the necessity of man's accepting his guilt, however, Miller is in danger of arguing "we are all guilty; therefore, none of us are guilty."

Two main symbols provide the background for the examples of personal cruelty and love destroyed by egotism which abound in Quentin's past. These images, a tower of a German concentration camp and the Committee on Un-American Activities, are in their own way both personifications and public extensions of these personal failings – the one in a physical and the other in an intellectual sense. The symbols gain their particular effectiveness from the realization that both institutions derive their power from the ready complicity not only of the "innocents" who stand by and watch but also of the victims who succumb still naively believing in the folly of opposition and the virtue of inactivity. Miller uses both of these symbols but particularly that of the camp tower to highlight literally these individual acts and thus show that in essence they both have their genesis in the same source. When Quentin's mother, Rose, discovers that her husband has lost all of their money in a stock crash, all that she can think about is, "My *bonds*." Where human understanding is called for, all that she can do is callously to degrade her husband in front of his son. Quentin looks up at the tower and thus establishes the connection, which Miller is at pains to enforce, between public and private violence. The bond of love, which Quentin as their son had imagined to be between them, is shattered under stress, thus contributing to his own distrust of love as a force and to his awareness of the guilt with which an insistence on innocence can be invested. He recalls, too, another incident of personal violence and "treachery" when Lou, a friend of his, is degraded by his wife. Lou, having been arraigned by the Committee on Un-American Activities, wants to publish a book which he has written. His wife feels that this will only serve to draw attention to him once again, this time perhaps with more serious results. She exclaims bitterly that if he were thrown out of his academic job he would be incapable of doing any other work. When Lou protests, she cuts him down with contempt, "This is hardly the time for illusions" (p. 37). The generic connection between this and the other instances of cruelty is enforced by the instant recall of Rose's vicious denunciation of Ike and the lighting of the camp tower.

It is this easy and instant recourse to treachery between those who should be united by love which sets Quentin searching for the origin of cruelty in his own life. He realizes that at an early age he had been made an accomplice of his mother in her shame at her husband's lack of sophistication. The stress which had been laid on his learning to write well had stood as a reproach to his illiterate father. He realizes now that he had been used as a weapon to strike at Ike. He remembers, too, an occasion on which he was tricked into staying at home while the rest of the family went to the sea. He was thus introduced to the mechanics of treachery at an early age, and the older Quentin is the victim of his own youth just as Maggie is the result of her sexually repressed youth. Nevertheless, he is not content with assembling the evidences of cruelty but rather strives to understand its nature and come to terms with the fact of its existence. The paradox which he discovers is that "innocence" cannot be erected as a goal for which to struggle, as an opposing force to this treachery which is itself a negation of love. For innocence possesses its own guilt which stems out of a wish for non-involvement. In an attempt to remain "innocent" he had avoided Micky, another friend of his who had been called before the

Committee. "I had a feeling it was something like that. I guess I didn't want to know any more ... not to see, to be innocent" (p. 43). He realizes that this "treachery" stems directly from self-interest whether it be Micky himself who decides to "name names" in the sacred name of truth and in effect to secure his own peace of mind, or those who build the concentration camp conscious only of a relief that it was not they who would be killed there.

After the Fall is a revolt against the simplistic responses of the dramatists of the 30's and 40's to social questions not fully understood. The absolute answers of socialism and universal love were in fact treatments for the symptoms and not the disease. These cures require a belief in perfectible man — man who with the will may return to his pristine state and secure a balance in society whose justice must be assumed to represent the norm. If men will sink their sectional differences, will ignore the dictates of self-interest and destructive egotism, they suggested, then all may be for the best in the best of all possible worlds. The theater of the 30's, in fact, believed in the perfectibility of man. In saying that he does not, Miller is hardly seeking election as a great iconoclast. *After the Fall* like a *A Clearing in the Forest* (1957) by Arthur Laurents and later *Who's Afraid of Virginia Woolf?* (1962) is devoted to challenging the basic premise of the social theater. It declares that man is not perfectible and that the sooner he recognizes it the better. In an age of disillusionment and uncertainty absolutes hold persuasive attractiveness. While it is true that immediate economic and social evils could be cured by this sense of corporate strength, however, it is equally true that the same panaceas were of no use for the underlying problems – the self-interest and economic and social cruelty which dominated the scene and which had its origin, not in any specific social system but rather in the hearts of men. Miller is concerned firstly with identifying this fact and then with the necessity of facing it as a fact of existence. This is man after the Fall, imperfect, self-centred but with the capacity to renew love even in the face of his imperfection.

Love remains the one possible answer, but it is a love aware of its own limitations and prepared to admit to the fact of individual and corporate cruelty as an inescapable legacy of the Fall rather than an inbuilt fault of society at large. This is not pessimism. To Miller a genuine optimism lies in a future based on an understanding of the present. He is no longer content with a world picture which sees man as the victim of a hostile society. To Miller man is a victim of himself and even the word "victim" is incorrectly applied since it implies an innocence which is no longer real.

These were facts which he had seen through a glass darkly in his earlier plays but which he had not fully developed nor even, one suspects, fully understood. In *All My Sons* universal love was apparently proffered as the golden hope of the age and yet the cruel selfishness of his characters left the audience painfully aware of some ill-defined insufficiency in that hope. That the conclusion grew out of the persecuting egotism of those surrounding Joe Keller was clear, but that the real reason for his acceptance of them all as "his sons" lay in the fact of their community of guilt is never fully examined. He dies, we see, because he realized that his responsibility extends beyond the family to man in general. What the Miller of *After the Fall* would have examined was that Joe was recognizing his community with man purely because he was recognizing his guilt. His death, necessary to *All My Sons* with its insistence on absolutes which was the legacy of a war situation, would have been unnecessary to the later Miller. To him, as we see in *After the Fall* and the later *Incident at Vichy* (1965), the necessity to recognize one's partnership with fellow man, one's "complicity," is sufficient in itself. The fact of death thereafter becomes irrelevant – a theatricality of little importance. Like Hawthorne before him, he recognizes guilt as a part of man's humanity. There is a connection in fact between Hawthorne's uncomprehending innocents and an innocence which, to Miller, is nothing more than a refusal to admit to the fact of guilt.

In effect, Miller is surely concerned, in *After the Fall*, with tying up the ends left dangling by his earlier plays. As we have seen, *All My Sons* stresses the cruelty even of those who hold "the truth." Claiming the necessity of love, they had initiated a cruel probing which if it led Joe to an understanding of his life nevertheless had its genesis in the selfishness of those who initiated it. In *After the Fall* Miller seems to be searching for the origin of this cruelty which was not obviously motivated in the former play and with stressing the need to accept a guilt which, while clear in the case of Joe, was less so in the case of the other characters. Similarly, he examines in this play the hollowness of success – a hollowness which many did not derive from such characters as Charley and Bernard in *Death of a Salesman*. In extending the line of *Death of a Salesman*, however, Miller was doing more than just borrowing the expressionistic technique. Quentin, in fact, is a successful Willy Loman made suddenly aware of the inadequacy of success and brought face to face with his "longings" in such a way as to be forced to contemplate their reality. He is a Willy Loman made finally to admit to his egotism and to the cruelty which this imposes on those around him. Quentin is, finally, a Willy Loman who has reached the height of society – the position, to be precise, of Bernard, Charley's son. This parallel is enforced not only by giving both characters the same profession but further by demonstrating their success in the legal profession by showing them both working on a brief to present before the Supreme Court. Whereas Bernard had evidenced no desire to examine the relevance of his success, however, Quentin senses its insufficiency and turns, as we have seen, to an examination of himself as a necessary prelude to taking up his life again after Maggie's death. He senses that success is a positive barrier between people. His first wife, Louise, complains of his concentration on his work to the exclusion of personal contact between them. He had considered his work and his success in that work to be of paramount importance and his relationship with his wife merely as an adjunct to that. He was obsessed, as Willy and his sons had been, with the future. As with them also, this concentration on the future destroys the human necessities of the present. "A future. And I've been carrying it around all my life, like a vase that must never be dropped. So you can't ever touch anybody" (p. 91). Maggie, too, is changed by success. When Quentin first meets her she was, he explains, not "defending anything, upholding anything, or accusing. She was just *there,* like a tree or a cat" (p. 67). In becoming successful, however, she goes beyond the frank acceptance of things and begins demanding. Selflessness gives way to egotism, and with egotism comes guilt and the need to blame others to retain the semblance of innocence. Whereas previously she had said, in Biff's words, "I know who I am," she ends her life in a drugged uncertainty which serves to highlight her failure to accept her role as both innocent victim and guilty persecutor. Quentin in his turn links himself to the cruelty which he had, in retrospect, discovered in others in confessing that there was a sense in which he was prepared to allow Maggie to die as he had been glad at Lou's death. Recognizing the signs of barbiturate poisoning, he delays taking action, feeling that to do so is to implicate himself in some way. He turns his back but discovers now, looking back, the source of this desire for non-involvement, this ultimate cruelty. He discovers in whose name he had turned his back. "And the name – yes, the name. In whose name do you ever turn your back ... but in your own? In Quentin's name. Always in your own blood-covered name you turn your back!" (p. 126). He recognizes finally the source of the personal violence which he has identified and in which he is himself implicated. He finds, in fact, that cruelty and violence can be defined in terms of self. They are a concentration on self to the exclusion and eventually to the extinction of others. And yet, having understood this, he is still faced with the apparently insoluble enigma that he had loved those whom he had hurt just as Rose had loved Ike, and Elsie, Lou. He recalls that after Elsie has viciously cut her husband down she had been immediately gentle and kind to him: "How tenderly she lifts him up! ... Now that he is ruined. Still, that could be a true kiss. Or is there no treason but only man, unblameable ..."[3] Reality, as he finds it, is a world of individuals in which the links which ought to exist have long since broken down. Love can temporarily link these "separate people" but eventually the inborn violence of man operates to fracture this relationship. Man is not capable of absolute love – that is a function which Quentin ascribes only to God. But man is capable of renewing love, knowing that defeat is necessary but knowing also that fear is not and that consciousness of man's double nature does not vitiate the value of that better part.

Quentin carries out this self-examination as a prelude to his marrying Holga, the girl he has recently met in Germany. Ironically, Holga represents the answer to the problems which perplex him. She takes him around a concentration camp and admits that she herself feels guilt for what has taken place there. Although originally unaware of the existence of such places, once she had been informed she felt that she could not turn her back: " ... no-one they didn't kill can be innocent again" (p. 32). She tells Quentin a story of her life which is in effect a parable. During the war, she tells him, she had lost her memory in a bombing raid. She wandered around and shied away from the violence which she saw around her: "Every day one turned away from people dying on the roads."[4] She tries to kill herself, but an injured soldier pulls her down from the bridge from which she was about to jump and leads her home. When there she has a dream that she has an idiot child and that the child is an image for her life. She realizes that even though the child is idiot and repulsive yet it is hers and she feels a necessity to embrace it. She does so and in future when she has the dream, "it somehow has the virtue now ... of being mine."[5] This is the answer which Quentin eventually discovers. However repulsive life appears to be, it is necessary, in Holga's words, to "take one's life in one's arms" (p. 33). Holga is not blind to the violence of man. She has learned to face up to it. She has learned from the facts of war what Quentin has to discover in the inability of love to overcome the cruelty which springs from egotism. "What burning cities taught her and the death of love taught me: – that we are very dangerous!" (p. 127). He accepts the image of the idiot child – a child who if he is bad is so by reason of his very nature and therefore needs all the more a love which does not baulk at the fact of his nature but rather renews constantly in the knowledge of its ultimate failure. Quentin walks to Holga at the end of the play and in doing so accepts his responsibility for his past cruelty but recognizes also that this stems from the nature of man and that the only crime is to stop trying. " ... the wish to kill is never killed, but with some gift of courage one may look into its face when it appears, and with a stroke of love – as to an idiot in the house – forgive it; again and again ... and forever?" (p. 127). The question mark at the end of that sentence emphasizes that there is no certainty that this is a reasonable basis on which to live but, to Quentin, it is all there is. "No, it's not certainty, I don't feel that. But it does seem feasible ... not to be afraid. Perhaps it's all one has" (p. 128).

This concept of acceptance which emerges as the necessary base for life is here clearly defined in Miller's work for the first time. In 1957, however, Arthur Laurents had in part anticipated him when he wrote *A Clearing in the Woods*. This play, first presented at the Belasco Theatre, New York City, was an expressionistic presentation of the struggle of a young woman against accepting those parts of her own character against which she rebelled. Her refusal to accept at first erects a barrier between her and those to whom she is naturally drawn. She refuses to accept that reality which does not correspond to her own dreams and wishes. In the end, however, Virginia, the protagonist, comes to accept the cruelty in her character and the limitations which life forces on her. She comes to accept dreams as dreams and reality as the only base for a life with integrity and without psychological disturbance and fear.

This is a play which also stands as a forerunner to *Who's Afraid of Virginia Woolf?* where Virginia – this time Virginia Woolf – again stands for an abandonment of dreams which is not an abandonment of hope. In that play, as in this, impotence is a function of the unreal world in which the characters live, and the punning references to sexual incompetence in both plays serve to highlight the sterility and psychological harm to be caused by this failure to accept. Laurents insists that "An end to dreams isn't an end to hope."[6] This is surely Miller's contention in *After the Fall* just as it is Albee's in *Who's Afraid of Virginia Woolf?* Miller, however, broadens the scope considerably beyond that which Laurent's play encompasses. There is one work, however, which is so close to Miller's play as to be justifiably regarded either as a source for it or as derived from a contemplation of the same facts. *The Fall* (La Chute) by Albert Camus was first published in 1956.

Like Quentin the protagonist of *The Fall* is a successful lawyer who comes to realize that his fame and success derive solely from egotism. Like Quentin also he starts with a desire to defend his innocence, a process which, as Miller indicates, is usually carried on at the expense of others.

From Camus, perhaps, we can derive the full meaning of the Christ symbolism which coalesces in *After the Fall* for the first time in Miller's work. In former plays there was nothing but a mere suggestion – a tree planted as a symbol of the son who gave his life in expiation in *All My Sons,* a man destroyed, partly by himself, partly by society, after working for his company for thirty-six years in *Death of a Salesman.* Here Quentin, a man hailed by his mother as the light of the world, clasps two light fixtures in a conscious crucifixion image. It is clear that he is expressing the powerful and selfless love necessary in life but more important still surely is the sense that Christ, too, like all other men, was guilty and guilty in the same way that Holga acknowledges her guilt. He bears the guilt of the survivor – the survivor of the massacre of the innocents:

Knowing what he knew, familiar with everything about man – ah, who would have believed that crime consists less in making others die than in not dying oneself! – brought face to face day and night with his innocent crime, he found it too hard for him to hold on and continue. It was better to have done with it, not to defend himself, to die, in order not to be the only one to live ...[7]

Holga had returned to the concentration camp "because I didn't die here" (p. 24). Quentin understands her reason, "survival can be hard to bear" (p. 25) – an interesting confession coming from a Jewish-American playwright. Like Quentin, Camus's protagonist, however, finally arrives at the necessity for acceptance, " ... I realized once and for all that I was not cured, that I was still cornered and that I had to make do with it as best I could. Ended the glorious life, but ended also the frenzy and the convulsions. I had to submit and admit my guilt. I had to live in the little ease."[8] The little ease of which he speaks is a cell in which it is impossible to either stand up straight or lie down. He accepts, therefore, that man's aspirations have their limits and that acceptance is the necessary conclusion of an honest self-examination.

Camus's *The Fall* is a confession rather than a novel; Miller's *After the Fall* is a confession rather than a play. The individual is, however, in both cases confessing on behalf of man. He is the Ancient Mariner condemned to repeat his experience, whether to a man met in a bar or to a psychiatrist, as a warning and a guide. They both underline the failure of success to serve anything but the ego, to mean anything but a conditional belief in innocence which when it dissipates leaves both protagonists alienated from their former existences. To secure a real place among mankind, like Hawthorne's characters, they have to stress the guilt which is their link with humanity. In *The Fall* Clamence keeps a stolen painting and arranges everything "so as to make myself an accomplice"[9] while Quentin leaves a note for his wife to read "in order to ... somehow join the condemned."[10]

Camus's account is aimed more at undermining complacency, at revealing the true springs of a success built on condescension and self-esteem. To Miller, however, the acceptance, wherein lies the only hope for a 'happy' life, is an acceptance of an implication in the violence and cruelty of man. It is an acknowledgement that this is man but that a constantly renewed love is the only response which can restore integrity and defeat fear.

In making the protagonist a lawyer, Miller was seeking something more than lucidity, just as was Camus in *The Fall* and Osborne in *Inadmissible Evidence*. The analytical probing of the confessional form calls for a combination of advocate and prosecutor, able to probe the central issue – guilt. Miller's long-standing obsession with this subject only truly receives full attention in this play. For it is only here that he penetrates beyond a concept of guilt as a legal or moral responsibility dependent on physical causality. The guilt which Quentin accepts transcends both the culpability of Eddie in *A View from the Bridge* and the egalitarian responsibility of *All My Sons*. It derives from his sense of abandonment and amounts to what seems virtually to be an existential viewpoint. For Quentin had "looked up one day – and the bench was empty. No judge in sight" (p. 13). He had realized that, in Sartre's words, he was condemned to be free: "Whether I open a book or think of marrying again, it's so damned clear I'm choosing what I do – and it cuts the strings between my hands and heaven" (p. 33). When Quentin accepts total responsibility as a natural corollary of total freedom, he is not far removed from the Sartre who proclaimed that he was as profoundly responsible for the war as though he had himself declared it. Nevertheless, the conclusion which Miller draws establishes a determinism which would not be accepted by an existentialist. For although he sees *After the Fall* as an examination of the "terrifying fact of choice," he accepts the idea that absolute freedom means absolute power and that absolute power necessarily leads to corruption, violence, and treachery. If this determinism makes retrospective sense of the savage idealism of Chris Keller in *All My Sons* and Stockman in Miller's version of *An Enemy of the People,* it does little to locate Miller either as a direct descendant of Nathaniel Taylor or as a disciple of Jean Paul Sartre.

What makes *After the Fall* finally such an unsatisfactory play is not the intrusion of personal detail but the fact that Miller fails to establish the credibility of his protagonist. The confessional form necessarily leads to a dominant character since the play ultimately consists of his thoughts and memories. So that Quentin's unbelievably pretentious language reveals itself not as a necessary aspect of his character but as a mark of Miller's submission to that intellectual self-indulgence which is an endemic danger of the play's form. The man who strikes his chest in confession may derive his satisfaction not so much from his admission of guilt as from the exquisite nature of the blow.

Miller's latest work, *Incident at Vichy,* serves merely to make more explicit the concerns of *After the Fall*. A group of men picked up by the Germans during the war sit in an outer office waiting to be called into a room by a professor who turns out to be an anthropologist. They anxiously cling to the hope that it is merely a document check, but the nervous suspicions of Lebeau, a painter, together with information smuggled to them by a waiter who has taken coffee to the Germans, makes it clear that they are here because they are Jews and that they are to be taken to Poland, not to do forced labour but to die. LeDuc, a psychiatrist, accepts this as true not because they are Germans or Fascists but "because they are people."[11] He thus identifies, as Quentin had in the former play, the origin of violence as being in man himself. He recognizes also that it is a fact of man's nature to require a victim. "Each man has his Jew; it is the other. And the Jews have their Jews,"[12] a fact highlighted here by the prejudice shown by the detainees towards a gypsy who has been brought in with them. So, too, Camus had stressed the same point: "Every man needs slaves as he needs fresh air."[13] LeDuc clashes with Von Berg, an Austrian nobleman arrested by mistake, and taunts him with the guilt of the survivor since it is clear that he will escape the purge. The taunt is neatly reversed, however, when Von Berg offers him his free pass. He accepts, "his hands springing to cover his eyes in the awareness of his own guilt."[14] This is *After the Fall* all over again even to the point of the necessity of acceptance. As LeDuc says before the moment of his own treachery, "I am only angry that I should have been born before the day when man has accepted his own nature; that he is *not* reasonable, that he is full of murder, that his ideals are only the little tax he pays for the right to hate and kill with a clear conscience."[15] Like Quentin, having accepted the fact of his own guilt, LeDuc accepts the responsibility and decides to live with it. By taking the pass from Von Berg, he endorses Quentin's refutation of those previous Miller heroes for whom guilt and the acknowledgement of it was only the prologue to the revolver or the speeding car. His recognition of idealism as merely a cover for cruelty does something belatedly to elucidate the character of Chris in *All My Sons*.

Incident at Vichy has little or nothing to add to *After the Fall*. Its characters, if less easily identifiable as ghosts from his own past, are nonetheless ineffectual, tending as they do to the stereotype. These two plays which appeared so uncharacteristically close to one another are two variations on the same theme. Poor theater they may be, but it is clear that thematically they represent a change in Miller's outlook: they investigate matters which the younger Miller was prepared to leave confusingly ambiguous. A case for their significance as social drama could readily be made in a period in which the world has signally failed to learn the lessons of the Second World War. According to Miller, it is time that man stopped kidding himself that violence and cruelty are the special preserves of any nation or political creed and in accepting this fact accept also the guilt and responsibility which this implies. If the earlier Miller had found guilt to be incapacitating, then this new Miller finds in an acceptance of its existence no reason for inactivity but rather a true basis for living.

NOTES

* When *After the Fall* was first produced at the Lincoln Centre, *The Saturday Evening Post* published the complete play in what it described as a pioneering effort for magazine publishing. When the final version of the play appeared in 'hard-back,' it became evident that several changes had been made. These changes are small in number but all serve to make the play less explicit. Thus it is interesting to note that in writing this paper several of the quotations which I considered central to the theme which Miller was developing in *The Saturday Evening Post* edition I found to be omitted in the final published version. Where this is true I have noted the fact in footnotes but have otherwise limited myself to the Secker and Warburg edition (London, 1965).

1 Arthur Miller, *After the Fall*, *The Saturday Evening Post* (Feb. 1, 1964), 44. This is omitted in the final published edition.

2 Arthur Miller, "A Foreword by the Author," *The Saturday Evening Post* (Feb. 1, 1964), 32.

3 *The Saturday Evening Post* (Feb. 1, 1964), 44. This passage is omitted in the final published text.

4 *Ibid.*, p. 40. Omitted from final text. All that remains is the dream of the idiot child.

5 *Ibid*. Omitted in the final printed version.

6 Arthur Laurents,. *A Clearing in the Woods* (New York, 1957), p. 169.

7 Albert Camus, *The Fall* (London, 1963), p. 63.

8 *Ibid.*, p. 80.

9 *Ibid.*, p. 107.

10 Miller, *After the Fall, The Saturday Evening Post* (Feb. 1, 1964), 47. Omitted from final printed version.

11 Arthur Miller, *Incident at Vichy* (London, 1965), p. 20

12 *Ibid.*, p. 66.

13 *The Fall*, p. 34.

14 *Incident at Vichy*, p. 69.

15 *Ibid.*, p. 65.

Arthur Miller's *The Crucible*: Background and Sources

ROBERT A. MARTIN

When *The Crucible* opened on January 22, 1953,[1] the term "witch-hunt" was nearly synonymous in the public mind with the Congressional investigations then being conducted into allegedly subversive activities. Arthur Miller's plays have always been closely identified with contemporary issues, and to many observers the parallel between the witchcraft trials at Salem, Massachusetts in 1692 and the current Congressional hearings was the central issue of the play.

Miller has said that he could not have written *The Crucible* at any other time,[2] a statement which reflects both his reaction to the McCarthy era and the creative process by which he finds his way to the thematic center of a play. If it is true, however, that a play cannot be successful in its own time unless it speaks to its own time, it is also true that a play cannot endure unless it speaks to new audiences in new times. The latter truism may apply particularly to *The Crucible,* which is presently being approached more and more frequently as a cultural and historical study rather than as a political allegory.

Although *The Crucible* was written in response to its own time, popular interest in the Salem witchcraft trials had actually begun to surface long before the emergence of McCarthyism. There were at least two other plays based on the witchcraft trials that were produced shortly before *The Crucible* opened: *Child's Play* by Florence Stevenson was produced in November, 1952 at the Oklahoma Civic Playhouse; and *The Witchfinders* by Louis O. Coxe appeared at about the same time in a studio production at the University of Minnesota.[3] Among numerous other works dealing with Salem witchcraft, a novel, *Peace, My Daughter* by Shirley Barker, had appeared as recently as 1949, and in the same year Marion L. Starkey had combined an interest in history and psychology to produce *The Devil in Massachusetts,* which was based on her extensive research of the original documents and records. Starkey's announced purpose was "to review the records in the light of the findings of modern psychology," and to supplement the work of earlier investigators by calling attention to "a number of vital primary sources of which they seem to have been ignorant."[4]

The events that eventually found their way into *The Crucible* are largely contained in the massive two volume record of the trials located in the Essex Country Archives at Salem, Massachusetts, where Miller went to do his research. Although he has been careful to point out in a prefatory note that *The Crucible* is not history in the academic sense, a study of the play and its sources indicates that Miller did his research carefully and well. He found in the records of the trials at Salem that between June 10 and September 22, 1692, nineteen men and women and two dogs were hanged for witchcraft, and one man was pressed to death for standing mute.[5] Before the affair ended, fifty-five people had confessed to being witches, and another hundred and fifty were in jail awaiting trial.

Focusing primarily upon the story of John Proctor, one of the nineteen who were hanged, Miller almost literally retells the story of a panic-stricken society that held a doctrinal belief in the existence of the Devil and the reality of witchcraft. The people of Salem did not, of course, invent a belief in witchcraft; they were, however, the inheritors of a witchcraft tradition that had a long and bloody history in their native England and throughout most of Europe. To the Puritans of Massachusetts, witchcraft was as real a manifestation of the Devil's efforts to overthrow "God's kingdom" as the periodic raids of his Indian disciples against the frontier settlements.

There were, surprisingly, few executions for witchcraft in Massachusetts before 1692. According to George Lyman Kittredge in his *Witchcraft in Old and New England,* "not more than half-a-dozen executions can be shown to have occurred."[6] But the people of Salem village in 1692 had recent and – to them – reliable evidence that the Devil was at work in the Massachusetts Bay Colony. In 1688 in Boston, four children of John Goodwin had been seriously afflicted by a "witch" named Glover, who was also an Irish washwoman. In spite of her hasty execution and the prayers of four of the most devout Boston ministers, the Goodwin children were possessed by spirits of the "invisible world" for some months afterward. One of the leading Puritan ministers of the time was Cotton Mather, who in 1689 published his observations on the incident in "Memorable Providences, Relating to Witchcrafts and Possession."[7] Although the work was intended to warn against witchcraft, Mather's account can also be read as a handbook of instructions for feigning possession by demonic spirits. Among numerous other manifestations and torments, Mather reported that the Goodwin children were most often afflicted by "fits":

Sometimes they would be Deaf, sometimes Dumb, and sometimes Blind, and often, all this at once. One while their Tongues would be drawn down their Throats; another-while they would be pull'd out upon their Chins, to a prodigious length. They would have their Mouths opened unto such a Wideness, that their Jaws went out of joint; and anon they would clap together again with a Force like that of a strong Spring Lock.[8]

Four years later, in February, 1692, the daughter and niece of the Reverend Samuel Parris of Salem village began to have "fits" very similar to those experienced by the Goodwin children as reported and described by Mather. According to Marion Starkey, Parris had a copy of Mather's book, and, in addition, "the Parrises had probably had first-hand experience of the case, since they appear to have been living in Boston at the time. The little girls might even have been taken to see the hanging."[9]

In spite of an apparent abundance of historical material, the play did not become dramatically conceivable for Miller until he came upon "a single fact" concerning Abigail Williams, the niece of Reverend Parris:

It was that Abigail Williams, the prime mover of the Salem hysteria, so far as the hysterical children were concerned, had a short time earlier been the house servant of the Proctors and now was crying out Elizabeth Proctor as a witch; but more – it was clear from the record that with entirely uncharacteristic fastidiousness she was refusing to include John Proctor, Elizabeth's husband, in her accusations despite the urgings of the prosecutors. Why? I searched the records of the trials in the courthouse at Salem but in no other instance could I find such a careful avoidance of the implicating stutter, the murderous, ambivalent answer to the sharp questions of the prosecutors. Only here, in Proctor's case, was there so clear an attempt to differentiate between a wife's culpability and a husband's.[10]

As in history, the play begins when the Reverend Samuel Parris begins to suspect that his daughter Betty has become ill because she and his niece Abigail Williams have "trafficked with spirits in the forest." The real danger Parris fears, however, is less from diabolical spirits than from the ruin that may fall upon him when his enemies learn that his daughter is suffering from the effects of witchcraft:

PARRIS There is a faction that is sworn to drive me from my pulpit. Do you understand that?
ABIGAIL I think so, sir.
PARRIS Now then, in the midst of such disruption, my own household is discovered to be the very center of some obscene practice. Abominations are done in the forest —
ABIGAIL It were sport, uncle![11]

As Miller relates at a later point in the play, Parris was a petty man who was historically in a state of continual bickering with his congregation over such matters as his salary, housing, and firewood. The irony of the above conversation in the play, however, is that while Parris is attempting to discover the "truth" to prevent it from damaging his already precarious reputation as Salem's minister, Abigail actually is telling him the historical truth when she says "it were sport." Whatever perverse motives may have subsequently prompted the adult citizens of Salem to cry "witch" upon their neighbors, the initiators of the Salem misfortune were young girls like Abigail Williams who began playing with spirits simply for the "sport" of it, as a release from an emotionally oppressive society. A portion of the actual trial testimony given in favor of Elizabeth Proctor (John Proctor's wife) by one Daniel Elliott suggests that initially, at least, not everyone accepted the girls' spectral visions without question:

the testimony of Daniel Elliott, aged 27 years or thereabouts, who testifieth and saith that I being at the house of lieutenant Ingersoll on the 28 of March, in the year 1692, there being present one of the afflicted persons which cried out and said, there's Goody Proctor. William Raiment being there present, told the girl he believed she lied, for he saw nothing; then Goody Ingersoll told the girl she told a lie, for there was nothing; then the girl said that she did it for sport, they must have some sport.[12] [punctuation added]

Miller's addition in *The Crucible* of an adulterous relationship between Abigail Williams and Proctor serves primarily as a dramatically imperative motive for Abigail's later charges of witchcraft against Elizabeth Proctor. Although it might appear that Miller is rewriting history for his own dramatic purposes by introducing a sexual relationship between Abigail and Proctor, his invention of the affair is psychologically and historically appropriate. As he makes clear in the prefatory note preceding the play, "dramatic purposes have sometimes required many characters to be fused into one; the number of girls ... has been reduced; Abigail's age has been raised; ... " Although Miller found that Abigail's refusal to testify against Proctor was the single historical and dramatic "fact" he was looking for, there are two additional considerations that make adultery and Abigail's altered age plausible within the historical context of the events.

The first is that Mary Warren, in the play and in history, was simultaneously an accuser in court and a servant in Proctor's household. If an adulterous affair was probable, it would more likely have occurred between Mary Warren and Proctor than between Abigail Williams and Proctor; but it could easily have occurred. At the time, Mary Warren was a fairly mature young woman who would have had the features Miller has represented in Abigail: every emotional and sexual impulse, as well as the opportunity to be involved with Proctor. Historically, it was Mary Warren who attempted to stop the proceedings as early as April 19 by stating during her examination in court that the afflicted girls "did but dissemble": "Afterwards she started up, and said I will speak and cried out, Oh! I am sorry for it, I am sorry for it, and wringed her hands, and fell a little while into a fit again and then came to speak, but immediately her teeth were set, and then she fell into a violent fit and cried out, oh Lord help me! Oh Good Lord save me!"[13] As in the play, the rest of the girls prevailed by immediately falling into fits and spontaneously accusing her of witchcraft. As her testimony of April 21 and later indicates, however, she soon returned to the side of her fellow accusers. On June 30, she testified:

The deposition of Mary Warren aged 20 years here testifieth. I have seen the apparition of John Proctor senior among the witches and he hath often tortured me by pinching me and biting me and choking me, and pressing me on my Stomach till the blood came out of my mouth and also I saw him torture Mis Pope and Mercy Lewis and John Indian upon the day of his examination and he hath also tempted me to write in his book, and to eat bread which he brought to me, which I refusing to do, Jno Proctor did most grievously torture me with a variety of tortures, almost Ready to kill me.[14]

Miller has reduced Mary Warren's lengthy and ambiguous trial testimony to four pages in the play by focusing on her difficulty in attempting to tell the truth after the proceedings were under way. The truth that Mary has to tell – "It were only sport in the beginning, sir" – is the same that Abigail tried to tell Parris earlier; but the telling has become compounded by the courtoom presence of Proctor, Parris, Hathorne and Danforth (two of the judges), the rest of the afflicted girls, and the spectators. In a scene taken directly from the trial records, Mary confesses that she and the other girls have been only pretending and that they have deceived the court. She has never seen the spirits or apparitions of the witches:

HATHORNE How could you think you saw them unless you saw them?
MARY WARREN I – I cannot tell how, but I did. I – I heard the other girls screaming, and you, Your Honor, you seemed to believe them, and I – It were only sport in the beginning, sir, but then the whole world cried spirits, and I – I promise you, Mr. Danforth, I only thought I saw them but I did not.[15]

The second, additional consideration is that although Miller has raised Abigail's age from her actual eleven to seventeen, and has reduced the number of girls in the play to five only, such alterations for purposes of dramatic motivation and compression do not significantly affect the psychological or historical validity of the play. As the trial records clearly establish, individual and family hostilities played a large role in much of the damaging testimony given against those accused of witchcraft. Of the ten girls who were most directly involved in crying out against the witches, only three – Betty Parris (nine years old), Abigail Williams (eleven years), and Ann Putnam (twelve years) – were below the age of sexual maturity. The rest were considerably older: Mary Walcott and Elizabeth Booth were both sixteen; Elizabeth Hubbard was seventeen; Susanna Sheldon was eighteen; Mercy Lewis was nineteen; Sarah Churchill and Mary Warren (Proctor's servant) were twenty. In a time when marriage and motherhood were not uncommon at the age of fourteen, the hypothesis of repressed sexuality emerging disguised into the emotionally charged atmosphere of witchcraft and Calvinism does not seem unlikely; it seems, on the contrary, an inevitable supposition. And it may be worth pointing out in this context that Abigail Williams was not the only one of the girls who refused to include John Proctor in her accusations against his wife, Elizabeth. In her examination of April 21, Mary Warren testified that her mistress was a witch and that "her master had told her that he had been about sometimes to make away with himself because of his wife's quarreling with him, ... " A few lines later the entry reads: "but she would not own that she knew her master to be a witch or wizzard."[16]

With the exception of Abigail and Proctor's adultery, the events and characters of *The Crucible* are not so much "invented" data in a fictional sense as highly compressed representations of the underlying forces of hatred, hysteria, and fear that paralyzed Salem during the spring and summer of 1692. And even in this context Abigail Williams's characterization in the play may be more restrained in the light of the records than Miller's dramatization suggests. For example, one of the major witnesses against John Proctor was twelve year old Ann Putnam, who testified on June 30 that "on the day of his examination I saw the apparition of Jno: Proctor senior go and afflict and most grievously torture the bodies of Mistress Pope, Mary Walcott, Mercy Lewis, Abigail Williams. ... "[17] In projecting several of the girls into Abigail, Miller has used the surface of the trial records to suggest that her hatred for Proctor's wife is a dramatic equivalent for the much wider spread hatred and tension that existed within the Salem community. Abigail, although morally corrupt, ironically insists upon her "good" name, and reveals at an early point in the play that she hates Elizabeth Proctor for ruining her reputation:

PARRIS [*to the point*] Abigail, is there any other cause than you have told me, for your being discharged from Goody Proctor's service? I have heard it said, and I tell you as I heard it, that she comes so rarely to the church this year for she will not sit so close to something soiled. What signified that remark?

ABIGAIL She hates me uncle, she must, for I would not be her slave. It's a bitter woman, a lying, cold, sniveling woman, and I will not work for such a woman![18]

On a larger scale, Miller brings together the forces of personal and social malfunction through the arrival of the Reverend John Hale, who appears, appropriately, in the midst of a bitter quarrel among Proctor, Parris, and Thomas Putnam over deeds and land boundaries. Hale, in life as in the play, had encountered witchcraft previously and was called to Salem to determine if the Devil was in fact responsible for the illness of the afflicted children. In the play, he conceives of himself, Miller says, "much as a young doctor on his first call":

[*He appears loaded down with half a dozen heavy books.*]
HALE Pray you, someone take these!
PARRIS [*delighted*] Mr. Hale! Oh! it's good to see you again! [*Taking some books*] My, they're heavy!
HALE [*setting down his books*] They must be; they are weighted with authority.[19]

Hale's entrance at this particular point in the play is significant in that he interrupts an argument based on private and secular interests to bring "authority" to the question of witchcraft. His confidence in himself and his subsequent examination of the girls and Tituba (Parris's slave who inadvertently started the entire affair) represent and foreshadow the arrival of outside religious authority in the community. As an outsider who has come to weigh the evidence, Hale also helps to elevate the issue from a local to a regional level, and from an unofficial to an official theological inquiry. His heavy books of authority also symbolically anticipate the heavy authority of the judges who, as he will realize too late, are as susceptible to misinterpreting testimony based on spectral evidence as he is:

HALE [*with a tasty love of intellectual pursuit*] Here is all the invisible world, caught, defined, and calculated. In these books the Devil stands stripped of all his brute disguises. Here are all your familiar spirits – your incubi and succubi; your witches that go by land, by air, and by sea; your wizards of the night and of the day. Have no fear now — we shall find him out if he has come among us, and I mean to crush him utterly if he has shown his face![20]

The Reverend Hale is an extremely interesting figure historically, and following the trials he set down an account of his repentance entitled "A Modest Inquiry into the Nature of Witchcraft" (Boston, 1702). Although he was at first as overly zealous in his pursuit of witches as everyone else, very much as Miller has portrayed him in *The Crucible,* Hale began to be tormented by doubts early in the proceedings. His uncertainty concerning the reliability of the witnesses and their testimony was considerably heightened when his own wife was also accused of being a witch. Hale appears to have been as tortured spiritually and as dedicated to the "middle way" in his later life as Miller has portrayed him in *The Crucible.* Five years after Salem, he wrote in his "Inquiry":

The middle way is commonly the way of truth. And if any can shew me a better middle way than I have here laid down, I shall be ready to embrace it: But the conviction must not be by vinegar or drollery, but by strength of argument. ... I have had a deep sence of the sad consequence of mistakes in matters Capital; and their impossibility of recovering when compleated. And what grief of heart it brings to a tender conscience, to have been unwittingly encouraging of the Sufferings of the innocent.[21]

Hale further commented that although he presently believed the executions to be the unfortunate result of human error, the integrity of the court officials was unquestionable: "I observed in the prosecution of these affairs, that there was in the Justices, Judges and others concerned, a conscientious endeavour to do the thing that was right. And to that end they consulted the Presidents [Precedents] of former times and precepts laid down by Learned Writers about Witchcraft."[22]

In *The Crucible*, Hale's examination of Tituba is very nearly an edited transcription of her testimony at the trial of Sarah Good, who is the first person Abigail accuses of consorting with the Devil. At the time of the trials, Sarah Good had long been an outcast member of the Salem community, "unpopular because of her slothfulness, her sullen temper, and her poverty; she had recently taken to begging, an occupation the Puritans detested."[23] When she was about to be hanged, her minister, the Reverend Nicholas Noyes, made a last appeal to her for a confession and said he knew she was a witch. Her prophetic reply was probably seen later as proof of her guilt when she said to Noyes: "you are a lyer; I am no more a Witch than you are a Wizard, and if you take away my Life, God will give you Blood to drink."[24] A few years after she was hanged, Reverend Noyes died as a result of a sudden and severe hemorrhage.

Largely through the Reverend Hale, Miller reflects the change that took place in Salem from an initial belief in the justice of the court to a suspicion that testimony based on spectral evidence was insufficient for execution. This transformation begins to reveal itself in Act Two, as Hale tells Francis Nurse that the court will clear his wife of the charges against her: "Believe me, Mr. Nurse, if Rebecca Nurse be tainted, then nothing's left to stop the whole green world from burning. Let you rest upon the justice of the court; the court will send her home, I know it."[25] By Act Three, however, Hale's confidence in the justice of the court has been badly shaken by the arrest and conviction of people like Rebecca Nurse who were highly respected members of the church and community. Hale, like his historical model, has discovered that "the whole green world" is burning indeed, and fears that he has helped to set the fire.

Partially as a result of Hale's preliminary investigation into the reality of Salem witchcraft, the Court of Oyer and Terminer was appointed to hear testimony and conduct the examinations. The members of the court immediately encountered a serious obstacle: namely, that although the Bible does not define witchcraft, it states unequivocally that "Thou shalt not suffer a witch to live" (Exodus 22:18). As Proctor attempts to save his wife from hanging, Hale attempts to save his conscience by demanding visible proof of the guilt of those who have been convicted on the basis of spectral testimony:

> HALE Excellency, I have signed seventy-two death warrants; I am a minister of the Lord, and I dare not take a life without there be a proof so immaculate no slightest qualm of conscience may doubt it.
>
> DANFORTH Mr. Hale, you surely do not doubt my justice.
>
> HALE I have this morning signed away the soul of Rebecca Nurse, Your Honor. I'll not conceal it, my hand shakes yet as with a wound![26]

At first, the witches who were brought to trial and convicted were generally old and eccentric women like Sarah Good who were of questionable character long before the trials began. But people like Rebecca Nurse and John Proctor were not. As Miller has Parris say to Judge Hathorne in Act Four: "it were another sort that hanged till now. Rebecca Nurse is no Bridget that lived three year with Bishop before she married him. John Proctor is not Isaac Ward that drank his family to ruin."[27] In late June, Rebecca Nurse was found guilty and sentenced to hang after an earlier verdict of "not guilty" was curiously reversed. Her minister, the Reverend Nicholas Noyes again, decided along with his congregation that she should be excommunicated for the good of the church. Miller seems to have been especially moved by her character and her almost unbelievable trial and conviction, as he indicates by his comments in the "Introduction" and his interpolated remarks in Act One. On Tuesday, July 19, 1692, she was hanged on Gallows Hill along with four others, all women. She was seventy-one years old. After the hanging, according to Starkey:

The bodies of the witches were thrust into a shallow grave in a crevice of Gallows Hill's outcropping of felsite. But the body of Rebecca did not remain there. Her children bided their time ... and at night when the crowds and the executioners had gone home again, they gathered up the body of their mother and took it home. Just where they laid it none can know, for this was a secret thing and not even Parris, whose parsonage was not a quarter of a mile up the road past the grove where the Nurses buried their dead, must see that a new grave had been opened and prayers said. This was the hour and the power of darkness when a son could not say where he had buried his mother.[28]

Historically, Proctor was even more of a victim of the laws of his time than Miller details in *The Crucible*. Although the real John Proctor fought against his arrest and conviction as fervently as anyone could under the circumstances, he, like Miller's Proctor, was adamant in his refusal to confess to witchcraft because he did not believe it existed. And although fifty-two of his friends and neighbors risked their own safety to sign a petition in his behalf, nothing was done to re-examine the evidence against him. Ironically, Proctor's wife – in whose interest he had originally become involved in the affair – had become pregnant and, although sentenced, would never hang. She was eventually released after enduring her husband's public execution, the birth of her child in prison, and the seizure and loss of all her possessions.

Under the law, the goods and property of witches could be confiscated after their trial and conviction. In Proctor's case, however, the sheriff did not wait for the trial or the conviction. A contemporary account of the seizure indicates that neither Proctor nor his wife were ever expected to return from prison:

John Proctor and his Wife being in Prison, the Sheriff came to his House and seized all the Goods, Provisions, and Cattle that he could come at, and sold some of the Cattle at half price, and killed others, and put them up for the West-Indies; threw out the Beer out of a Barrel, and carried away the Barrel; emptied a Pot of Broath, and took away the Pot, and left nothing in the House for the support of the Children: No part of the said Goods are known to be returned.[29]

(The Proctors had five children, the youngest of whom were three and seven.) Along with three other men and one woman, John Proctor was hanged on August 19. On September 22, seven more witches and one wizard were hanged, and then the executions suddenly ended.

Miller has symbolized all the judges of the witchcraft trials in the figures of Danforth and Hathorne (Nathaniel Hawthorne's ancestor), and presented them as being more "official" in a legal sense than their historical models actually were. None of the judges in the trials had any legal training, and, apparently, neither had anyone else who was administering the law in the Massachusetts Bay Colony. According to Starkey, the curious nature of the trials was in part due to the Puritans' limited understanding of the law, their contempt for lawyers, and their nearly total reliance on the Bible as a guide for all matters of legal and moral authority:

The Puritans had a low opinion of lawyers and did not permit the professional practice of law in the colony. In effect the administration of the law was in the hands of laymen, most of them second-generation colonists who had an incomplete grasp of current principles of English jurisdiction. For that matter, this chosen people, this community which submitted itself to the direct rule of God, looked less to England for its precepts than to God's ancient and holy word. So far as was practicable the Puritans were living by a legal system that antedated the Magna Carta by at least two millennia, the Decalogue and the tribal laws codified in the Pentateuch.[30]

As historians occasionally have pointed out, the executions did not stop because the people in Massachusetts suddenly ceased to believe in either the Devil or witchcraft; they stopped, simply and ironically, because of a legal question. There never was any doubt for most people living in New England in 1692 whether or not witchcraft was real or whether witches should be executed; the question centered around the reliability of spectral evidence coming from the testimony of the afflicted. It was largely through the determinations of Increase Mather and fourteen other Boston ministers that such testimony was declared to be insufficient for conviction and therefore became inadmissable as evidence. It was better, they concluded, to allow ten witches to escape than to hang one innocent person. In late October, Governor Phips officially dismissed the Court of Oyer and Terminer, and – although the trials continued through the following April – in May, 1693 he issued a proclamation discharging all the remaining "witches" and pardoning those who had fled the colony rather than face arrest, trial, and certain conviction.

Miller has said that if he were to rewrite *The Crucible,* he would make an open thematic issue of the evil he now believes to be represented by the Salem judges. His altered viewpoint toward the play may be accounted for partially as a reconsideration of his intensive examination of the trial records which, he has said, do not "reveal any mitigation of the unrelieved, straightforward, and absolute dedication to evil displayed by the judges of these trials and the prosecutors. After days of study it became quite incredible how perfect they were in this respect."[31]

Miller's subsequent view of evil, however, did not come entirely from his study of the trial records. Between writing *The Crucible* in 1952 and producing the "Introduction" to the *Collected Plays* in 1957, he underwent a personal crucible when he appeared before the House Un-American Activities Committee in 1956. Although the experience was understandably not without its effect on his later attitude toward Congressional "witchhunters," it should, nevertheless, be considered in relation to his comments on the judges and evil quoted above. A more accurate reflection of Miller's attitude while writing *The Crucible* appears perhaps most clearly in the account published in February, 1953 of his thoughts while standing on the rock at Gallows Hill:

Here hung Rebecca, John Proctor, George Jacobs – people more real to me than the living can ever be. The sense of a terrible marvel again; that people could have such a belief in themselves and in the rightness of their consciences as to give their lives rather than say what they thought was false. Or, perhaps, they only feared Hell so much? Yet, Rebecca said, and it is written in the record, "I cannot belie myself." And she knew it would kill her. ... The rock stands forever in Salem. They knew who they were. Nineteen.[32]

Like the rock at Salem, *The Crucible* has endured beyond the immediate events of its own time. If it was originally seen as a political allegory, it is presently seen by contemporary audiences almost entirely as a distinguished American play by an equally distinguished American playwright. As one of the most frequently produced plays in the American theater, *The Crucible* has attained a life of its own; one that both interprets and defines the cultural and historical background of American society. Given the general lack of plays in the American theater that have seriously undertaken to explore the meaning and significance of the American past in relation to the present, *The Crucible* stands virtually alone as a dramatically coherent rendition of one of the most terrifying chapters in American history.

NOTES

1 *The Crucible* opened at the Martin Beck Theater in New York City. Directed by Jed Harris, the cast included Arthur Kennedy as John Proctor, E.G. Marshall as the Reverend John Hale, and Beatrice Straight as Elizabeth Proctor. After 197 performances, the play closed on July 11, 1953.

2 John and Alice Griffin, "Arthur Miller Discusses *The Crucible*," *Theatre Arts* 37 (October, 1953), 33.

3 Dennis Welland, *Arthur Miller* (New York, 1961), p. 74.

4 Marion L. Starkey, *The Devil in Massachusetts* (New York, 1949), p. 12; hereafter cited as *The Devil*.

5 For this and other information of an historical and factual nature, I am indebted to *What Happened in Salem?*, ed. David Levin (New York, 1960), hereafter cited as *Salem*; *Narratives of the Witchcraft Cases, 1648–1706*, ed. George Lincoln Burr (New York, 1914), hereafter cited as *Narratives*; and *Salem Witchcraft* by Charles W. Upham (Boston, 1867). I have also drawn upon material located in the Essex County Archives, particularly the Works Progress Administration transcript of *Salem Witchcraft, 1692* on file in the Essex County Court House at Salem. For a perspective of the events as social history, see Paul Boyer and Stephen Nissenbaum, *Salem Possessed: The Social Origins of Witchcraft* (Cambridge, Massachusetts, 1974).

6 George Lyman Kittredge, *Witchcraft in Old and New England* (Cambridge, Massachusetts, 1929), p. 367. Frederick C. Drake, however, in "Witchcraft in the American Colonies, 1647–62," documents by names, dates, and places twenty executions for witchcraft between 1647–62, the majority of which took place in Massachusetts and Connecticut. Only two executions, Drake says, took place in the colonies between 1662 and 1691, one of which was the result of the Goodwin case in Boston in 1688 (*American Quarterly* 20 [1968], 694–725).

7 Cotton Mather, "Memorable Providences...," (Boston, 1689); rpt. in Burr, *Narratives*, pp. 93–143.

8 Burr, *Narratives*, p. 101.

9 Starkey, *The Devil*, p. 24.

10 Arthur Miller, *Arthur Miller's Collected Plays* (New York, 1957), p. 41; herein-
after cited as C.P. Present-day Salem is not where the witchcraft began in 1692.
The town of Danvers, originally called "Salem Village," is the location of
Miller's play and the historical site in Essex County where the tragedy began.
Danvers, or Salem Village, is a few miles northwest of present-day Salem,
which was then called "Salem Town."

11 *C.P.*, p. 231.

12 Levin, *Salem*, p. 64.

13 *Ibid.*, pp. 52–53.

14 *Ibid.*, pp. 61.

15 *C.P.*, pp. 302–303.

16 Levin, *Salem*, p. 56.

17 *Ibid.*, pp. 60–61.

18 .*C.P.*, p. 232.

19. *Ibid.*, p. 251.

20 *Ibid.*, p. 253. *Incubi, succubi*: in the mythology of witchcraft, incubi are evil
spirits capable of assuming the human male form to have sexual intercourse
with women at night, while succubi assume the female form to have sexual intercourse with men in their sleep.

21 Burr, *Narratives*, pp. 404–405. Hale's account was written in 1697; published in
1702 after his death.

22 Burr, *Narratives*, p. 415.

23 Levin, *Salem*, p. xviii.

24 Burr, *Narratives*, p. 358.

25 *C.P.*, p. 277.

26 *Ibid.*, p. 297.

27 *Ibid.*, p. 316.

28 Starkey, *The Devil*, p. 177.

29 Burr, *Narratives*, p. 361.

30 Starkey, *The Devil*, p. 36. In addition to Starkey's conclusion, George Lincoln
Burr has noted that "in these trials of 1692 the jurors were chosen from among
church-members only, not, as later, from all who had the property to make them
voters under the new charter." *Narratives*, p. 362, n. 2.

31 *C.P.*, pp. 42–43.

32 Arthur Miller, "Journey to 'The Crucible,'" *New York Times*, February 8, 1953,
Sec. 2, p. 3. Miller's admiration for the "Salem Nineteen" is presumably also
extended to the twentieth person who died there – the eighty year old Giles Corey,
who was pressed to death on September 19 for standing mute before the judges and
the court. "Pressing" involved placing rocks on the accused's chest until he died
or consented to enter a plea and stand trial. Tradition has it that Corey's last words

were "more weight," just before he died, but a less heroic end was recorded by a contemporary who probably witnessed the gruesome procedure: "In pressing[,] his Tongue being prest out of his Mouth, the Sheriff with his Cane forced it in again, when he was dying. He was the first in New-England, that was ever prest to Death." Burr, *Narratives,* p. 367.

Arthur Miller's *Incident At Vichy*: A Sartrean Interpretation

LAWRENCE D. LOWENTHAL

In 1944, just after Paris was liberated from the Nazi occupation, Jean Paul Sartre sat at the Café de Flore on the Left Bank and wrote *Anti Semite and Jew (Réflexions sur la Question Juive)*, a fascinating and controversial analysis of Europe's most terrifying problem. Twenty years later, America's leading dramatist, Arthur Miller, wrote a long, one-act play about the holocaust, called *Incident at Vichy*. Although Ronald Hayman, an English critic, recently suggested that "a good case could be made for calling Arthur Miller the most Sartrean of living playwrights,"[1] no critic has yet pointed out that *Vichy* is an explicit dramatic rendition of Sartre's treatise on Jews, as well as a clear structural example of Sartre's definition of the existential "theatre of situation."

This affinity between Sartre and Miller is understandable when one considers the existential development of Miller's later plays. Beginning with *The Misfits*, Miller's works begin to shift the tragic perspective from man's remediable alienation from society to man's hopeless alienation from the universe and from himself. *After the Fall, Incident at Vichy*, and *The Price* are all organized around "absurdist" themes of metaphysical anxiety, personal solitude, and moral ambivalence. Quite clearly, one presumes, the accumulated impact of international and personal tragedies has strained Miller's faith in man's ability to overcome social and spiritual diseases. Miller no longer has any illusion about a "Grand Design" whose revelation will enable man to live harmoniously as a social being. His characters now grope alone for values to sustain their dissipating lives and each value, once discovered, slips again into ambiguity. Most frightening of all is the realization that human corruption, once attributed to conscious deviation from recognizable moral norms, is now seen as an irresistible impulse in the heart of man. The theme of universal guilt becomes increasingly and despairingly affirmed. But Miller's belief in original sin in a world without God does not preclude the possibility of personal redemption, for Miller shares Sartre's insistence on free will and the possibility of "transcendence" or the re-creation of self through a succession of choices.

Miller's existential concerns are clearly delineated in *Vichy,* a play that reminds us immediately of Sartre's "The Wall" and *The Victors.* In all these works a fundamental Sartrean thesis is dramatized: "A man's secret, the very frontier of his freedom is his power of resistance to torture and death."[2]

Structurally, *Vichy* answers Sartre's call for "situational drama" which, he hoped, would replace the outmoded drama of "character" so prevalent in the contemporary bourgeois theatre. In a famous article, "Forgers of Myth," written in 1946, Sartre described situational drama as "short and violent, sometimes reduced to the dimensions of a single long act":[3] "A single set, a few entrances, a few exits, intense arguments among the characters who defend their individual rights with passion....[4]

Each character is displayed as a free being, entirely indeterminate, who must choose his own being when confronted with certain necessities."[5] Men do not have "ready made" natures, consistent throughout alternating circumstances – a primary assumption in the theatre of character – but are rather naked wills, pure, free choices whose passion unites with action.

The characters in *Vichy* are not simply "types" or "public speakers with a symbolic role" as one critic maintains;[6] on the contrary they are dynamic, fluid, undetermined beings, "freedoms caught in a trap," to use a Sartrean phrase. We know nothing about them, aside from their professions, until they reveal themselves through their choices of behavior, and their choices often prove to be surprising. They are all faced with undeniable limits to these choices, but within these limits they are always free to act. The Jew can resist or submit; the German can murder or rebel. The structural movement of the play is existential in that individual possibilities for evading choice are methodically decreased. As each Jew is taken into the dreaded office, the option to revolt becomes more difficult. The traditional palliatives of reason, civilization, political ideology, and culture which ordinarily stand between man and the absurd are dispelled, one by one, until each character is made to face the realities of torture and irrational death.

Miller's play, though existentialist in theme, is rationalistic in structure. Like Sartre, Miller writes about the absurd in coherent terms. Miller's intention is still to explore "sheer process itself. How things connected,"[7] and although his discovery of cause and effect patterns no longer reveals "the hidden laws of the gods" with any certainty, the disasters in the play do not spring from a mysterious void as they do in the absurdist plays of Beckett and Ionesco. The central crisis is, of course, precipitated by Nazism, but Miller's analysis of the cause of this evil is more existential than political or sociological, and is expressed in terms of the Sartrean concepts of Nothingness and Dread.

Sartrean "dread" is a state-of-being arising from one's confrontation with "contingency," or the inherent meaninglessness of the physical world. Sartre's vision of ontological chaos or the absurd is most graphically described in *Nausea,* his first novel. As Roquentin, the narrator, sits idly on a park bench, he sees the root of a chestnut tree suddenly ooze into viscosity before his eyes. Flowing obscenely beyond its bounds, it shape, its position amidst other physical objects, the tree suddenly loses its essence as a tree and becomes merely substance, *there,* without reason or justification. The tree's abandonment of its *a priori* essence compels Roquentin to acknowledge the general fact of the world's contingency: "I mean that one cannot define existence as necessity. ... Everything is gratuitous. ... When you realize this, your heart turns upside down and everything begins to float."[8] Roquentin's awareness that "existence comes before essence" is the starting point of Sartre's philosophy. Beginning as an undefinable consciousness in a world of innately undefinable objects, man finds himself responsible for imposing himself on the world and creating a reason for his existence. The realization of his superfluity leaves man forlorn because "neither within him nor without does he find anything to cling to. He can't start making excuses for himself."[9]

Roquentin's psychic epiphany in *Nausea* is paralleled in *Incident at Vichy* by the phenomenon of Nazism. Both events undermine all assumptions about the necessity of human existence. The Nazis are the fulfillment of Ivan Karamazov's cry, "everything is permitted." Their boundless evil is like Roquentin's oozing tree. Like the tree's outrageous proliferation which shatters the theory that essence precedes existence, the Nazis' refusal to abide by the rules of civilization makes a mockery of all illusions about moral behavior, social order, and humanist conceptions of man. If civilized people like the Germans can suddenly become uncivilized monsters, then one's belief in the continuity of human essence is destroyed. As Von Berg says, "What one used to conceive a human being to be will have no room on this earth."[10] The effect of this transformation stuns those who retain the civilized codes, now seen as absurdly fragile artifices, and arouses the sense of "nausea" that afflicts Roquentin. Von Berg is the first to recognize the implication of the Nazi power. When told of the death camps in Poland, he says, "I find it the most believable atrocity I have heard." When asked why, he replies: "Because it is so inconceivably vile. That is their power, to do the inconceivable; it paralyzes the rest of us" (p. 61). The Nazis are like Camus's "plague" which falls upon our safe and ordered lives and alienates us from all harmonious connections with the universe. In the wake of their attack on civilization lies the void, the disintegrated wreckage of all human constructs against the threat of chaos. "Who can ever save us," cries Von Berg after his awakening (p. 107).

But Von Berg's plea is, of course, the starting point for existential ethics, for if man can no longer find refuge in external deities and beliefs, he must look for sanctions within himself. Since existence is neither inherently necessary or predefined, man is free in that he is permanently in flux; his capacity for self definition is therefore illimitable: "Man is nothing but that which he makes of himself," Sartre writes, "that is the first principle of existentialism."[11] The only solution to the devastation wrecked upon human security by the plague is a responsible and free human action, an end in itself, which will momentarily solidify the relentless flow of our inner and outer being. But it is precisely this obligation that causes dread in man. As Sartre says, "Man is condemned to be free." The constant necessity to reassert and redefine values, projects, and commitments – the perpetual challenge to justify one's life – produces anguish, the feeling that results when we confront "the absolute openness of our future, the nothingness in the center of which we live."[12] Rather than commit himself to responsible actions without recourse to outside justification, man clings instead to "bad faith," that "lie in the soul", as Sartre calls it, which enables him to flee from responsibility into determinism.

Bad faith appears in a variety of forms: the coward abandons freedom by fabricating excuses for his condition; the masochist accepts the congealed image imposed upon him by the Other; the "salaud" claims special rights to existence in accord with a fabricated, *a priori* system of values and assumptions. The persecutors and victims in Miller's play clearly illustrate one or more of these types.

The Nazi, to begin with, is the most violent example of Sartre's concept of the anti-Semite – the most dangerous man of "bad faith." If the phenomenon of Nazism illuminates the horror of contingency to the naive civilized man, Nazism itself can be seen as a flight from the same Nothingness. The Nazi is incapable of accepting his condition of freedom. He flees from consciousness which reveals to him the contingency of the human conditon, the openness of all truth, the limitless and elusive possibilities of his self image, and chooses instead "impenetrability," the durability of a stone.[13] He cannot tolerate the continual suspension of his existence but wishes "to exist all at once and right away" (p. 19). Sartre's concept is clearly expressed by Von Berg's analysis of the Germans, who assiduously "despise everything that is not German": "They do these things not because they are Germans but because they are nothing. It is the hallmark of our age – the less you exist the more important it it to make a clear impression" (p. 61).

Fleeing from Nothingness, the Germans find refuge in the "durable stone" of Nazi ideology. Their lives, as a result, far from being gratuitous, become absolutely necessary: they have "rights," like Lucien, the anti-Semite in Sartre's short story "The Childhood of a Leader," but these "rights" can only be affirmed by denying them to other people. Like the actors in Genet's *The Balcony* who need the cooperation of the Other in order for the game of illusion to be maintained, the Nazi needs the Jew to affirm his illusion of personal necessity. "If the Jew did not exist," Sartre says, "the anti-Semite would have to invent him" (p. 13).

Anti-Semitism, therefore, is an ontological phenomena in that it reveals a yearning for a cohesive sense of being, a passion for essence. Because one's essence, however, is continuously nihilated by the Nothingness that separates man from what he was and what he wants to be, the anti-Semite must repress his consciousness and thereby convert a false assumption into a sacred belief. To achieve this aim, the anti-Semite divides the world into a Manichean duality of good and evil – gentiles and Jews – and to sustain this duality he must be constantly alert, wary of any sudden, rational intrusion into his fabrication.

Anti-Semitism is thus a freely chosen project which crystalizes the world and the individual anti-Semite's place in it. He no longer fears isolation, ego deflation, or purposelessness; he belongs not only to his country, a condition forever barred to the alien Jew, but also to the community of anti-Semites to which he clings. His essence is clearly defined, tangible, and, in his own mind, empirically defensible.

The Professor in *Vichy* is the clearest example of the Nazis' "bad faith." Armed with the scientific conclusions of the "Race Institute," the Professor's function is to separate "inferiors" like Jews and gypsies from the superior race. His "rights" as a superior person, sanctioned to live whereas other people are not, are never questioned: "Science is not capricious," he tells the Major, "My degree is in racial anthropology" (p. 65). The Professor is a "salaud" and he fits Sartre's description of the anti-Semite as a "destroyer in function, a sadist with a pure heart. ... He knows that he is wicked, but since he does evil for the sake of Good, since a whole people waits for deliverance at his hands, he looks upon himself as a sanctified evil-doer" (p. 50). The Professor's "bad faith" extends beyond his scientific assertion of "rights and duties" to a disavowal of personal responsibility for the acts he performs: "I will not continue without you, Major. The Army's responsibility is quite as great as mine here (p. 67). By diffusing all responsibility, the Professor hopes to deindividualize himself; he seeks facelessness in the collective unit of the Nazi apparatus because, even though he is scientifically convinced of his "rights" as a German, he is unwilling to stand alone and assume the consequences of his assertion.

The Jews themselves all face an existential crisis: "The Jew remains the stranger, the intruder, the unassimilated at the heart of our society," Sartre writes (p. 83). As Sartre says: "To be a Jew is to be thrown into – to be abandoned to – the situation of a Jew" (p. 88). This particular situation of the Jew is to be looked at by the anti-Semite. This "look" of the other is the essence of Sartre's concept of Being-for-Others – a mode of existence clearly illustrated by the Jew's relationship with his enemy. "Conflict," Sartre says, "is the original meaning of Being-for-Others."[14] One's consciousness, Sartre says, is unreflective of itself and needs the presence not only of objects but of the

Other's subjectivity to realize its structure of being. We determine ourselves according to the other's image of us. But the confrontation between two individuals results in a struggle to undermine the freedom of each since the Other's look is unfortunately negative and enslaving.

The presence of the Other is Sartre's version of the fall, since the Other cuts off man's freedom and renders him vulnerable to feelings of shame and ossification. The loss of innocence is the consciousness of being seen and the consequent guilt one feels in the "look" of the Other. The Other freezes our possibilities for transcendence by imposing on us a "Nature," an outside, an objective identity. We are no longer in process but are fixed in the jelled image of the Other's gaze. Because the "look" is reciprocative, human relations become a relentless, see-saw battle of wills, each person attempting to wriggle out of the Medusa stare of the Other in a desperate effort to regain freedom. The antagonists often collapse into the bad faith of sadism and masochism in order to end the struggle.

In the Jew–anti-Semite confrontation, the anti-Semite sadistically objectifies the Jew in order to justify his own existence, while the Jew often submits to this manipulation in order to escape the struggle toward transcendence. But the masochistic Jew will always feel anguish because he knows that within his violently narrow sphere he is free to make choices. If nothing else, he is free to determine his attitude toward uncontrollable circumstances. In his situation, therefore, the Jew can either act authentically by maintaining a "lucid consciousness" of the situation and assuming the risks and responsibilities it involves (meaning, to defy the gaze of the anti-Semite), or inauthentically by escaping into the "bad faith" of cowardice and masochism.

Marchand, the wealthy merchant, acts inauthentically by removing himself from his fellow Jews and indirectly denying his Jewishness. Similar to Birenshatz in Sartre's novel, *The Reprieve,* Marchand is disgusted by the Jewishness of others and considers himself to be purely French. But, as Sartre says, "If the Jew has decided that his race does not exist, it is up to him to prove it: for a Jew cannot choose not to be a Jew" (p. 89). The Nazis release Marchand, presumably because they still consider him useful, but once they choose to manifest his "race" all his efforts to repudiate their "look" will be in vain.

Both Miller and Sartre agree that a Jew cannot be defined by religion, race, or national identity: one is a Jew if a gentile says one is a Jew, a thesis Miller previously affirmed in his novel *Focus*. Quite simply, Sartre says, "what makes the Jew is his concrete situation, what unites him to other Jews is the identity of their situation" (p. 145). The look of the gentile circumscribes the situation of a Jew and defines the choices he is compelled to make. In *Vichy* the Jews are thrust into their Jewishness. The victims in the play, aside from the religious old man, are either indifferent or hostile to their Jewishness. Each considers himself French, and each identifies himself with his profession or political ideology rather than his religion. There is no feeling of unity in their mutual crisis and even their physical movements on stage lead away from their fellow victims toward a brooding isolation. What unites them technically into a "we" consciousness is simply the fact that the Nazi, or the "third" as Sartre would call him, looks upon them hostilely as a collective unit. The Jew experiences the "look" of the anti-Semite as a community alienation, but his sense of "community" ironically arouses only fear and antagonism.

The artist Lebeau, for example, is a masochist who feels a Kafkaesque sense of guilt because he is a Jew and is driven by his humiliation and despair into a death wish. He waits for slaughter like a naughty child waits for parental punishment: "I don't know. Maybe it's that they keep saying such terrible things about us, and you can't answer. And after years of it you ... I wouldn't say you believe it, but ... you do, a little" (p. 80). Sartre points out that this kind of inferiority complex is not actually received from the outside, but that the Jew "creates this complex when he chooses to live out his situation in an unauthentic manner. He has allowed himself to be persuaded by the anti-Semites; he is the first victim of their propaganda (p. 94). Lebeau accepts the image of himself that he sees reflected in the eyes of the Other, and instead of transcending the Other's gaze, he allows himself to be paralyzed and destroyed. He relinquishes his freedom as a man in order to sink into the blissful passivity of a Thing. Like the Nazi, who solidifies himself in the role of "Superior One," Lebeau escapes his crisis by falling into the stone-like posture of "victim." His struggle ends in resigned submission.

Bayard, the communist, can suppress his panic only by depersonalizing himself. He is the Sartrean "man of seriousness," like Brunet, the dedicated party worker in *Roads to Freedom,* whose individual fate will be redeemed by the inevitable proletarian victory. Bayard, too, is guilty of "bad faith": like the Professor he abdicates his freedom by dissolving his individuality in a collective mass, and by turning back on the existential present for the theoretical proletarian revolt in the future. Von Berg's pointed assertion that most Nazis are from the working class damages Bayard's thesis, but he continues to delude himself in the absence of any other defense. Without his communistic idealism, Bayard explains, "I wouldn't have the strength to walk through that door" (p. 54). Like Sartre's Brunet, Bayard is an attractive character, strong, alert and ideologically sincere, but his absolute belief in historical determinism compromises his authenticity.

Monceau, an actor, puts the reality of the Absurd at a distance by fabricating an image for himself as he does on stage. He believes he can flee from his crisis into the illusion of a role. Believing that the Nazis are like dangerous animals who can sniff out the fear in their victims, he will *act* as if he is unafraid, for salvation lies simply in the ability to convince one's executioners that one is not a victim. Monceau refuses to acknowledge the absence of reason in their plight and chooses instead to delude himself into believing the Nazis cannot be as monstrous as people say and that civilization has not ended, despite all the evidence to the contrary: "I go on the assumption that if I obey the law with dignity I will live in peace" (p. 82). Pushed by Leduc to the extremity of his illusion, Monceau finally admits that if the world is mad, there is nothing he can do but submit to its madness, a conclusion which draws from Leduc the despairing remark: "Your heart is conquered territory, mister" (p. 83).

Like Lebeau, Monceau succumbs to the temptation of "impenetrability." He, too, is masochistic, an object to be casually destroyed by the hostile Other. His "bad faith" lies in his refusal to acknowledge the mutability of the world, its potentiality for alteration through human action. But action demands revolt, and, as in the case of Lebeau, the role of rebel proves more terrifying to him than the role of victim.

The dramatic core of the play is the moral debate between the psychiatrist Leduc, the German Major, and Von Berg. Their arguments revolve around Miller's central question: What is the nature and possibility of responsibility in a world acknowledged to be absurd? The German Major, according to his statements to Leduc, is a decent man who despises Nazi brutality and madness, but in order for him to protest against this evil he would have to sacrifice his life. Furthermore, his sacrifice would change absolutely nothing because, as he tells Leduc, "We would all be replaced by tomorrow morning, wouldn't we?" (p. 85). All that he would gain from helping Leduc escape would be Leduc's love and respect, but the Major cannot accept this reward as adequate compensation because, "Nothing of that kind is left, don't you understand that yet?" (p. 86).

The Major's "bad faith" is similar to Monceau's: Both men relinquish their freedom by submitting to what they insist is an overwhelming determinism. "There are no persons anymore, don't you see that? There will never be persons again," the Major shouts (p. 87). Responsibility and ethics in a fallen world become meaningless words to the Major, but his plea of helplessness is merely an evasion of his own tormenting moral impulses.

The Major, like Garcin in Sartre's *No Exit*, is guilty of essentialism. He tries to convince Leduc that he has an essence of decency which circumstances cannot violate. "Captain, I would only like to say that … this is all as inconceivable to me as it is to you. Can you believe that?" (p. 85). But Miller, like Sartre, insists on defining character through action. Since essence is never given but rather chosen and constantly renewed, a man *is* what he *does,* and all the Major's civilized instincts are nullified by his uncivilized acts. "I'd believe it if you shot yourself," Leduc replies. "And better yet, if you took a few of them with you" (p. 85).

Deprived of his decent "nature" by the scornful "Look" of Leduc, the Major now tries to ensnare a new being completely outside himself. Exploding with hystierical fury, he hurls himself into the role of anti-Semite by making the Jews cower under his pistol: "Like dogs, Jew-dogs – look at him – with his paws folded. Look what happens when I yell at him, Dog" (p. 87). Submitting to the lure of sadism, the Major now decides to be nothing but the fear he inspires in others. By conforming his words and gestures to the disquieting image he sees in the eyes of his victim, he achieves a solid reality and momentarily dispels his anguish.

The Major's sadistic "bad faith" is further reinforced when he skillfully challenges Leduc's assumption of moral superiority. By forcing Leduc to admit that his innocence is coincident with his present role of victim, the Major makes clear the circumstantial nature of morality. When asked by the Major if he would refuse to be released while his fellow Jews were kept prisoners, Leduc is forced to answer "no." It becomes clear that the foundation for moral stability is precarious, and even decent men like Leduc would rather survive in disgrace than die with honor. Under these circumstances, the efficacy of individual moral action becomes buried in an infinite chain of destructive power: an executioner like the Major is himself a victim, acting in response to a gun pointing at his head. In a crisis situation, when individual moral action can only be equated with self destruction and when evil is seen as a constant in human relations, all rational motives for decency decay and the world collapses into moral anarchy.

Up to this point, Miller seems to have presented a nihilistic vision. Von Berg, however, is Miller's answer to despair. Like Sartre's Orestes in *The Flies,* he is the existential hero who wrenches himself from passivity to engagement by freely committing a sacrificial act. Von Berg's act is absurd in that it has no rational basis, but it elevates him to moral authenticity. His rebellion annihilates the nausea brought on by his understanding of the Nazi plague and his realization of his personal complicity in the holocaust, a realization unknown to him until his conversation with Leduc toward the end of the play. Leduc convinces the apparently innocent Von Berg that he harbors in his heart, unknown to himself, "a dislike, if not hatred of Jews," not like an ordinary anti-Semite, but simply as a human being who must somehow objectify his need to despise "that stranger, that agony we cannot feel, that death we look at like a cold abstraction" (p. 105). For Von Berg, the Jew fulfills Heidegger's concept of "the one" upon whom we thrust off the threat of death: "one dies," we say, never imagining the statement to apply to ourselves. "Each man has his Jew; it is the other," Leduc says. "And the Jews have their Jews" (p. 105). The hunger for survival makes accomplices of us all.

Von Berg's sacrifice, however, eradicates his guilt as victimizer and confirms his previously untested assertion that "there are people who would find it easier to die than stain one finger with this murder" (p. 104). Von Berg's present action throws Leduc's accusation of complicity into the irrelevant past.

Von Berg, in effect, becomes what he does: by dying in Leduc's place he translates his guilt into active responsibility and becomes Leduc's "Jew."

Leduc is now stained by Von Berg's gift of life and must carry on the existential cycle of transmuting his guilt into redemptive action. He is free, like all men, to transcend his present action by choosing a new and redeeming project. If Leduc fights in the Resistance, he will modify the guilt brought on by Von Berg's sacrifice: the death of the weak aristocrat will then be justified by the services of the strong combat officer. Until he performs that action, however, Leduc will feel as morally debased as the Major who also saves his life at the expense of the Other.

Von Berg is the only triumphant character in the play since death will cut him off at his highest point and permanently fix his essence as martyr. His act frees him from alienation and imposes a moral coherence upon his previously contingent world.

The varied threads of the intellectual and emotional debate finally crystallize around the concrete act of Von Berg. A moral norm is unequivocally established: One's life must submit to one's conscience, despite the absence of any external moral criteria. All the characters in the play, particularly the Major, are judged by Von Berg's "Look," and since Von Berg will die, his look becomes uneradicable. Of course the possibility of the Major's moral transcendence in the eyes of others continues to exist, but under the implacable gaze of Von Berg the Major can never alter his constitution as a degraded object.

The play thus represents in its total action the essence of Sartre's philosophy, which was, and still is, the demand for authenticity, or the moral awakening to individual responsibility. But if Miller follows Sartre in the general theme, structure, and dynamics of his play, his implied conclusion to the threat of anti-Semitism differs radically from Sartre's *Anti-Semite and Jew*. Ironically, Sartre offers an optimistic proposal to the problem while Miller remains doubtful and pessimistic. In the twenty-one years between the publication of *Being and Nothingness* and the production of *Incident at Vichy* the two writers have exchanged philosophic positions — Miller subscribing to Sartre's corrosive analysis of human relations in *Being and Nothingess* and Sartre affirming Miller's former belief in human solidarity.

Despite Sartre's analysis of anti-Semitism as a cowardly search for being and, therefore, an ontological problem, he nevertheless concludes that the Jew's dilemma is social and consequently remediable.

Sartre's ordinarily complex and tough-minded Marxism seems simplistic and contradictory in *Anti-Semite and Jew*. While allowing for the freedom of the anti-Semite, Sartre nevertheless believes that an alteration of the anti-Semite's situation will consequently alter his choice of being. Existential free will and socialist determinism are unsatisfactorily mixed. With the advent of the Marxist state, Sartre predicts, all members would feel a mutual bond of solidarity because they would all be engaged in a common enterprise, and anti-Semitism would naturally disappear. Man's fear of being would be overcome by the benevolent leadership of the unbiased proletarian, the abolition of private ownership of land, and the consequent elimination of class struggles.

As Sartre's political activism increased, Miller's early leftist enthusiasm diminished. Leduc undoubtedly speaks for the playwright when he insists that "man is not reasonable, that he is full of murder, that his ideals are only the little tax he pays for the right to hate and kill with a clear conscience" (p. 104). Leduc's description might well fit the brutal characters in Sartre's early play *No Exit*, that grim dramatization of human interaction as outlined in *Being and Nothingness*. Since the void at the heart of being is a static condition, man's attempts to escape it through sadism and masochism cannot be expected to change.

Understandably, *Incident at Vichy* has been attacked by left wing critics. Eric Mottram has accused Miller of expounding nihilistic despair: "Miller can only see the present repeated endlessly as the future ... Miller can suggest no argument for the future based on social change, through economic legislation, education and sexual understanding."[15] Miller would answer that he is still a liberal, but his faith in the efficacy of social reform has diminished since man's evil, he now feels, is directly related to his fear of existence, an unalterable condition even in the Marxist "utopia."

Tom F. Driver, writing from a theological perspective, criticizes Miller's loss of faith in a "universal moral sanction" and his subsequent failure to discover a conceivable basis for a new one.[16] Miller does offer a "lesson" in *Incident at Vichy* however: If man can awaken to his complicity in evil, he can exchange his guilt for responsibility, as does Von Berg. But Miller admits that "it is immensely difficult to be human precisely because we cannot detect our own hostility in our own actions. It is tragic, fatal blindness. ..."[17] Driver describes the existential nature of Miller's conclusions:

There being no objective good and evil, and no imperative other than conscience, man himself must be made to bear the full burden of creating his values and living up to them. The immensity of this task is beyond human capacity ... to insist upon it without reference to ultimate truth is to create a situation productive of despair.[18]

Obviously, however, this moral task is not "beyond human capacity" since Von Berg succeeds in fulfilling it. It is well to remember that Miller based his play on a true story.

Undeniably, Miller's moral imperative is difficult. His attack on Jewish victims like Lebeau and Monceau, who willingly submit to their destruction, may seem callous, especially since Miller concedes the terrible plight of the escaped Jew in occupied Europe. But in the claustrophobic intensity of the drama, Miller succeeds in turning us against these inauthentic characters. He strips away all extenuating circumstances and brings each man into an irreducible conflict with his fate. There is no mitigation of the harsh necessity to choose ourselves, especially since Miller seems to agree with the Sartrean ethic that what one chooses for oneself, one chooses for all men. Miller is, in essence, dramatizing Sartre's famous account of the freedom one felt in France during the Occupation, "When the choice each of us made of our life was an authentic choice because it was made face to face with death."[19] Man is always capable of saying "no," even to his torturer.

Von Berg chooses to say "no" to the men and circumstances that threaten to degrade him, and he therefore fits Miller's definition of the tragic hero in his early essay, "Tragedy and the Common Man." Although the play is grim, it is not "productive of despair" since the heroic action of a frightened and delicate man sets the norm for all the characters. If Miller now seems pessimistic about Mankind, he is still optimistic about individual man. Solidarity between two individuals is achieved; a gentile has broken through the ontological barrier that makes an enemy or an object of the Jew; and guilt has been eradicated through heroic action. If it is clear at the end that Evil is unredeemable and that the horror just witnessed will be repeated after the arrival of new prisoners, the cycle of complicity has been momentarily broken and the human reaffirmed.

Eric Mottram has negatively described the climax of *Vichy* as "an act of courage and love within the context of nihilism."[20] But is this statement not an apt description of some of the most powerful of modern tragedies?

NOTES

1 "Arthur Miller," *Encounter,* November 1970, p. 73.

2 Quoted *ibid.,* p. 74.

3 "Forgers of Myth," in *Playwrights on Playwriting,* ed. Toby Cole, New York, 1960, p. 123.

4 *Ibid.,* p. 122.

5 *Ibid.,* p. 117.

6 Robert Brustein, *Seasons of Discontent,* New York, 1967, p. 260.

7 "The Shadows of the Gods," in *American Playwrights on Drama,* ed. Horst Frenz, New York, 1965, p. 139.

8 *Nausea,* Norfolk, Conn., undated, p. 176.

9 "Existentialism," in *A Casebook on Existentialism,* ed. William Spanos, New York, 1964, p. 282.

10 *Incident at Vichy,* New York, 1967, p. 61. Subsequent references are cited in the text.

11 "Existentialism," p. 278.

12 Maurice Cranston, *Jean Paul Sartre*, New York, 1962, p. 49.

13 *Anti-Semite and Jew*, trans. George J. Becker, New York, 1962, p. 18. Subsequent references are cited in the text.

14 *Being and Nothingness*, trans. Hazel Barnes, New York, 1956, p. 367.

15 "Arthur Miller: The Development of a Political Dramatist in America," in *Arthur Miller: A Collection of Critical Essays*, ed. Robert W. Corrigan, Englewood Cliffs, New Jersey, 1969, pp. 55-6.

16 "Strength and Weakness in Arthur Miller," *Arthur Miller*, ed. Robert Corrigan, p. 65.

17 "Our Guilt for the World's Evil," quoted by Leonard Moss, *Arthur Miller*, New Haven, 1967, p. 97.

18 Driver, p. 66.

19 Quoted by William Barrett, "Jean Paul Sartre," in *On Contemporary Literature*, ed. Richard Kostelanetz, New York, 1964, p. 557.

20 Mottram, p. 54.

Part Three

Edward Albee
1928–

Tragic Vision in *The Zoo Story*

ROBERT B. BENNETT

While the conclusion to *The Zoo Story* has met with the approval of some readers and the disapproval of others, the meaning of the protagonist's death has not been disputed. The consensus has been that Albee intends us to understand Jerry's death as a Christ-like sacrifice. Rose Zimbardo and George Wellwarth praise the symbolism. Martin Esslin and Brian Way complain that the play's ending loses absurdist rigor and degenerates into sentimentality.[1] Similarly Lee Baxandall argues that when Albee resorts to aesthetic solutions, which are symbolically instead of historically meaningful, he does not offer a solution viable in drama, "the most socially rooted of the arts."[2]

Apparently unheeded by all these viewpoints are Albee's stage directions. These, it seems to me, are included in order to prevent us and the actor who plays Jerry from either sentimentalizing his death scene or regarding it purely as a Christ-like sacrifice. Albee writes:

Oh, Peter, I was so afraid I'd drive you away. (*He laughs as best he can*) You don't know how afraid I was you'd go away and leave me. ... Peter ... thank you. I came unto you (*He laughs, so faintly*) and you have comforted me. Dear Peter.[3]

The biblical phrasing and the expression of thanks and affection would, by themselves, be sentimental. Laughter, however, is an expression not of compassion, but of psychic distance. Moreover, Jerry's going on to praise Peter for being an animal like the rest of us ("You're an animal, too" [p. 49]) may be laughable and depressing, but it is not melodramatic; and his scornfully mimicking Peter in his dying breath should discourage us from accusing Jerry of emotional over-indulgence. At the same time, however, Jerry clearly wants to believe that a God exists and that love is possible; and he has witnessed what seem to be similar longings in the other persons in his rooming-house. Indeed,

Jerry is not a hardened absurdist;[4] and if Albee's stage directions are followed, there will be supplication along with mimicry in his ambivalent last words. Jerry hopes that his death is possibly sacrificial and that he has created by his act an effect beyond itself; but he is not so spiritually entranced as to fail to realize that his Christ-like self-sacrifice for Peter's regeneration – what Baxandall means presumably by his "aestheticism of symbolic transcendence" (p. 98) – may possibly be no more than a glorified front to a suicide. In other words Jerry, and Albee, are as conscious of the frailty of the symbolic solution as Baxandall is.

To regard the dramatic experience of *The Zoo Story* as embodying a doctrinally absolute statement underestimates the play's complexity. Albee does not here presume the absurdist's certainty that all is meaningless nor the social protester's certainty that he knows what is wrong and how to correct it.[5] Rather, in the manner of tragedy, this play tests and questions, by the experience it presents, the propositions of religion and philosophy. Through Jerry, Albee asks how we can tell whether spiritual love is a genuine human faculty or an illusion. Jerry hopes that man is a spiritual creature, expects that he is no more than an animal with illusory and frustrated spiritual longings, and fears that man may have lost even his animal instincts as a result of social conditioning. At the time of the play Jerry is consumed by a need to resolve these doubts; and, to borrow Arthur Miller's description of the tragic hero, he "is ready to lay down his life, if need be, to secure ... his personal dignity."[6]

Jerry's concern about his personal dignity is more cosmic than social, and is centered in the question, "If we can so misunderstand, well then, why have we invented the word love in the first place?" (p. 36). Jerry realizes that if man is incapable of loving, he cannot be blamed for not loving. On this level of perception, Jerry sees Peter as man (*Homo sapiens*) to be understood by comparison with animal and vegetable nature. Jerry does not pigeonhole Peter as the affluent-New-York-businessman; this label is merely the superficial and illusory identity that he sees standing in the way of Peter's self-knowledge. Whereas Michael Rutenberg sees Jerry as a social critic like Vance Packard,[7] I find him less obviously but more importantly a philosopher like Hamlet. Just as Hamlet questions why the Creator has given us "godlike reason/To fust in us unus'd" (IV.iv.33–39),[8] so Jerry wonders why man possesses the urge for spiritual communion if there is no worldy way to express and fulfill it. If love can only "fust in us unus'd," he seems to say, then man is "a beast, no more."

The dramatic power of tragedy usually depends heavily upon the playwright's giving expression to a full complex of feelings and perceptions within the protagonist toward himself and his world. These will have been generated by an experience that has jarred him from a conventional pattern of existence. In *The Zoo Story* the three attitudes of love, hate, and indifference provide the general frames of reference for the conflicting forces within Jerry himself and between Jerry and Peter. Kindness proceeds from spiritual nature; cruelty from animal nature; and indifference from social conditioning which reduces one's personality, Jerry suggests, to the level of a vegetable. Jerry, as author of the incident, tries to shape his actions according to the hypothesis that kindness (love) and cruelty (hate) in combination form the teaching emotion, an emotion which can harmonize the elements of spirit and body in man, and resolve the tensions that divide his amphibian nature. The seeming antithesis between the separate emotions of love and hate dissolves, Jerry has learned, when both are understood to be expressions of passionate commitment that together vie against the inclination toward apathy in the effort to define what man is or what he can become. Although one probably first thinks of the play as a conflict between the loving-hating Jerry and the indifferent Peter, I shall try to show that indifference has not been foreign to Jerry's nature, either in his past or in the present, and that the play is also importantly a conflict of all three attitudes within Jerry himself. As is true of most tragedies, there is no clear resolution in this play's conclusion. Death ends the struggle but does not definitively answer the questions, although the final projection is admittedly bleak.

In order fully to understand *The Zoo Story* as tragedy, we must first reassess some of the common assumptions that, if accepted, undermine the play's basic dynamics and reduce the play from a dramatic experience to a philosophical lesson. Frequently Jerry is spoken of as a symbol "meaning" something instead of a human being who is doing and feeling something. "The old pigeonhole bit" of calling Jerry a Christ figure or "a universal symbol of alienated modern man"[9] automatically sets a critical distance between us and Jerry, and makes genuine sympathy for him impossible. We have already seen the inadequacy of a strict reading of Jerry as Christ-like. This is an image to which he consciously aspires but not one that he uncritically accepts as achieved or even as valid. The symbol, thus, remains subordinate to and less than the experience. Those who suggest that Jerry is "alienated modern man" incapable of love not only limit the play's vision but seriously misrepresent it. While their argument rightly observes that Jerry in the past has not been able to love "the little ladies" or his lonely compeers in the rooming-house, it must assume, in order to sustain its point, that Jerry, contrary to his claim, has learned nothing from his experience with the dog, and that he shows no love in his relationship with Peter. It must interpret Jerry's sharing with Peter his most personal feelings, thoughts, and experiences as insincere or as yielding to an irresistible impulse rather than, in the way Albee's stage directions urge, as an honest and difficult giving of himself. In general, studies have discussed Jerry as if his nature were frozen, not vital and developing. Jerry's comment, "every once in a while I like to talk to somebody, really *talk*" (p. 17), has encouraged critical inferences such as, "Jerry, weary of the indecisive encounters with the Peters ..." (Baxandall, "Theater of Edward Albee," p. 88), which see his present action as part of an habitual effort to make contact. But Jerry's own account of his past indicates that what he is doing with Peter is as new to him as it is to Peter. When Jerry describes the colored queen who leaves his door open and the woman who cries behind her closed door, we realize that he observed and did not respond to their passive invitations for a relief from loneliness. Similarly Jerry never saw the prostitutes more than once. Jerry's intense assault on Peter is in striking contrast to his former aloofness. The intervening event between his past and present that causes this change is his collective encounter with the landlady and the dog. This is an experience of tragic awakening which shapes his vision of man and possesses his spirit.

Jerry differs from Peter and from us not in his complex human nature but in his particular tragic experience; and his plight sets in bold relief a universal human problem. Two experiences, his lifelong poverty and the recent rooming-house episode, separate Jerry from Peter. Jerry's poverty has made him more aware than Peter of a spiritual side to his nature that needs fulfillment. Preoccupation with the paraphernalia of society, says *The Zoo Story* (in a manner that reminds us of *Everyman*), encourages man to ignore the existential loneliness of his human condition and, hence, stifles his initiative to seek spiritual fulfillment. The traditional tragic situation in which alienation from society brings suffering and spiritual awareness is present here in the colored queen, the weeping woman, and the little ladies, as well as in Jerry. It is because these characters manifest in their actions an intense spiritual longing, a sensitivity not evident in Peter, that Jerry holds the existence of God and love possible ("with making money with your body which is an act of love ... WITH GOD WHO IS A COLORED QUEEN ... WHO IS A WOMAN WHO CRIES WITH DETERMINATION BEHIND HER CLOSED DOOR" [p. 35]). But whereas poverty has simply stimulated an awareness of spiritual privation, the encounter with the landlady and the dog has gone farther by jolting Jerry with the suggestion that the fault for his loneliness lies not with God, the stars, or society, but with himself. The actions of his two assailants not only force Jerry to recognize his own resistance to involvement, but also suggest to him a possible method for overcoming such resistance in others. The landlady made advances of love to Jerry, so far as her level of being could approach it, and Jerry responded with the same wish to be rid of her that Peter has toward him. The dog made advances that Jerry describes as antipathy and, on reflection, possibly love; and it received a similar resistance from Jerry. Jerry fed and poisoned the dog to get it to leave him *alone*. Critics impose a conventional symbolism on the dog's behavior, ignoring Jerry's unconventional perception; and they miss the point of the encounter. Rutenberg writes:

The symbolism, unmistakably, is that the dog represents that vicious aspect of society which attacks whenever Jerry tries to gain entrance. The dog never attacks when Jerry leaves the premises, only when he enters. Later in the play Peter "will respond to the invasion of his 'property' with the same ferocity the dog has shown," clearly illustrating this animalistic reaction to an invasion of one's private thoughts. (*Edward Albee*, p. 31)

Perhaps the dog was protecting his domain (which is an animal trait people possess, not a feature of society which dogs have picked up), but Jerry believes and tries to explain to Peter that the dog's attempt to bite him was probably an act of love. The parallels between the dog and Peter that Rutenberg, quoting Zimbardo, draws are misleading (*Edward Albee*, p. 13). The dog attacks Jerry of its own initiative. Peter, left to his own initiative, would have walked home. His defense of the bench comes only after Jerry's calculated efforts to provoke at least an animal response in Peter. There is nothing in the play's final action which relates to an invasion of Peter's private thoughts, about which Jerry has ceased to concern himself since Peter's reaction to Jerry's long monologue. The parallels that do exist are between the dog's attack on Jerry and Jerry's assault on Peter, and between Jerry's attempts to keep the dog away and Peter's efforts to avoid involvement with Jerry. For Rutenberg's symbolic formula to work, Peter would have to knock Jerry off the bench the moment Jerry sits down. Albee's point is that Jerry has worked Peter out of his social mold as a vegetable into an animal state that is at least Peter's own self. The importance to Jerry of the assaults of the landlady and the dog is that together they have had effects outside of themselves. They have aroused in Jerry strong feelings, a violent antipathy toward the landlady and a love for the dog, curiously counter-balancing the feelings they have shown him. They have possessed Jerry with an idea of communication that he must test. And apparently they have dispossessed him of the rooming-house, just as he will dispossess Peter of the bench. Quickly, as if embarrassed to admit it, Jerry tells Peter toward the end of his narrative, "I have not returned" (p. 35). Their invasion of Jerry's private space has made it impossible for him to remain spiritually isolated, aware only of his own loneliness and his own needs.

Yet, however illuminating Jerry's experience with the dog has been, it has concluded unsatisfactorily. After claiming they made contact, Jerry says in apparent contradiction, "We had made many attempts at contact, and we had failed" (p. 35). Ironically, what seems to have happened is that their actions have resulted not in a meeting of minds but in a transference of attitudes. The dog has received Jerry's message in the feeding and poisoning and now leaves him alone, and Jerry, believing now that the dog attacked him out of affection, loves the animal! Jerry has socially conditioned the dog to indifference at the same time that the dog has engendered in him a compelling desire for establishing a relationship. The change, of course, is not the one Jerry ultimately hoped for: " ... I loved the dog now, and I wanted him to love me. ... I don't really know why I expected the dog to understand anything, much less

my motivations ... I hoped that the dog would understand" (p. 34). Jerry seems
to sustain his hope for a spiritual communion by concluding he expected too
much of the dog, limited as it is by its animal nature. If his longing can ever be
fulfilled, it must be through communion with a person.

Jerry brings from his rooming-house experience more than a pain-pleasure
teaching technique. Having his own indifference toward others revealed to
him, he has learned a compassionate explanation for others' indifference
toward him that allows at least a part of him to feel affection and sympathy for
Peter. Indifference, which gives the impression of irresponsible neglect,
complacency, selfishness, and presumptuous superiority, may actually be the
embarrassed response of one who wants but does not know how to share
feelings with others. Jerry's description of his final relationship with the dog is
suggestive of a much broader human situation: "We regard each other with a
mixture of sadness and suspicion, and then we *feign* indifference" (p. 35, my
italics). Jerry realizes that the family man Peter, who spends his free time alone
on a park bench, is as lonely as he is, though suffering less because he is more
lost.[10] Jerry approaches Peter, then, as an enlightened brother and not, as
Wellwarth (p. 323) and Nilan (p. 59) claim, as a polar opposite.

Neither hope nor despair totally governs Jerry at the opening of the play. The
new and driving hope generated by the rooming-house incident counters but by
no means eliminates his "great weariness," his old and ingrained fear of
involvement and responsibility. Jerry's hope is evident in his passionate
displays of love and hate for Peter; his indifference, in his mocking and
patronizing manner. The former attitude seeks to establish a kinship while the
latter longs simply for death. On the surface it looks as if death has been Jerry's
primary objective; his early prophecy of what Peter would see on TV and his
retrospective "could I have planned all this? ... I think I did" (p. 48) encourage
this assumption. It is more accurate, though, to see Jerry at the start expecting
and half hoping to die but hoping more to establish a relationship on spiritual
rather than physical terms. Jerry's anger and disappointment when Peter fails to
respond with loving understanding to his confessional narrative are directly
proportional to the degree to which his passionate hope has overweighed his
detached expectation; and Albee's stage directions indicate that the conclusion
of Jerry's story and the period immediately following are the moments of
greatest emotional intensity in the play.

To this point I have tried to demonstrate Jerry's basic and complex humanity,
and the conditions and experiences that have raised him to a special level of
sensitivity and awareness. There remains, though, in claiming for Jerry a tragic
status, the need to admire his encounter with Peter as a skillful and honest
attempt to resolve the basic tensions within himself and, by extension, within
man. For if his effort is either facile or fundamentally misguided, or if his
feelings are maudlin and excessive, his state is less than tragic.

An answer to critics' complaints that Jerry does not carry on a real conversation with Peter provides us with a means for examining Jerry's effort in specific terms.[11] For in Peter, Albee has effectively dramatized his belief that "the sentences people make half the time bear absolutely no resemblance to what people think."[12] Peter, at his present level of sensitivity, is not able to "really talk." And Jerry knows that he cannot genuinely communicate with Peter until he has shown him that "normal conversation" is typically a rhetorical exercise designed to avoid self-expression. In order to establish real contact with Peter, therefore, Jerry himself must "go a very long distance out of his way to come back a short distance correctly." His verbal assault is the pedagogical tool by which he hopes to make Peter aware of the enslaving formula of polite conversation. With this awareness, he hopes, will come a willingness from Peter to say what he feels and thus to establish a spiritual union in which conversation will become a sharing of selves. Up through the story of the dog, Jerry moves the conversation toward greater and greater directness. When, however, Peter proves himself incapable of responding openly to Jerry's narrative, Jerry removes himself from an intensely spiritual to a less demanding physical level of confrontation. By doing this, Jerry brings Peter finally to a level where he can unite feeling and words in his angry cry, "You're a bum ... that's what you are" (p. 43). It is Peter's most honestly felt statement in the play, however inadequate it may be as a description of Jerry.

Jerry resorts to the rhetorical more than the denotative power of language to excite emotion and stimulate thought in Peter. The nature and effect of Jerry's rhetorical approach have been largely ignored or poorly understood. Zimbardo says that "words, when they do penetrate Peter's surface, merely cause him to throw up further barriers to contact" ("Symbolism," p. 13). It is true that Peter resists the total commitment Jerry demands of him, which implicitly is to give up all his external tokens of identity, his occupation, family, and material wealth; but it is equally true that without his verbal stripping, Jerry could never have brought Peter to the level of animal commitment that he achieves at the end. Peter's almost cordial reaction to Jerry's tickling would have been unthinkable without the prior establishment of a personal bond. Robert Wallace, arguing against Tom Driver's position that the plot is implausible because any normal person would not have put up with Jerry, says the reason Peter stays is that he has been captivated by Jerry as storyteller and is interested in finding out what happened at the zoo.[13] While the mystery surrounding the zoo is an enticement for staying, Jerry, before the narrative of the dog, is not for the most part telling a story nor is he desperately holding out the incident at the zoo as a lure to Peter. If Albee had made the story about the zoo the only thing holding Peter, I would agree with Driver's complaint of implausibility.

It is, however, through a skillful verbal application of the teaching principle, kindness and cruelty combined, that Jerry keeps Peter listening to him. First coercing and then cajoling, insulting then flattering, Jerry keeps Peter constantly off balance emotionally while he probes into Peter's personal life. The process gradually strips away Peter's formal defenses and establishes a bond of intimacy through shared information that makes Peter even forget at points that he is talking with a complete stranger. Jerry's approach is effective theater because it is spontaneous and improvisational; Jerry takes whatever details he can grasp about Peter and, combining the pain-pleasure formula with a fine psychological reading of his pupil, he works his effect. Consider, for example, the following sequence. Jerry, after some undirected small talk, watches Peter light his pipe and comments, "Well, boy; you're not going to get lung cancer, are you?" (p. 13). Peter, although initially annoyed by the personal and physical implications of the comment, is on reflection pleased by Jerry's apparent respect for pipe smokers. The pipe is an identity symbol for Peter. But Jerry deflates the impression and strips away the status symbol immediately by suggesting the physical reality, the likelihood of cancer of the mouth. Yet before Peter can let his irritation and discomfort motivate him to leave, Jerry plays once again to his ego by eliciting from Peter the term *prosthesis* and praising him for being an educated man and, with a cynicism that escapes Peter, a reader of *Time*. Jerry follows essentially the same pattern in probing Peter about his family, pets, occupation, and income. As the process develops, Peter is held less by Jerry's superficial – and calculated – flattery than by the pleasure of sharing personal concerns with another, although the initial rendering of facts and feelings each time is painful.

Once Jerry has involved himself with Peter, he can and must proceed to the more difficult task of involving Peter with him. He must subject himself to the pain-pleasure experience. It is painful for Jerry to tell Peter the embarrassing and degrading personal details of his life;[14] and his occasionally cavalier tone, a feigned indifference, helps him to endure the process. Equally intimidating to Jerry is his knowledge that in trusting himself to Peter's understanding he runs the risk, should Peter fail him, of facing an even deeper isolation. We see Jerry's anxiety reflected in his shift from an immobile stance while he quizzes Peter to a pacing about as he tells about his life. Jerry during this period ceases to mock Peter so insistently, and the pretended affection and calculated scorn of the earlier part of the play yield now to more genuine sympathy and at points to more genuine anger as Jerry comes to expect greater sensitivity from Peter. As Jerry frees Peter from the tyranny of a code of polite behavior, the desired likelihood that Peter will act according to his own wishes increases; whereas earlier Jerry would manipulate Peter against his wishes through a hollow rhetorical trick ("Do you mind if we talk?"), now he holds him more through an exercise of Peter's own will. Admittedly Jerry still lures Peter as if he were a child with the promise of the story about the zoo, but there is an adult directness in his challenge, "You don't *have* to listen. Nobody is holding you here;

remember that. Keep that in your mind" (p. 29); and Jerry commences the narrative which culminates his attempts at establishing a spiritual kinship only when he can feel that Peter's continued presence is due to willing involvement and not to customary politeness.

Throughout the entire process of educating Peter, Jerry has to keep control over himself as well; and it is with an heroic effort that he prevents his own conflicting thoughts and emotions from spoiling his systematic approach. In probing Peter for the banal details of his conventional existence, Jerry is in danger of being so uninterested in the information that he will not summon enough energy to pursue his assault. Once, when Peter inquires about what he is to see on TV, Jerry glides into a revery on his anticipated death from which he is barely able to emerge and continue his probe of Peter's life. When Jerry begins to tell Peter his history, the danger shifts to his having too little distance from himself to take Peter's perception of his life sympathetically into account. Jerry becomes surprisingly angry at Peter's kindly intended gauche presumptions: "Oh, I thought you lived in the village" (p. 21), and "Well, it seems perfectly simple to me" (p. 25). Jerry's sharp retort to the latter of these remarks so alienates Peter that Jerry, frightened by Peter's anger, has quickly to apologize in order to prevent him from walking away.

Jerry's account and interpretation of his encounter with the dog climaxes his attempt to make spiritual contact with Peter, that is, to achieve a meeting of the minds, sympathy, and love. He knows that if the story succeeds in removing all the remaining barriers of ignorance and insensitivity that still separate Peter from him, he will no longer need to manipulate Peter, who will then be spiritually free, and he will also have resolved his own emotional conflicts. During his climactic personal monologue, Jerry rarely protects himself with an air of cynical indifference. Here, except in the stylizing and partially ironic scriptural phraseology with which he frames the account, Jerry entrusts to Peter a confession and vision essentially untouched by euphemistic or distancing language. As Jerry brings his long monologue to a close, we see a playing out of the pain-pleasure principle on its most abstract, spiritual level, objectified physically in Jerry's passing from intense exhaustion to exhilaration. Albee's stage directions reveal to us the course of Jerry's feelings and involvement:

Jerry *is abnormally tense now ... Much faster now, and like a conspirator ...* Jerry *sighs the next word* [People] *heavily ... Here* Jerry *seems to fall into almost grotesque fatigue ... then* Jerry *wearily finishes* [and at the end of the story] Jerry *moves to* Peter's *bench and sits down beside him. ...* Jerry *is suddenly cheerful.* (pp. 34–36)

Jerry's sitting down, sharing the bench with Peter, is clearly a physical manifestation of a spiritual union he hopes now exists.

Jerry has excited Peter, stunned him, and moved him to tears; but by placing himself totally at Peter's mercy at the same time, Jerry has demanded more than Peter, even in his emotionally and intellectually heightened state, can provide. Peter is frightened because he has not comprehended with his whole being Jerry's metaphysics of possession. "Ownership" to Jerry means spiritual kinship, not legal or physical possession. Jerry is initially furious at Peter's refusal to admit that he understands Jerry's message, and Peter's shaken state indicates that he does in fact understand a great deal. Baxandall ("Theater of Edward Albee," p. 88) and Zimbardo ("Symbolism," p. 15) are partly right in contending that Peter lies. But if Jerry's vision of a spiritual union as the highest bliss were valid, then Peter would embrace it if he really understood it. The fact that he resists proves that he understands only what will be lost, not what will be gained. Jerry retreats to his great weariness after Peter, still in panic, cries, "I don't understand you, or your landlady, or *her* dog" (p. 37, my italics). That Peter would still perceive the dog as belonging to the landlady in whose physical possession it remains leaves Jerry with the feeling not only that Peter has not understood his vision ("*Her* dog! I thought it was my ... "), but that the vision itself is probably an illusion ("No, No, you're right") and that man's conception of himself as a spiritual being is a presumption or wish without foundation in experience.

Jerry's spiritual commitment really ends here, for from this moment he ceases to aspire toward realizing a spiritual nature in Peter and seeks only to verify his earlier projection, spoken quizzically, that Peter is "an animal man" (p. 18). Jerry's tickling and hitting are simply a reduction from spiritual to physical terms of his kindness-and-cruelty mode of instruction. Free will is no longer an urgent concern to Jerry since he seeks only to prove Peter an animal; and with little emotional strain he manipulates Peter to his desired catastrophe.

When Jerry thanks Peter for comforting him, we cannot know, nor need we think that Jerry knows, to what degree each of the various impulses inside him – his suicidal weariness, his wish to be remembered, and his selfless desire to save Peter from a death-in-life existence – contributes to whatever satisfction he finds in dying in this manner. But we do know that Jerry has chosen no easy way to die. In tragic defiance of the existential loneliness that seems to be humanity's lot, Jerry has marshalled heroic resources of courage, energy, manipulative cleverness, and sensitivity in an effort to realize an idea of kinship. The play's tragic affirmation emerges more from the powers Jerry manifests in his quest than from the result he obtains.

The play's story is bizarre, but so are most tragedies. Its mode is tragic realism, not social realism. The incident provides Albee a context for exploring the limits of human aspiration and potential for love. Jerry is an extremist in ideals, like most tragic heroes, and he does not place a modest demand upon Peter or himself; he seeks a total commitment. Realism is sufficiently present for us to identify with the characters, but it properly is a dramatic tool, not an end in itself. *The Zoo Story* aims to excite feelings in us, as we experience the play sympathetically, that we seldom, if ever, exercise because we are not confronted with situations of such intensity in our own lives. These feelings, moreover, accompany and gain their legitimacy from the enlightening vision of human nature worked out in experiential terms. The play is modest in scope, but it possesses a resonance and power that one finds only in tragedy.

NOTES

1 Zimbardo, "Symbolism and Naturalism in Edward Albee's *The Zoo Story*," *Twentieth Century Literature* 8 (April 1962), 15; Wellwarth, *The Theater of Protest and Paradox*, 2nd ed. (New York, 1971), p. 322; Esslin, *The Theatre of the Absurd*, 2nd ed. (Garden City, New York, 1969), p. 267; Way, "Albee and the Absurd," in *American Theatre*, ed. J.R. Brown and Bernard Harris (New York, 1967), p. 204.

2 "The Theater of Edward Albee," in *The Modern American Theater*, ed. Alvin Kernan (Englewood Cliffs, New Jersey, 1967), p. 98.

3 Edward Albee, *The American Dream* and *The Zoo Story* (New York, 1959), p. 48. All page references are from this edition.

4 Spokesmen for *The Zoo Story* as absurdist theater include Esslin, *Theatre of the Absurd*, p. 267; Charles R. Lyons, "Two Projections of the Isolation of the Human Soul: Brecht and Albee," *Drama Survey* 4 (Summer 1965), 121. Way sees the play as a confusion of absurdist and social protest drama ("Albee and the Absurd," p. 204). Spokesmen against the absurdist designation include Michael Rutenberg, *Edward Albee: Playwright in Protest* (New York, 1969), p. 11; and Thomas B. Morgan, "Angry Playwright in a Soft Spell," *Life*, 26 May 1967, p. 97.

5 The majority of critics, including Rutenberg, Baxandall, and Morgan, read *The Zoo Story* as a social tract.

6 From "Tragedy and the Common Man," *New York Times*, 27 Feb. 1949, II, pp. 1, 3; rpt. in *Death of a Salesman: Text and Criticism*, ed. Gerald Weales (New York, 1967), pp. 143–47.

7 *Edward Albee*, pp. 16 and 20.

8 *The Riverside Shakespeare* (Boston, 1974), p. 1172.

9 Mary M. Nilan, "Albee's *The Zoo Story*: Alienated Man and the Nature of Love," *Modern Drama* 16 (1973), 58.

10 Cf. Arthur Miller's comparison of Biff and Hap Loman, *Death of a Salesman*, p. 19.

11 Robert Wallace, "Albee's Attack on Fiction," *Modern Drama* 16 (1973), 53.

12 Quoted in Melvyn Gussow, "Albee: Odd Man In on Broadway," *Newsweek*, 4 Feb. 1963, p. 50.

13 Wallace, "Albee's Attack on Fiction," p. 49; Driver, "What's the Matter with Edward Albee?" in *The Modern American Theater, op. cit.*, p. 99.

14 I differ with Rutenberg's position, which seems to be widely held, that Jerry is "in [a] fervor to spill out his own lonely feelings" (*Edward Albee*, p. 19).

Games People Play in *Who's Afraid of Virginia Woolf?*

JOY FLASCH

Games People Play by Eric Berne, M.D.,[1] was published in July, 1964, and is now in its thirtieth printing. Appealing to man's interest in himself, Berne elaborates on a system of individual and social psychiatry based on game analysis and group therapy introduced in a previous volume, *Transactional Analysis in Psychotherapy*. The current work shows how people can lead more constructive lives by analyzing their behavior in terms of games.

Who's Afraid of Virginia Woolf? by Edward Albee won the New York Drama Critics' Circle Award and the Tony Award as the best play of the 1962–63 season. The screen version won top honors at the 1967 Academy Awards presentations and was paid similar tribute in England. Like all successful drama, it sheds light on human nature, revealing the dark inner recesses of the self.

Berne's psychology of human relationships makes an interesting backdrop for Albee's characters, so possessed with problems of a psychological nature. After reading the two works, one can hardly resist playing the game Berne calls "Psychiatry"[2] as he considers the "games" people play in *Who's Afraid of Virginia Woolf?*[3]

According to Berne, when one is a member of a group of two or more people, he structures his time in one of five ways, which he gives in order of complexity: (1) Rituals, (2) Pastimes, (3) Games, (4) Intimacy, and (5) Activity. The forms of social intercourse apropos to this study are Pastimes and Games. Pastimes are "semi-ritualistic, simple, complementary transactions arranged around a single field of material, whose primary object is to structure an interval of time."[4] They may take the form of "chit-chat" or may become more serious. They differ from games in that they are candid; they may involve contest but not conflict. Games are defined as "transactions, often repetitious, superficially plausible, with a concealed motivation."[5] They are basically dishonest but their outcomes are dramatic. The word *Game,* in this sense, does not necessarily imply fun or enjoyment, although the moves are designed to yield the maximum permissible satisfaction at each step. The essential feature of the *game* is its payoff. Thus, in "Schlemiel" one makes messes and then apologizes, but the payoff or purpose of the game is to obtain the forgiveness which is forced by the apology. Berne designates Games as being of first, second, or third degree in intensity. A First-Degree Game is socially acceptable; a Second-Degree Game does not cause irremediable damage, but the players prefer to conceal it from the public; a Third-Degree Game is played "for keeps" and usually ends in the hospital, courtroom, or morgue.[6] In playing games, individuals assume certain positions or roles, which Berne calls Parent, Adult, and Child roles. Each has a legitimate place in a full life, but when one or the other disturbs the healthy balance, analysis and reorganization are needed. Colloquial epithets are used for game titles because they are precise and carry dynamic meaning. Thus, "verbalizing projected anal aggression" is named simply "Ain't It Awful."[7]

Act I of *Who's Afraid of Virginia Woolf?* is entitled "Fun and Games." Actually, there are few party games in this act; there are, however, many variations of the games described by Berne in his analysis of human relationships. The game entered into most frequently is "Blemish." This is played from the depressive Child position, "I am no good" and is protectively transformed into the Parent position "They are no good" in order to gain negative reassurance for the player.[8] Martha initiates a First-Degree Game of "Blemish." Her history professor husband George is a "cluck" because he complains of the late hour at which they have returned from her father's party, a "Dumbbell" because he fails to recognize her inebriated imitation of Bette Davis. He can't do anything right, not even mix well with the other guests at the party. When he ignores her rendition of the song "Who's Afraid of Virginia Woolf?" she shifts to Second Degree "Blemish": " ... you make me puke!"

For awhile George frustrates her by refusing to play, but eventually he indulges in a round of First-Degree "Blemish." She chews ice cubes like a cocker spaniel; furthermore, he is six years younger than she – he always has been and he always will be. Happy that George will play, Martha asks for a kiss. He moves ahead by turning her down.

Martha switches the game to "Sweetheart." The second most common game played in marital groups, according to Berne, it combines derogatory comments with loving epithets.[9] Martha calls George "lover" and talks baby talk ("I'm firsty"). When he is disgusted with her drinking, she announces, "Look, sweetheart, I can drink you under any goddamn table you want. ... "

The doorbell announcing their two a.m. guests prompts George to join the game: "All right, love ... whatever love wants." He infuriates Martha by warning her not to start the two-handed make-believe game which they have played for several years, "Bringing Up Baby."[10] He then combines "Sweet-heart" and "Blemish," adroitly timing his reference to "love" as a yowling "subhuman monster" so that she screams a particularly vulgar epithet just as he opens the door for their guests. The first round is his.

Martha starts round two of "Blemish" immediately. She tells Nick and Honey, the new biology instructor and his wife, to ignore "old sour puss." George retaliates by playing "Blemish" with the guests she has invited. He imitates Honey's silly giggle and completes every sentence Nick begins. He then opens a game of "Ain't It Awful"[11] as they make small talk about the faculty party, but Nick kills it by playing "Sunny Side Up"[12] – it seems he enjoyed the party. George switches the Game to a variation of "Courtroom"[13] as he tells the guests how difficult it is being married to the daughter of the college president. Martha states her case: *some* men would consider it the chance of a lifetime.

When the women leave the room, Nick attempts the Pastime of "Man-Talk,"[14] but George prefers a subtle game of "Blemish." Nick, a novice at Games compared to George, loses his temper, so George shifts to the Parent role, informing Nick that "Musical beds is the faculty sport around here." He toys with Nick like a cat with a mouse, releasing him momentarily only under Nick's threats, as he inquires innocently about Nick's age, his weight, his wife's age, her slim hips, Nick's theory about "chromozones." He also casually drops Martha's age (108).

Nick and Honey's Parent-Child relationship is obvious throughout the play. He asks often how she feels and she replies with "the echo of a whine, a long-practiced tone." Occasionally they shift positions. Honey initiates "Tell Them, Dear," and he responds with the parallel games of "Aw Shucks, Fellows." She beams while Nick "admits" that he had his master's degree at nineteen and was intercollegiate state middleweight champion.

Berne points out that, as in any game, the players become "increasingly adept with practice. Wasteful moves are eliminated, and more and more purpose is condensed into each move. ... Certain intermediate, precautionary or concessional moves can be elided, giving a high degree of elegance to the relationship."[15] Thus, Martha, an old "pro," pounces on Nick's success story as the perfect companionpiece for George's failures these many years. She skillfully maneuvers into "Let's You and Him Fight"[16] coupled with "Blemish" as she insults George:

George is bogged down in the History Department. He's an old bog in the History Department, that's what George is. A bog. ... A fen. ... A G.D. swamp. Ha, ha, ha Ha! A Swamp! Hey, swamp! Hey swampy!

An equally experienced player, George responds with, "Yes, Martha? Can I get you something?" She orders him to light a cigarette for her, and he scores by switching the Game to a combination of anti-"Sweetheart," Silent Type and anti-"Schlemiel,"[17] to which she can find no reply:

No ... there are limits. ... Now ... I'll hold your hand when it's dark and you're afraid of the bogey man, and I'll tote your gin bottles out after midnight, so no one'll see ... but I will not light your cigarette. And that, as they say, is that.

Martha begins her version of "The Stocking Game"[18] by changing to a dress in which she looks most voluptuous. Her real objective is to move into "Now I've Got You, You Son of a Bitch," making George the loser. Berne describes this game in terms of a poker game in which one player gets an unbeatable hand but is more interested in the fact that his opponent is at his mercy than he is in good poker or making money.[19] George counters Martha's move by inviting Honey for a walk in the garden. At this, Martha changes the Game to "Blemish," entertaining Nick and Honey with a blow-by-blow account of a boxing match between George and herself, which had ended with his landing flat on his back in a huckleberry bush. George walks out and returns with a new party game he has been saving for just such a special occasion. He points a short-barreled shotgun at Martha's head and pulls the trigger. A large red and yellow Chinese parasol shoots out. Martha howls with laughter at his original and forceful play as she asks joyously, "Where'd you get that, you bastard?" She is so pleased that she invites George to make love, but he has played Games with her too long to think she will trade a Game for Intimacy. He scores as he rejects her invitation with, "What are we going to have ... blue games for the guests?"

Recovering her poise, Martha moves into Second-Degree Games of "Blemish" with George and "The Stocking Game" with Nick, while George plays "Blemish" with Nick. He attacks his "chromosome theory" which, according to George, will make every man look like Nick. He announces that in protest he will fight Nick to the death, one-handed, the other hand protecting that portion of his anatomy threatened by Nick and his cohorts who are out to "assure the sterility of the imperfect." Martha applauds George's aggressiveness, and she is delighted when Nick responds with some un-inhibited "body language": they are playing her game, "Let's You and Him Fight."

She loses her advantage, however, when Honey innocently asks about their son. Now George knows that Martha has broken their rule about keeping "Bringing Up Baby" a two-handed Game. He forces her to talk about their "son," and she scores with a vicious round of Third-Degree "Blemish" in which she says that George dislikes their son because he is not sure he is the father. Hurt deeply, George makes a comeback by announcing that that is the one thing in the world he is sure of, a skillful play that evokes congratulations from Martha.

When George calls Martha's father a white mouse with beady red eyes, she changes the Game to "Courtroom," spelling out George's inadequacies compared with her father's virtues. She calls George "A great ... big ... fat ... Flop!" and nearly scores the winning point here as George breaks a liquor bottle, clutching the jagged top, and pleads with her to stop. Sensing the nearness of victory, Martha orates triumphantly on her favorite subject, George:

... who's married to the President's daughter, who's expected to *be* somebody, not just nobody, some bookworm, somebody who's so damn ... contemplative, he can't make anything out of himself, somebody without the *guts* to make anybody proud of him. ... All Right, George!

But her speech gives him time to rally, and he drowns out her tirade by singing vigorously, "Who's Afraid of Virginia Woolf?"

Act II, "Walpurgisnacht," opens with George and Nick alternating the Pastime of "Man-Talk" with the Game of "Blemish." Both seem compelled to talk about their past. The difference in their Game-playing ability is revealed, however, as the drunken novice Nick tells the truth while the drunken professional George hides the truth. George skillfully draws Nick out, then admits: " ... you represent a direct and pertinent threat to my lifehood, and I want to get the goods on you." Nick enjoys a Game of "Look, Ma, No Hands,"[20] while George sagaciously plays "Stupid,"[21] the thesis of which is "I laugh with you at my own stupidity" in order that I may play more effectively. Nick is having such fun joking about "plowing pertinent wives" and considering Martha as the "biggest goose in the gaggle" that he fails to recognize George's warning that he's treading in the quicksand of truth – not part of the Game.

Martha and George are now ready for Third-Degree "Blemish." He accuses her of cornering their son until he ran away, and she plays "The Stocking Game" with Nick as they indulge in a very sexy dance. George does not take the bait. He plays "Sweetheart," encouraging her to "do her stuff." She jokes about his novel, actually the true story of how he had killed both of his parents accidentally as a teenager. Martha scores as George yells, "The Game Is Over! ... I'll Kill You!" He tries to choke her, but Nick pulls him away.

Regaining his composure, George announces:

Well! That's one game. What shall we do now, hunh? Oh come on ... let's think of something else. We've played Humiliate the Host ... we've gone through that one. ... There are other games. How about ... how about Hump the Hostess? Hunh?? How about that?

When the only response to this proposal is Martha's giggle, George suggests another game first, "Get the Guests." He volunteers to be "It" and tells them a story, the story Nick and confided during their truth session: that he had married Honey when she had an "hysterical pregnancy," that his father-in-law had been a preacher who ran a "traveling clip joint," that Nick puts up with his mousy "brandy gargler" mainly because she has money. "Get the Guests" concludes with Honey getting sick, Nick vowing revenge, and Martha congratulating George on his game of "pigmy hunting." George and Martha then intensify their Game of Third-Degree "Blemish," slashing each other with painful truths and accusations which culminate in their declaration of total war.

Martha flings herself into a Third-Degree version of "The Stocking Game" with Nick. She warns George that she is necking with one of their guests, but George chooses to play "Corner."[22] He replies unconcernedly, "Oh, that's nice. Which one?" Pushed to the limit, Martha hardly knows what to do. She repeats her statement, but when George tells Nick and her to go on about their business, she knows she is "cornered" if she backs out. She cannot concede the Game to George. Her only resort is to complete "The Stocking Game" she has started with Nick. When they leave the room, George hurls the book he has supposedly been reading against the wall. But suddenly he knows how he can top the move Martha has made. He will "kill" their son and thus end for all time the Game she loves most, "Bringing Up Baby."

Much of Act III, "The Exorcism," is played on the expressionistic level as the games are pushed to Third-Degree intensity. Martha engages in "Blemish" and "Now I've Got You, You Son of a Bitch" to needle Nick about his lack of success in the bedroom as she orders him around and calls him "Houseboy." George enters with a big bunch of snapdragons, and he and Martha assume adolescent poses and talk baby-talk. When Nick interrupts their play, they both turn on him.

George announces one last game, the finale of "Bringing Up Baby." Sensing his intensity, Martha pleads, "No more games. ... please. It's games I don't want. No more games." Assuming a Parent role, George strokes her hair and assures her that as the original game girl she will love this one. When she reaches out to him, he slaps her hand, then her face, and tells her he is going to make her performance look like an Easter pageant. He wants her on her feet and slugging; he wants her mad; he wants an equal battle; this one will be to the death.

Playing "Hospitable Host," he tells them all:

I think we've been having a ... a real good evening ... all things considered. ... We've sat around and got to know each other, and had fun and games. ...

Combining variations of Third-Degree 'Blemish," "Courtroom," and "Bringing Up Baby," he forces Martha to tell the life story of their child. When she stops, he takes over: poor Martha does have problems – a husband who is a "younger-than-she-is bog," alcoholism, a father who couldn't care less about her, a son who "could not tolerate the slashing, braying residue that called itself his MOTHER!" Martha protests hysterically while George solemnly chants in Latin. The Game is climaxed by George's announcement that a telegram has arrived: their son has been killed in an automobile accident. He registers a decisive victory as Martha quivers with rage and loss, howls, moans, pleads, threatens. Disgusted with her "poor sportsmanship," George tells her, "You know the rules, Martha! For Christ's Sake, You Know the Rules!" Because she has talked about their "son" to someone else, he has the right to kill him if he wishes. For the first time, Nick understands the extent to which the Games have gone.

Nick and Honey go home and George and Martha are alone. The Games are over. Martha makes a feeble attempt to resume them, but George will not play. He puts his hand on her shoulder and sings softly,

Who's afraid of Virginia Woolf,
  Virginia Woolf,
  Virginia Woolf,

And looking into the cold light of the new day, Martha confesses, "I ... am ... George. ... I ... am. ... " George nods, slowly. There is silence as the curtain closes.

Albee's inference is that George and Martha will attempt to face reality, their fears, and the past experiences which have warped them into human beings with feelings of guilt and failure. They will attempt to put aside the destructive Games which have taken the place of true Intimacy. It will be difficult, perhaps impossible. As Berne points out, some Games are necessary for the maintenance of health in certain people.

These people's psychic stability is so precarious, and their positions are so tenuously maintained, that to deprive them of their games may plunge them into irreversible despair and even psychosis. ... This is often observed in marital situations when the psychiatric improvement of one spouse (i.e., the abandonment of destructive games) leads to rapid deterioration in the other spouse, to whom the games were of paramount importance in maintaining equilibrium. ... Fortunately, the rewards of game-free intimacy, which is or should be the most perfect form of human living, are so great that even precariously balanced personalities can safely and joyfully relinquish their games if an appropriate partner can be found for the better relationship.[23]

Whether or not this better relationship is possible for George and Martha,

Albee does not state explicitly. Psychologist Berne points out that there may be no hope for the human race in general to achieve anything more than "togetherness," but there is hope for individual members. The good life he pictures would be well worth the difficult struggle to give up the Games which have become so much a part of life for George and Martha, for people the world over:

For certain fortunate people there is something which transcends all classifications of behavior, and that is awareness; something which rises above the programing of the past, and that is spontaneity; and something that is more rewarding than games, and that is intimacy.[24]

NOTES

1 Formerly Consultant in Psychiatry to the Surgeon General, U.S. Army, Dr. Berne is now lecturer at the University of California Medical School and Chairman of the San Francisco Social Psychiatry Seminars.

2 Players assume the role of psychiatrist, based on the position "I am a healer." Eric Berne, *Games People Play* (New York, 1966), p. 154.

3 The subject of this paper was suggested to the writer by Dr. Clifton Warren, Professor of Humanities, Central State College, Edmund, Oklahoma.

4 Berne, p. 41.

5 Berne, p. 48.

6 Berne, p. 64.

7 Berne, p. 71.

8 Berne, pp. 112–113.

9 Berne, p. 109.

10 *Who's Afraid of Virginia Woolf?* (New York 1966), p. 205.

11 The player is covertly gratified at the satisfactions he can wring from his misfortunes. Berne, pp. 111–112.

12 The player is quite happy about everything – most disconcerting to a complainer. Berne, p. 45.

13 "Courtroom" is essentially three-handed, with a plaintiff, defendant, and judge, or perhaps an audience as jury. Berne, p. 96.

14 The title reveals the object of the game. Berne, p. 42.

15 Berne, p. 55.

16 The Albee version is a slight variation of the description given by Berne (p. 124), but essentially the procedure is that the woman maneuvers or challenges two men into fighting, with the implication or promise that she will surrender herself to the winner.

17 Berne's example is, "You can tell derogatory anecdotes about me, but please don't call me 'Sweetheart.'" (p. 109).

18 The obvious characteristic is exhibitionism calculated to arouse men sexually and make other women angry (or in this instance, a husband). Berne, p. 129.
19 Berne, p. 85.
20 This game is similar to "Aw Shucks, Fellows." Berne, p. 42.
21 Berne, p. 157.
22 What Player A wants is to be coaxed out of his position. Player B knows this but pretends he doesn't, thus cornering Player A. Berne, pp. 92–93.
23 Berne, p. 62.

Curiouser and Curiouser:
A Study of Edward Albee's
Tiny Alice

C.W.E. BIGSBY

When *Tiny Alice* first appeared in New York its reception was something less than ecstatic. The general impression was that Albee had moved over to join that school of the deliberately boring and repulsive then in process of being identified as *Camp*. At best it was thought to be a personal therapy paralleled perhaps by Tennessee Williams' *Camino Real*; at worst it was a confidence trick pulled on the world in general and the drama critics in particular. Certainly Albee's bland assurance in a note to the published version that the play was "less opaque in reading than it would be in any single viewing" was an incredible admission of failure on the part of a dramatist. Nevertheless for all its weaknesses *Tiny Alice* does serve to demonstrate Albee's commitment to continuing experimentation. Yet while he consciously abandons the formula which had so nearly won him a Pulitzer Prize it is clear also that thematically speaking *Tiny Alice* represents a logical step forward from *Who's Afraid of Virginia Woolf?* So that a close examination of the play, while not redeeming its validity on the stage, does reveal Albee's continuing fascination with the theme of reality and illusion, and his concern with refining his own definition of these terms.

If the need to face reality was the main principle which emerged from *Who's Afraid of Virginia Woolf?* then Albee had done little to define exactly what he meant by reality in that play. *Tiny Alice* remedies this and in fact attempts a definition which is in many ways anti-Platonic. The illusions of *Who's Afraid of Virginia Woolf?* had been largely the Faustian distractions of sensuality and sterile scholarship. He had made no attempt, however, to integrate the metaphysical world into this picture nor to assess its validity as a part of the reality to which he urged his characters. *Tiny Alice* continues to urge the acceptance of reality as a way to some kind of secular salvation but in doing so Albee clearly rejects the validity of metaphysical abstractions, identifying them as an expression of man's fear of facing the reality of the human condition.

The plot can be stated fairly simply. Miss Alice, a young but apparently eccentric semi-recluse, wishes to leave a large sum of money to the church. She accordingly sends her lawyer to a Cardinal who, on promise of the money, agrees to send a young lay-brother, brother Julian, to Miss Alice to arrange terms. When Julian goes to the castle in which Miss Alice lives it becomes apparent that she, in conjunction with the lawyer and her butler, is part of a conspiracy aimed at seducing him away from the church. A marriage is arranged between Alice and Julian at which the Cardinal officiates. After the marriage, their mission apparently completed, they leave, having first shot Julian when he refuses to accept their version of reality. He dies clinging onto a model of the castle which has dominated the stage throughout most of the play.

The origin of Julian's early acceptance of the metaphysical world as a kind of supra-reality is outlined by Albee by means of quasi-parables. It becomes apparent that the impulse to predicate an abstraction in his case and by implication in others, derives from the harshness of the facts of the temporal world. Julian describes, for example, the situation of a person finding himself locked inside a closet in an attic. In order to retain sanity that person is forced to predicate the existence of somebody who can eventually open the door and release him. As Julian says, "My faith and my sanity ... are one and the same."[1] The need to personify the abstraction to which the mind gives existence results in a belief in a god. Similarly in another story/parable Julian describes the moment in his childhood when he had first felt the need for this predication which is clearly seen by Albee as a form of escapism. He had been severely injured in a fall and his calls for help had gone unanswered. Gradually his call changes from a cry for his grandfather to a plea to God, whose non-appearance is accountable and who is the personification of the need to be helped. The abstraction is thus seen as a compensation for the apparent inadequacies of the temporal world and man's fear of loneliness. It provides an apparent escape from the insistent facts of the world. So that if man cannot avoid birth or the aging process it seems to Julian that the invention of an afterlife voids the relevance of death.

Julian is chosen as a good subject by the conspirators, apparently, because of his genuine regard for reality as opposed to appearance. At one stage in his life he had lost his faith. He had gone to an asylum, not so much to seek for his lost faith as to escape the fact of the loss. His position as lay-brother emphasises his failure to accept even now.

Tiny Alice in fact amounts to Albee's attempt to define reality and reject the escapism of intellectual abstraction. He chooses religion as a specific example of the belief in an abstraction which stems from a fear of immediate reality although, as the lawyer points out, he could have chosen predestination, fate or chance. To convince the audience of the necessity of facing this reality he uses what are close to being Platonic arguments to endorse an anti-Platonic conclusion. The central symbol of a play which presents a morass of symbols, is that of the 'model' castle which dominates most of the scenes in the play. The play is concerned with the 'conversion' of Julian from a belief in abstraction, which would have relieved him of responsibility, to a knowledge of reality as represented by the model. This would seem to be an equivalent of a rise in the Platonic scale in so far as it involves the realisation that what he formerly took for originals are in fact only images or copies. This necessitates his acceptance, in symbolic terms, of the 'model' castle as the 'real' one and the larger version as merely a projection of it. It is significant that Plato's word for the ultimate form was 'paradigm' which was also the word for an architect's model. While Plato's model was seen as an abstraction, however, Albee here turns the tables and literally cuts Plato down to size.

The world of reality is, however, almost by definition, unattractive to those who have lived sufficiently long with illusion. The sort of trauma which faces Julian when he is urged to accept the apparently diminutive 'model' as being reality is comparable to that which faced Plato's man in the cave.[2] Far from seeing reality as a means of perceiving more clearly, it is seen as a restriction on perception and is rejected as such, " ... they would laugh at him and say that he had gone up only to come back with his sight ruined; it was worth no one's while even to attempt the ascent."[3] While it is clear that Plato's idea of reality differs in kind from Albee's one feels that they would both concur in Plato's statement that the function of knowledge is "to know the truth about reality."[4]

In *Tiny Alice* the conspiracy is clearly devoted to the end of convincing Julian that he should accept this apparent diminution of his concept of reality. "Don't personify the abstraction, Julian," the lawyer urges him, "limit it, demean it. Only the mouse, the toy ... is all that can be worshipped." (*T.A.*, p. 107.) The role of the conspirators is clearly the same as that assigned in Plato's *Republic* to those 'philosophers' who, having glimpsed reality, were bound to descend into the cave with the message. To Plato reality and truth were synonymous. It is hardly surprising, therefore, to find that Alice, who finally becomes identified with the forces of reality, derives her name from the Old German word for 'truth.'

Alice, in fact, is herself identifiable with the model castle. She is a more acceptable form of the reality to which the conspirators must urge Julian. She is a lure, a symbol of the reality to which Julian must marry himself. "Julian, I have tried to be ... her. No; I have tried to be ... what I thought she might, what might make you happy, what you might use, as a ... what? ... We must ... represent, draw pictures, reduce or enlarge to ... to what we can understand." (*T.A.*, p. 161.) Although she is closely identified with the model – to the extent even that the conspirators speak to it and give it the name of Alice – she is still its servant. She does have an identity outside of her symbolic role, however. She even regrets her function just indeed as had Plato's 'philosophers' whose very unwillingness had been their chief qualification. "I have tried very hard to be careful, to obey, to withhold my ... nature? I have tried so hard to be good, but I'm ... such a stranger ... here." (*T.A.*, p. 92.)

In urging the rejection of a non-temporal god it is clear that, as in *Who's Afraid of Virginia Woolf?*, Albee is suggesting that man is his own god and that the paraphernalia of religion may be as appropriately applied to the finite as to the non-finite world. Clearly the marriage of Julian and Alice is parallel to the marriage with the church at which Julian, only a lay-brother, had balked. It is his inability to accept the general view of "God as older brother, scout leader" (*T.A.*, p. 106) which makes him an ideal subject for, as the conspirators realise, he "Is walking on the edge of an abyss, but is balancing. Can be pushed ... over, back to the asylums/ ... Or over ... to the Truth." (*T.A.*, p. 106.) If he cannot accept the God of society then they are ready to offer him a 'true' God. The butler insists, "there is *some*thing. There is a *true God*." (*T.A.*, p. 107.) It is the lawyer, however, who identifies it, "There is Alice, Julian. That can be understood. Only the mouse in the model. Just that." (*T.A.*, p. 107.) When Julian dies he suffers the martyrdom for which he had always longed but it is a martyrdom for the new religion of man – a religion founded on truth and reality. He dies with his back to the model and in a reversal of his former 'conversion' his cry for God now changes to a cry for Alice, "ABSTRACTION ... ABSTRACTION! ... Art coming to me. How long wilt thou forget me, O Lord? ... I accept thee, Alice, for thou art come to me. God, Alice ... I accept thy will." (*T.A.*, pp. 189–190.) This religion even has its own ritual, although this is founded securely on the mundane but real world. "Bring me my slippers, the sacramental wine, my cookie." (*T.A.*, p. 187.) In the light of this concept of a religion founded on the observable world Julian's earlier experience while in the asylum becomes strongly relevant. He describes an experience which he cannot positively identify as being hallucinatory or real. He describes his sexual relations with a woman who believed herself to be the Virgin Mary and who subsequently claimed herself to be pregnant with the Son of God. This represents, in fact, Albee's attempt to build up a mythology around the secular religion which he had in part formulated in his earlier plays. This concentration on the physical stands also in stark contrast to a religion which is no more than a codification of the abstract need to escape. The woman is indeed not the Virgin Mary of this religion in which impregnation is an act of faith and an intellectual concept. She is rather the Virgin Mary of a new religion in which impregnation is an animal fact of "the taste of blood and rich earth in the mouth, sweet sweaty slipping ... ejaculation." (*T.A.*, p. 62.) This act, in fact, is the summation of the contrast between the two worlds which Albee brings into confrontation. The one is an abstraction, a belief which gives validity to escapism; the other is an acceptance of the physical base of life and the need to build an approach to existence on that base. Even the physical structure of the asylum suggests a material parallel to the "many mansions" of heaven. Here, Julian tells us, there are many "sections-buildings" just as in the castle there are many rooms. Thus despite the fact that he had gone to the asylum to escape it is here that he encounters the first intimations of the falsity of his beliefs.

Julian's death is pointedly a crucifixion, "His arms are wide, should resemble a crucifixion ... JULIAN dies, head bows, body relaxes some, arms stay wide in crucifixion." (*T.A.*, p. 190.) This crucifixion is enacted, however, against the model castle which has come to be referred to as Alice and which is the epitome of reality and truth. In the moments before his death Julian recognises the inversion of his values which has resulted from his contact with Alice, a conversion which results in his dying for a religion of man rather than for that of an extra-temporal god. In comparing a phrenological head, which Albee has rather pointedly left on stage throughout most of the play, with Alice he realises that his compulsion had always been to make the abstract real and the rest unreal; to see man, in fact, in terms of this head with its eyes focused on some far horizon rather than as a creature of flesh and blood existing in a concrete world:

Is that the ... awful humor? Art thou the true arms, when the warm flesh I touched ... rested against, was ... nothing? And she ... was not real? Is thy stare the true look? Unblinking, outward, through, to some horizon? And her eyes ... warm, accepting, were they ... not real? Art thou my bride ... Ah God! Is that the humor? THE ABSTRACT? ... REAL? THE REST? ... FALSE? ... It is what I have wanted, have insisted on. Have nagged ... for. IS THIS MY PRIESTHOOD, THEN? THIS WORLD? (*T.A.*, pp. 188–189.)

It is significant that once again, as in *The Zoo Story* and *Who's Afraid of Virginia Woolf?*, violence is presented as the catalyst necessary for this conversion. Like Bellow, Albee seems to believe that truth comes "in blows." Before the lawyer shoots him Julian is still determined to escape, to go back to the asylum which, although it had contained the seed of his new faith, had been seen by him at the time as a refuge from that faith. When he has been shot, however, his mind reverts to the image of the person shut up in the attic closet and he admits, what he would not have admitted before, that "No one will come" (*T.A.*, p. 176). He arrives at a realisation which one might take as a justification for Albee's obsessive insistence on the necessity of violence, "Consciousness, then, is pain" (*T.A.*, p. 181).

If the symbolic pattern of *Tiny Alice* is essentially Platonic the dilemma which that pattern highlights is, as he has shown in his previous plays, a central one to modern society. It is interesting to see, in fact, just how closely Julian matches the archetypal neurotic in retreat from reality as outlined by a pioneer in psychology, Alfred Adler. The very precision of this parallel, in fact, tends to grant to Albee's creation the general application which is clearly his aim. Adler terms escapism 'safeguarding through distance.' His description of the neurotic fits Julian's situation precisely. Unable to face the world as it is Julian had retreated into religious faith in early childhood. In an attempt to compensate and obsessed by the fact of death he longs for a martyrdom which will reinstate his superiority. He longs, as he says, to "shout my humility from the roof" (*T.A.*, p. 119). As Adler says in describing the neurotic's situation:

The neurotic's faulty picture of the world is constantly being so shaken by reality that he feels threatened from many sides. Consequently he narrows down his sphere of activity; he always presents pedantically the same opinions and the same attitudes which he accepted early in his life. Eventually, as a result of the "narrowing down" process, he shows an inferiority complex with all its consequences. Then, in order to escape this inferiority complex and because he finally sees himself threatened by the problem of death, he convulsively contructs a superiority complex.[5]

His references to the past, his concern with death and his choice of religion are all recognised by Adler as symptoms of this desire to "safeguard through distance," "To think about the past is an unobtrusive, and therefore popular, means of shirking. Also, fear of death or disease. ... The consolation of religion with the hereafter can have the same effect, by making a person see his actual goal only in the hereafter and the existence on earth as a very superfluous endeavor. ... "[6]

If Albee is concerned here with describing the dilemma of modern society in retreat from reality the title would seem to suggest that he saw a fellow spirit in Lewis Carroll. While it is clear that Alice's wonderland, as an escape from 'dull reality,' can be seen as a parallel to Julian's wonderland of religion, it would be unwise to press the parallel too closely. For while Carroll's literally 'tiny' Alice is clearly a part of the illusory world, Albee's tiny Alice is herself the symbol of reality. If Carroll insists on returning his protagonist to the real world at the end of his books it is not without a nostalgic glance back over his shoulder to his wonderland. There is no such nostalgic glance in Albee. Julian has to relinquish the abstract which is his retreat from reality. In doing so he abandons the robes of the church for the clothes of ordinary life, a change which symbolises his shift of identity. This assumption of identity as a function of commitment to an abstraction is reminiscent of Nigel Dennis's satire on the great abstracts of modern society, *Cards of Identity* (1956). Here too a conspiracy of three effect a change of identity in a man lured to their mansion by the prospect of monetary gain – a change signified here, as in *Tiny Alice*, by a physical change of clothes. To Dennis, also, religion is one of those projections whereby man escapes from the immediate reality of his situation and accepts a ready-made identity. It is an escape, moreover, which implies a denial of intellect as it does a denial of reality. In Dennis's ironical words, "God is worshipped as a solid only by backward people; once educated, the mind reaches out for what cannot be grasped, recognises only what cannot be seen: sophistry adores a vacuum,"[7] or, more succinctly as he puts it in his unabashed satire on religion, *The Making of Moo* (1957), "You have nothing to lose but your brains."[8]

In a sense also *Tiny Alice* can be seen as Albee's prose version of Eliot's *The Cocktail Party* (1949). In this play Eliot had presented a similar conspiracy of three designed to 'save,' in this case, four people. He makes a distinction, however, between a reconciliation to the human condition which leads to a comatose contentment and a true confrontation with the apocalyptic vision. One character alone chooses to confront the stark reality of her situation. Celia, while convinced that man is alone and that "the dreamer is no more real than his dreams," pursues the vision, the ecstasy which she feels to be present behind the projected shadows. She chooses what Julia, one of the conspirators, calls 'transhumanisation.' Such a process brings her into confrontation with solitariness and forces her to relinquish her artificial personality. She ceases to see reality as an extension of her own dreams. She accepts a re-definition of that reality which in turn destroys the escapist nature of her life and leads on to her literal crucifixion. When she makes this decision it is consecrated by the conspirators in a champagne toast, just as is Julian's decision in *Tiny Alice*. To confront the apocalyptic vision, to accept the limitation of reality which that involves and yet to pursue a sense of ecstasy is to invite crucifixion but this is presented by both Eliot and Albee as a better conclusion and purpose than the trivia of social posturing. Celia turns her back on a phantasmal world where people are shaped by the roles they play, just as the great abstractions shape Albee's Cardinal and even Genet's Bishop. When Julian faces crucifixion in *Tiny Alice* it is with a similar, if tardy, understanding of the true nature of things. He is urged "to accept ... our ecstasy" (*T.A.*, p. 165). The play concludes with his realisation that reality is not an aspect of a defined role or an extension of individual desires but rather the immediate result of choices made in the context of a concrete world whose only premise and conclusion is ultimate death.

Thus the abstract fear of *Who's Afraid of Virginia Woolf?* is here crystallised in Julian's perception of the terrifying loneliness of man. Used to the projections of his own sensibilities he has come to accept a diminution of his concept of reality. As Goetz had said in Sartre's *Lucifer and the Lord* (1951), "God is the loneliness of man ... If God exists, man is nothing."[9] So too Albee is insisting that man's freedom and identity depend on his ability to discount reliance on an abstraction which is the creation of his own metaphysical solitude. But if Julian dies in the moment of comprehension, in doing so he is consecrating a myth. He becomes, like Jerry in *The Zoo Story,* a martyr. But Albee's myth lacks the fundamental requirement of simplicity while his sensitive probing of his chosen theme constantly verges on the merely esoteric.

Camino Real is perhaps a useful play to invoke in the context of this study for even Tennessee Williams has come to regard his expressionistic nightmare more as a piece of personal therapy than compelling drama. Perhaps every dramatist has a right to a *Tiny Alice* just as a drama professor once told Williams that every artist has a right to paint his nudes. Unfortunately Albee's next play, *Malcolm,* evidences much the same opacity. Based on Purdy's surrealistic novel it seemed to Robert Brustein, writing in *The New Republic,* to confirm the tendency of Albee's plays to "get more abstract and incoherent until he is finally reduced, as here, to a nervous plucking at broken strings."[10] Nevertheless it is clear that without the radical approach of an Albee the American theater would be in danger of stagnating once again. For if he is capable of grotesque misjudgement, as in *Tiny Alice* and, apparently, in *Malcolm,* then he is also capable of the achievement of *The Zoo Story* and *Who's Afraid of Virginia Woolf?* Neither can *Tiny Alice* justifiably be called regressive for it evidences both Albee's continuing concern with stylistic experimentation and his determination to examine every aspect of his chosen theme. So long as Albee remains committed to extending the range of drama itself and so long as he refuses to pander, as he himself puts it, to a supposed need for "self-congratulation and reassurance"[11] then he is in danger of losing the sympathy of his audiences. But by the same token it is only through the courage of such a dramatist that American drama can ever hope to realize its full potential.

NOTES

1 Edward Albee, *Tiny Alice* (New York, 1965), p. 45. All further references to this play are abbreviated to *T.A.* and incorporated in the text.
2 Plato describes the difference between reality and illusion by means of the simile of the cave. At the bottom of a cave, which has an entrance to daylight, men are fastened so that they can only look at a huge screen on the back wall. On this screen the images of men and objects are projected by a fire built in the entrance to the cavern. He posits the difficulty of one of this number when suddenly released and confronted with true reality and the unwillingness of those others to accept the validity of a reality which would seem more diminutive than the images to which they are used.
3 Plato, *The Republic of Plato,* trans. with introduction and notes F.M. Cornford (London, 1955), pp. 225–226.
4 *Ibid.,* p. 180.
5 Alfred Adler, *The Individual Psychology of Alfred Adler,* ed. H.L. Ansbacher and R.R. Ansbacher (London, 1958), p. 277.

6 *Ibid.*, p. 277.

7 Nigel Dennis, *Two Plays and a Preface* (London, 1958), p. 7.

8 *Ibid.*, p. 194.

9 Jean-Paul Sartre, *Lucifer and the Lord,* trans. Kitty Black (London, 1952), p. 133.

10 Robert Brustein, "Albee's Allegory of Innocence," *The New Republic,* January 29, 1966, p. 36.

11 Edward Albee, "Which Theatre is the Absurd One?" in John Gassner, *Directions in Modern Theatre and Drama* (New York, 1965), p. 334.

Death as a Mirror of Life: Edward Albee's *All Over*

ROBBIE ODOM MOSES

The critic Richmond Crinkley erred in judging Albee's *All Over* (1971) to be a "play about the end of the haute monde," and "an elegy for a particularly sterile social milieu."[1] The import of *All Over* is not restricted to a single social class, nor does the play sound, as critics like Martin Gottfried[2] and Jack Kroll[3] thought, the death-knell of Albee as a dynamic playwright. In addition to being, as Henry Hewes[4] attests, an honest and realistic reflection of contemporaneity, *All Over* confronts, as the title suggests, the endemic trait of all living organisms. Death, the great leveler to a poet like William Cullen Bryant, is, for Albee, man's final confrontation with life. In the play, death is tantamount to a metaphysical conceit, with the death of the body being but one thematic strain. The famous man, whose dying is both a public event for the press and the crowd awaiting word of his demise, and a private ritual for the circle of intimates assembled for the vigil, is the instrument through which Albee explores some issues attendant to dying and death. The age at which a person becomes aware of death is an idea examined that is important to the development of psychological maturity. Knowing her husband as a thorough man with almost as much knowledge about law as Best Friend, Wife forces the lawyer into a deeper meaning of death when she dismisses fifteen, "the age we all become philosophers,"[5] as the age when he became aware of personal extinction: "No, no, when you were aware of it for yourself, when you knew you were at the top of the roller-coaster ride, when you knew half of it was probably over and you were on your *way* to it" (*AO*, pp. 90–91). Best Friend reveals that the awareness of the inevitability of death came at thirty-eight and reflected itself, for him, in the making of a will.

The modern tendency to dehumanize death is another issue broached in the play. The man's removal from the hospital to his former residence, Mistress relates, occurred in obedience to his instructed need to die in familiar surroundings: "He *said* ... *here*. When it becomes hopeless ... no, is that what he said? Pointless! When it becomes pointless, he said ... have me brought here. I want a wood fire, and a ceiling I have memorized, the knowledge of what I could walk about in, *were* I to. I want to leave from some place ... I have known" (*AO*, p. 10). Wife articulates the growing concern about the loss of human dignity in the prolongation of life solely by machine. Despite Daughter's and Nurse's protests over moving her husband from the hospital, she recognized that a network of tubes and wires obscures humanness and does not constitute life: "A city seen from the air? The rail lines and the roads? Or, an octopus: the body of the beast, the tentacles electrical controls, recorders, modulators, breath and heart and brain waves, and the tubes!, in either arm and in the nostrils. Where had he gone!? In all that ... equipment. I thought for a moment *he* was keeping *it* functioning. Tubes and wires" (*AO*, p. 9). Anticipating the appearance of a book like Marya Mannes's *Last Rights* (1973) popularizing the issue, Albee in this play forcefully combats resignation to dehumanized and degrading death.

The dying Husband-Father-Lover-Best Friend concealed behind the screen is also the "other" whose rendezvous with death forces the watch to stare the Great Spectre in the face. For Doctor, "Death is such an old disease" (*AO*, p. 24) with which he has long been familiar. During his sixty years of practice in which he has presided at the deaths of both the Wife's and the husband's parents, Doctor has found his niche within the cycle of life: "I'm rather like a priest: you have me for the limits, for birth and dying, *and* for the minor cuts and scratches in between. If that nagging cough keeps nagging, now it's not *me* opens up the throat or the chest; not *me*. I send you on to *other* men ... and very quickly. I am the most ... general of practitioners" (*AO*, p. 25). Moreover, from his residency on death row, Doctor has a specific, intimate knowledge of the impact of imminent death: "I would be with them, and they were alone in the death cells, no access to each other, and the buggery was over, had it ever begun, the buggery and the rest; and there were some, in the final weeks, who had abandoned sex, masturbation, to God, or fear, or some enveloping withdrawal, but not all; some ... some made love to themselves in a frenzy – indeed, I treated more than one who was bleeding from it, from so much – and several confided to me that their masturbation image was their executioner ... some fancy of how he looked" (*AO*, p. 30). In addition, the doctor is personally acquainted with this close relationship between death and love. He admits that his young grandson's thrust of ' "Eighty-six! Man, that means going out!' " into his consciousness made him realize that the old, like the condemned, fight against extinction by embracing the source of their end, the young: "You see: I suddenly loved my executioners ... well, figurative; and in the way of ... nestling up against them, huddling close – for we do seek warmth, affection even, from those who tell us we are going to die, or when" (*AO*, pp. 31–32).

Doctor's present attendance upon death leaves him exhausted and makes him "suddenly feel quite old" (*AO*, p. 98). To a man too old to retire, death is but the end of the act of dying; it is "All over" (*AO*, p. 111).

For Nurse, who has spent forty years attending the family of the dying man, death prompts reflections upon the deaths of famous men and upon the human need for participation in the suffering of dying. The Wife's mention of Dr. Dey as the husband's obstetrician, who subsequently perished on the Titanic, activates Nurse's disclosure that the doctor actually died by committing suicide at his Maine hunting lodge after discovering that he had terminal cancer. The story of his death aboard the luckless ship, she reveals, was a fiction invented by his wife and corroborated by his mistress – herself. Nurse approves of elected death in hopeless situations, but resents being deprived of the hope to thwart death when public figures like both Kennedys and King undergo a curtailed dying stage:

It happened so fast; all people could figure for themselves was they'd been clubbed in the face by history. Even poor Bobby; he took the longest, but everybody knew he was dead before he died. Christ, that loathsome doctor on the tube kept telling us. "There's no chance at *all* as I see it; the hemorrhaging, the bullet where it is... No chance. No chance." Jesus, you couldn't even *hope*. It was a disgusting night; it made me want to be young, and a man, and violent and unreasonable – rage so that it meant something. Pope John was the last one the public could share in – two weeks of the vilest agony, and conscious to the very end, unsedated, because it was something his God wanted him to experience. I don't know, maybe a bullet *is* better. In spite of everything. (*AO*, pp. 41–2)

Nurse has her own acid test for gauging the prominence of a man: "That's the final test of fame, isn't it, the degree of it: which is newsworthy, the act of dying itself, or merely the death" (*AO*, p. 41). The agonized dying of a famous man, she thinks, is a cleansing, healing public event; but death, she tells Son, comes all too soon. She recommends a diet of eggs, fish, fruit, raw vegetables, two whiskies before dinner, a glass of good burgundy with it, and sex before bedtime to sustain life "until it's proper time for you to die. No point in rushing it" (*AO*, p. 73). Death, for Nurse, is a natural event that one directs only when all hope for the good life is gone.

Death moves across Best Friend, Son, and Daughter with unequal breath. The dying of his friend and client produces a preoccupation with formality and ritual in Best Friend. He reminds the daughter that it is her obligation to participate in the ritual; whether she knows if she wants to be there is irrelevant: "It's not required that you *do* know. It *is* more or less required that you *be* ... I think: here. Family. Isn't it one of our customs? That if a man has not outlived his wife and children – will not outlive them ... they gather?" (*AO*, p. 6). As an

attorney, he insists that they will follow whatever instructions are contained in
the unopened papers entrusted to him by the dying man; yet he threatens Wife
with court action if she persists in being adamant about burial rather than
cremation. Wife, however, reminds him that a human being with whom he has
shared life is his concern, not some legality: "We are talking of *my husband*.
Surely you've not forgotten. You were a guest in our house – in the days when
we *had* a house together. We entertained you. Here! You and your wife spent
Christmas with us; many times!" (*AO*, p. 93). Best Friend's encounter with the
death of "other" also causes him to become introspective and confess a type of
dying that had occurred within himself when he found his former wife growing
more progressively insane: "It was after I decided not to get the divorce, that
year ... until I committed her. Each thing, each ... incident – uprooting all the
roses, her hands so torn, so ... killing the doves and finches ... setting fire to her
hair ... all ... all those times, those things I knew were pathetic and not wanton,
I watched myself withdraw, step back and close down some portion of ... "
(*AO*, p. 15).

For Son, the dying of his father both awes and disturbs him. His shout of "I
WANT TO TALK TO HIM!" (*AO*, p. 32) reveals a need for a more intimate
and immediate experience with the death of the giver and shaper of his life.
When Doctor informs them that the man's heart resumed beating after
stopping, Son is overwhelmed with the mystery of death: "Just think: it could
have been finished then. I don't mean anything but the wonder of it" (*AO*, p.
67). Although his mother rebukes him for becoming emotionally disturbed at
the sight of a bathroom, Son had momentarily rediscovered in that inner
sanctum of strops and witch hazel masculinity the father-hero of his youth. His
sobbing provokes the contempt of his mother who is furious that death does not
recall for him the honors his father has received or the bedside vigil his father
conducted when he was ill: "No! Not any of it! Give us you, and you find a
BATHROOM ... MOVING?" (*AO*, p. 80). Uncharacteristically defending her
brother, Daughter berates their mother for ridiculing him: "Why couldn't you
have just left him alone? He's spent his grown life getting set against
everything, fobbing it all off, covering his shit as best he can, and so what if the
sight of one unexpected, ludicrous thing collapses it all? So *what*! It's proof,
isn't it? Isn't it proof he's not as ... little as you said he was? It is, you know"
(*AO*, p. 83).

Death holds no great mystique for Daughter; she will simply "sit it out" (*AO*,
p. 17). Despite his fame, her father is proving "*he's* mortal enough," a fact that
she anticipates with relief: "Well, I'll be glad when he's gone – no, no, not for
the horrid reasons, not for all of your mistakes about me, but simply that the
tintype can be thrown away, the sturdy group, and I can be what I choose to be
with only half of the disapproval, not longer the public" (*AO*, p. 59). The vigil
produces both ennui and hostility in Daughter. Telling her brother "I feel like a

child, rebellious, misunderstood and known oh, so very well; sated and ... empty" (*AO*, p. 58), she acts the role of the defender of the family by accusing Mistress of being a golddigger contaminating the "Puritan moral soul" (*AO*, p. 59) of this dynasty founded by the self-made, famous father, and of being the burier of husbands. Toward her mother who assaults her with the degradation of living with an undivorced liquor store owner engaged in Mafia-like political affairs and of being beaten by him, the daughter feels rage and contempt. She slaps her mother across the face, an insult returned, for taunting her about her paternity. Thinking her mother and the mistress are hypocrites with smug, excluding attitudes, daughter finds their hysterical laughter of fright disgusting: "*Stop it, stop it; stop it, you fucking bitches!*" (*AO*, p. 48). Death, for Daughter, is the occasion for lashing out and condemning. She scorns her mother with "You make me as sick as I make you" (*AO*, p. 83), and she belittles her brother: "You never were much good at anything" (*AO*, p. 65). However, her anguished questions of "Do *you* love *me*?" (*AO*, p. 50), directed to her mother, and "Does *anyone* love me?" (*AO*, p. 51) reveal self-condemnation on the Daughter's part and the real, but denied need for love.

For Wife and Mistress, the dying of the man they share surfaces autobiographical reminiscences and promotes an artificial unity. Her lover's approaching death makes Mistress very much aware of her status within his life. Adherence to ritual becomes very important for her. Ritual had prescribed her role as an outsider making it impossible for her to erase the man's need to spend Christmas with his family in the early years of their relationship. Ritual, she relates, had also prevented her from accompanying him for some time to the banquets at which he spoke or to the ceremonies conferring honorary doctorates. The ritual of death, however, is not to be denied to her; she will be part of the watch and the funeral: "I'll *be* there, dressed in my gray and white, a friend of the family. There'll be none of your Italian melodrama, with all the buzz as to who is that stranger off to one side, that woman in black whom nobody knows, wailing louder than the widow and the family put together. None of that. I have always known my place, and I shall know it then" (*AO*, pp. 71–2). Mistress believes that dying is a time for suffering on the part of the loved ones; at the same time, this man's dying gives his mistress of some twenty years a feeling of power and superiority. Brooking no challenge to her authority for bringing him to this particular room to die, Mistress exults in her dominion over the family: "You have my *word* for it; yes, you have only my word ... for so very much ... if he loved you, for example ... any more. You *all* have my word, and that is all" (*AO*, p. 10). In the women's power struggle over the flames, the method Mistress claims he instructed, and the worms, the wife's preference, Mistress obdurately insists that cremation will prevail: "Oh, Christ; you people! You will go by what I tell you; finally; as I have told you" (*AO*, p. 23).

This vigil with death prompts recollections of death; but in these reminiscences, Mistress' feelings of superiority break through. Her story of the dying mother with two children battling over her will, which she tells Daughter, is no veiled allegory or prophecy about her and her brother, is a vehicle for self-adulation: "But all of this is to tell you that I'm not an intruder in the dollar sense. I've more than enough – I was born with it. Don't you people ever take the trouble to scout? And I told your father I wanted nothing beyond his company ... *and* love. He agreed with me, you'll be distressed to know, said *you needed it*. So, I am not your platinum blonde with the chewing gum and the sequined dress" (*AO*, p. 70). Mistress' revelation about her two dead husbands, given in response to Daughter's jibe of "How many men have you gone through, hunh? No divorces, you just bury them" (*AO*, p. 64), is partly a testimony to her superior capacity to love and to suffer, and a probe into dying and death:

No divorces, I just bury them? Well, what would you have me do? I know, you meant it as a way of speaking; you were trying to be unkind, but keep it in mind should your lover be rid of his wife, marry you, and die. You've been a woman, but you haven't been a wife. It isn't very nice, you know, to get it all at once — for both my deaths were sudden: heart attack, and car. Well, maybe it's better than ... this. It's all done at once, and you're empty; you go from that to grief without the intervening pain. You can't suffer with a man because he's dead; his dying, yes. The only horror in participating ... (*Thinks better of it*) ... well, another time. (*AO*, pp. 68–9)

Mistress' narrative of the three men, "my own two husbands ... and yours" (*AO*, p. 86), and of the one boy she loved is a certification of a fuller sexuality than she thinks Wife possesses. The boy with the smooth swimmer's body had, she relates, "a penis I could not dismiss from my mind when I was not with him – I am not one of your ladies who pretends these things are of no account" (*AO*, p. 86). The death watch, for Mistress, is primarily a means to justify her role that enables her to fulfil needs for the man that his family could not supply.

For Wife, the imminent death of her husband is the "waiting out a marriage of fifty years" (*AO*, p. 18), which ushers in thoughts of beginnings and endings. Her refrain of "The little girl I was when he came to me" (*AO*, p. 19) is a requiem for dead expectations. At eighteen, she relates, her Prince Charming came to her rich uncle's house and made her feel secure. He was "done with the university, missing the war in France, twenty-four, already started on his fortune – just begun, but straight ahead, and clear" (*AO*, p. 104), but the promising beginning ended before his end: "And two years after that we were married; and thirty years later ... he met *you*. Quick history. Ah, well" (*AO*, p. 105). In this end of his life, Wife explains to Daughter that those who loved him have a place in the vigil: "This woman [Mistress] loves my husband – as I do – and she has made him happy; as I have. She is good, and decent, and she is not moved by envy and self-loathing" (*AO*, p. 50). Nevertheless, she will maintain her wifely prerogatives about burial: "I *will* do battle with you there, no matter what you tell me, no matter what an envelope may say, I will have my way. Not a question of faith, or a repugnance; merely an act of will" (*AO*, p. 79). Death, for Wife, re-established her primacy: "My rationale has been perfectly simple: you may lose your husband while he is alive, but when he is not, then he is yours again" (*AO*, p. 92). Death the restorer, however, is also the destroyer of the die that Wife thinks was never properly impressed upon his son: "Well ... I can't expect you to be the son of your father and *be* much; it's too great a *burden*; but to be so little is ... " (*AO*, p. 80). Despising her children for the failures they have made of their lives, Wife wants the mold broken through death: "I hope you never marry ... *either* of you! Let the line end where it is ... at its zenith" (*AO*, p. 81).

Besides confronting basic issues dealing with death and portraying encounters with the experience of death, Albee's *All Over* exposes a more insidious kind of death. In the play, Mistress's relation of her lover's objection to the use of the verb "to be" in connection with death is no mere semantic indulgence on the part of the playwright. Her report of their conversation provides valuable insights into Albee's concern with death:

He put down his fork, one lunch, at *my* house ... what had we been talking about? Maeterlinck and that plagiarism business, I seem to recall, and we had done with that and we were examining our salads, when all at once he said to me "I wish people wouldn't say that other people 'are dead.'" I asked him why, as much as anything to know what had turned him to it, and he pointed out that the verb to be was not, to his mind, appropriate to a state of ... non-being. That one cannot ... *be* dead. He said his objection was a quirk – that the grammarians would scoff – but that one could be dying, or have died ... but could not ... be ... dead. (*AO*, p. 4)

Death in this play encompasses those who have died, those who are dying, and those who *are* dead to life. Albee's deathbed scene shares traits that Carla Gottlieb has found to be characteristic of twentieth-century paintings interpreting death by depicting the deceased in the background with the survivors occupying the foreground, and by showing the participants turned away from the dead person and from one another. "Faced with death," Gottlieb concludes, "the family bonds fall apart, revealing their superficial character."[6] In *All Over*, death is a mirror reflecting family ties built upon rancor, resentment, and rivalry. The severity of the familial animosity surfaces when Wife searches for the correct words for killing parents and children: "What *is* it if you kill your daughter? It's matricide if *she* kills *you*, and infanticide if you do her in when she's a tot, but what if she's all grown up and beginning to wrinkle? Justifiable homicide, I suppose" (*AO*, p. 95). The story of Wife's aunt who "died when she was twenty-six – died in the heart, that is, or whatever portion of the brain controls the spirit; she went on, all the appearances, was snuffed out, finally at sixty-two in a car crash" (AO, p. 51) is lost on these survivors who have been ghouls battening on the flesh and spirit of the dying man, having themselves long since ceased to live.

Long before the dying man expires, rigor mortis has overtaken the attendants. Although the names of the characters represent human relationships,[7] they also signify in this play a cessation of growth. Receiving identity only through their relationship with the dying man, they have become rigid in their unchanging roles. The son can only be Son, representing no loss, Best Friend tells him, if he should decide to leave his father's firm. At fifty-two, Son is still the child, he confesses sadly, unable to compete with either father or mother: "Not up to you, mother; never was" (AO, p. 82). The others are equally atrophied. The lawyer will propose to and be turned down by his best friend's wife with whom he found comfort during that "secret time I fear that everyone knew of" (AO, p. 15). He will still remain detached, incapable of responding to an encounter with his discharged wife with anything other than the memory of a clanking bracelet, or incapable of comprehending why the Son would interpret his statement of expendability with the firm as disaffection: "Did I say I didn't *care* for you? I thought I said I'd feel no loss if you were gone. I'm pretty much out of loss" (AO, p. 61). Fixed in her role, Mistress confesses that Wife's decision not to divorce her husband was salubrious for her: "Glad you didn't, I think; it would have forced him to marry me ... or not. Move off" (AO, p. 37). Nevertheless, she will assume a widow's role. With her touch of class, she will avoid traveling with touring widows and will embark instead on her own special kind of pilgrimage: "I *shall* go away; I *know* that; but it won't be to places unfamiliar, either. There are different kinds of pain, and being once more where one has been, and shared, *must* be easier than being where one *cannot* ever ... I think what I shall do is go to where I've been, *we've* been, but I shall do it out of focus" (AO, p. 101). A week in Copenhagen when the Tivoli is closed and Christmas in Venice are among the shrines on the itinerary. The daughter, too, is imprisoned within her role as progeny of the dying man who, she feels, was stolen by the mistress and inexcusably lost by her mother. Daughter will always be the child refusing to eat in order to punish her parents: "I'm not your usual masochist, in spite of what *she* thinks. I mean, a broken rib really *hurts*, and everybody over twelve knows what a black eye on a lady *means*. I don't fancy any of that, but I do care an awful lot about the guilt I can produce in those that do the hurting" (AO, p. 62).

There is, indeed, as Son says, "enough death going here" (AO, p. 58) in a woman who conceives of herself only as a wife: "I function as a wife, and you – don't misunderstand me — you do not. Married twice, yes, you were, but I doubt that your husband took a mistress, for you were *that*, too. And no man who has a mistress for his wife will take a wife as mistress. We're different kinds; whether I had children or not, I would always be a wife and mother, a symbol of stability rather than refuge" (*AO*, p. 85). In this encounter with death, however, Wife discovers embers of life at the age of seventy-one. Wife's discovery that "we love to *be* loved, and when it's taken away ... then why *not* rage ... or pule" (*AO*, p. 109) is an honest admission of the selfishness within human nature, and she refuses to allow Best Friend to hide behind the cloak of insanity as an absolution from responsibility and commitment to his former wife. Aware that the loss of love is death and that divorce is a form of murder, Wife accuses Best Friend of spiritual homicide: "fucking – as it is called in public by everyone these days – is not what got at her; yours and mine, I mean. Divorce: leave *alone*: So don't tell *me* you don't believe in murder" (*AO*, p. 32). Moreover, Wife has, she admits, repressed the human condition: "I know I want to feel something. I'm waiting to, and I have no idea what I'm storing up. You make a lot of adjustments over the years, if only to avoid being eaten away. Anger, resentment, loss, self-pity – *and* self-loathing – loneliness. You can't live with all that in the consciousness very long, so, you put it under, *or* it gets well, and you're never sure which" (*AO*, p. 102). In Wife's unconscious are the sparks of the "Something [that] *must* be stirring" (*AO*, p. 102). The childhood time of the dream she had while napping on the couch, along with the dry goods store-living room setting of the action occurring in the dream, suggests that she is revisiting and taking stock of her life. In the dream, she is shopping for a certain kind of thread (the thread of life) and finds on the familiar shelves instead only canned goods and bottles of catsup (her hermetically sealed psychic existence).

From the unconscious comes the revelation that hers has been a death-in-life existence. From this brush with mortality comes the realization that death, even if selfishly so, causes one to turn inward and recognize the emptiness of disguised vitality. Although Wife had anticipated no death-shaking changes in a life she describes as "comfortable, interesting, and useful" (*AO*, p. 102), Wife becomes unfixed and discards pretense. Refusing to settle for companionship instead of love, she will not marry Best Friend. No longer pretending that she has resigned herself to separation from her husband, she brands Mistress as usurper and vehemently shouts "I LOVE MY HUSBAND!!" (*AO*, p. 108). With Mistress, Wife has freed herself from being among the condemned embracing the executioner, but she is still bound within the inflexibility of being unable to view Son and Daughter as other than disappointing offspring. She will probably continue to vilify them for failing to live up to their father. Nevertheless, the "Worst might be," as Wife realizes, "if there's nothing there any more, if everything has been accepted" (*AO*, p. 102). Wife's confession that she cries "BECAUSE ... I'M ... UNHAPPY!" (*AO*, p. 110) reveals that death has been the crisis reviving her dead soul and inaugurating at least a provisional growth into personhood that allows for a more honest confrontation with life. By partially exhuming the buried life,

Wife has learned at least to dog-paddle to keep from drowning in a sea of inauthenticity.

On one level, the death of the Husband-Father-Lover-Best Friend in *All Over* is the climax to a death watch characterized by friction and hostility among the enlarged family preoccupied with recollections of deaths and dying. On another level, the play uses death as a mirror reflecting the extent of life within the survivors. For Albee, death, then, is a metaphor for the quality of life. The irony in this play is that there is more life in the dead man than in the survivors. If all reports are true, the dying man exhibits a healthy attitude toward death that reflects a genuine, loving assumption of the moral condition. He has talked about death, made provisions and requests for a friendly place to die, and even joked about death. Mistress's disclosure that he had instructed her "not to snatch [his] heart from the flames," because "it is not a tasty organ" (*AO*, p. 21) is no disparagement, as Douglas Watt implies,[8] of the man's sanity. Through this oblique reference to Trelawny's romantic account of the cremation of Shelley, the sense of humor on the part of a literate man who received doctorates and spoke of Maeterlinck – who himself wrote about the deplorable practice of prolonging the agony of dying and expressed a preference for cremation – is revealed. Death, in *All Over,* is a measurement of life.

NOTES

1 Richmond Crinkley, "The Development of Edward Albee," *National Review,* 1 June 1971, 603.
2 Martin Gottfried, "Theatre: Albee's 'All Over' ' ... talked to death,'" *Women's Wear Daily,* 29 March 1971, rpt. in *New York Theatre Critics' Reviews,* 32 (April 1971), 322–23.
3 Jack Kroll, "Theater: The Disconnection," *Newsweek,* 5 April 1971, 52.
4 Henry Hewes, "The Theater: Death Prattle," *Saturday Review,* 17 April 1971, 54.
5 Edward Albee, *All Over* (New York, Atheneum, 1971), p. 90. All subsequent quotations from this edition are cited in the text. Unspaced periods occurring in quotations are Albee's.
6 Carla Gottlieb, "Modern Art and Death," in *The Meaning of Death,* ed. Herman Feifel (New York, 1959), p. 181.
7 Noting the familial base of Albee's play, Harold Lenz, in his article "At sixes and Sevens – A Modern Theatre Structure" appearing in *Forum,* 11 (Summer–Fall 1973, Winter 1974), 72–79, asserts that the seven characters represent the family life of modern man. Dr. Lenz further suggests that the names of the characters, along with the press, represent Society united by a profit-motive bond in that all are potential inheritors of the dying man.
8 Douglas Watt, "Albee's 'All Over' Is Glacial Drama About a Death Watch," *New*

York Daily News, 29 March 1971, rpt. in *New York Theatre Critics' Reviews*, 32 (April 1971), 323.
9 Maurice Maeterlinck, *Death*, trans. Alexander Teixeira De Mattos (New York, 1912), pp. 16, 27.

Albee's *Seascape*: An Adult Fairy Tale

LUCINA P. GABBARD

Edward Albee's *Seascape* is obviously not a realistic play. When the two great lizards slide onto the stage, behaving like ordinary married human beings and speaking perfect English, realism is immediately dispelled. Encounters between human beings and talking animals are the stuff of fairy tales. Bruno Bettelheim, in *The Uses of Enchantment,* describes a fairy tale as a work of art which teaches about inner problems[1] through the language of symbols[2] and, therefore, communicates various depths of meaning to various levels of the personality at various times.[3] This is the method of *Seascape.*

The play's principal concern is the realization of the proximity of death that comes with the passing of middle age. Albee depicts the adjustments that this realization entails, adjustments made difficult in the twentieth century by a tendency to deny mortality. Sigmund Freud spoke of this denial as an inner struggle between Eros and Thanatos which he viewed as the wellspring of all neuroses. Friedrich Nietzsche wrote about the need for a oneness that would embody the affirmation of death as well as life. More recently, Norman O. Brown has maintained that constructing "a human consciousness" capable of accepting death "is a task for the joint efforts of" psychoanalysis, philosophy, and art.[4] *Seascape* takes up this cause and earns importance because of it.

Symbols are the play's basic medium. Through symbolism the title announces that death is a part of the flux of life. A seascape is a view of the sea whose ever-moving waters are the meeting place between air and ground, heaven and earth, life and death. The waters of the sea are both the source and the goal of life. Returning to the sea is like returning to the birth waters of mother's womb; it is the symbolic equivalent of death.[5] The seascape is also vast: its final shore is beyond sight; its horizon is beyond reach. So is the flux of life; man is the product of continuous evolution – unstoppable in its insistent progress. The sea is also deep and dark; beneath its bright ripples are undercurrents, eddies, unseen life, and unplumbed depths. So is man's awareness merely the outer rim of an inner self that seethes with the buried life of the subconscious. Thus, the play intertwines three levels of meaning, ingeniously allowing each to add insight to the other. All three are condensed in the symbol of the lizards who come up from the sea. They concretize the evolution of mankind from water animals, the emergence of the individual embryo from its watery womb, and the return to consciousness of the repressed self.

All these levels of meaning can be communicated simultaneously when the fairy-tale events of the play are interpreted as an initiation rite. Joseph L. Henderson, in *Man and His Symbols,* explains the rites of passage and their associated symbols which, he says, can relate to the movement from any stage of life to any other – childhood to adolescence to maturity to old age to death. Moreover, the symbols of these rites are known to appear in the unconscious mind of man just as they did in ancient rituals.[6] One set of symbols that apply to this final stage of life, Henderson calls "symbols of transcendence" which concern "man's release from ... any confining pattern of existence, as he moves toward a superior ... stage" of his development. They provide for a union between the conscious and the unconscious contents of the mind.[7] The experience is usually presided over by a "feminine (i.e., anima) figure" who fosters a "spirit of compassion,"[8] and it occurs between middle age and old age when people are contemplating ways to spend their retirement – whether to travel or to stay home, to work or to play.[9] Often during this time the subject has dreams which incorporate a piece of wood, natural wood which represents primordial origins and, thus, links "contemporary existence to the distant origins of human life." Other subjects dream of being in a strange, lonely place "near a body of water." Such places are stops on a continuing journey which symbolizes the need for release.[10] The journey usually features an encounter with an animal that can live either on land or in the sea – a water pig, a lizard, a snake, or a fish. The amphibian quality of the animal is the universal symbol of transcendence. "These creatures, figuratively coming from the depths of the ancient Earth Mother, are symbolic denizens of the collective unconscious."[11] The full power of transcendence also incorporates symbols of flight. Thus, the "lower transcendence from the underworld snake-consciousness" passes "through the medium of earthly reality" and into the "superhuman or transpersonal reality" of winged flight.[12] In archaic patterns, the symbols of this final transcendence may have been winged horses or dragons or even wild birds. But Henderson says that today they can be jet planes or space rockets which also represent freedom from gravity. He notes that this final initiation begins in submission and moves through containment to further liberation. He warns, however, that the opportunity to experience these rites is not automatic; it must be understood and grasped. The individual who does "reconciles the conflicting elements of his personality" and strikes "a balance that makes him truly human, and truly master of himself."[13]

Other writers concur with Henderson and elaborate his statements. Joseph Campbell, in *Hero With A Thousand Faces,* calls this opportunity to be initiated "the call to adventure." He tells a fairy tale in which a frog heralds the call – to life, death, adventure, or self-realization. Regardless of the "stage or grade of life, the call rings up the curtain, always, on a mystery of transfiguration – a rite, or moment of spiritual passage, which, when complete, amounts to a dying and a birth."[14] Julius Heuscher, in his psychiatric approach to fairy tales, cites the story of the beautiful Czechoslovakian princess Zlatovlaska, who is won by a lowly cook, Yirik. This fairy tale introduces the "three realms of the physical world: earth, water, and air" which Yirik must befriend to gain his end, and it points out that death must be accepted as well as life if a true "spiritual awakening" is to occur, if a "wedding of the spirit or *animus* with the soul or *anima*" is to take place.[15] A third relevant comment comes from Carl Jung: "In myths and fairy tales, as in dreams, the psyche tells its own story, and the interplay of the archetype is revealed in its natural setting as 'formation, transformation/the eternal Mind's eternal recreation.'"[16]

Familiarity with the archetype of initiation and the symbols of transcendence facilitates their recognition in the events of *Seascape*. Albee's play begins on a deserted sand dune in the bright sun.[17] The barrenness of the sand dune seems to suggest the absence of fertility at life's end. Traditionally, sand also represents time and life's journey. In this context, Albee's characters have travelled to the edge of the sands of time – the sea, home of the waters of life and death. The bright sunlight is associated with rebirth. According to J.E. Cirlot, the Moon becomes fragmented in its cycles, but the Sun can cross the heavens and descend without dissolving. "Hence, the death of the Sun necessarily implies the idea of resurrection and actually comes to be regarded as a death which is not a true death."[18]

Within this setting are Charlie and Nancy, whose names, perhaps by accident, identify them as representatives of the masculine and feminine spirits: the name *Charlie* implies manliness, strength and vigor; *Nancy,* a variation of Anne, suggests grace and mercy. The conversation of Charlie and Nancy tells of their presence in the retirement years. They speak of the long way they have come – the children, the sharing of much time, the prospects of settling in "old folks' cities" (p. 10). Nancy even verbalizes their awareness of approaching death. Twice she reminds Charlie that they "are not going to live forever" (p. 11). Their attitudes display a wish to stop their journey through time. Nancy wants to become a "seaside nomad" (p. 5), to "go around the world and never leave the beach" (p. 6). Charlie, on the other hand, wants to do "nothing" (p. 8); he feels he has earned "a little rest" (p. 10). Each in his own way, therefore, rejects continuing. She wants to treadmill it on the shores of life, and he wants to halt where he is. Their reluctance to continue is demonstrated symbolically as well. At the opening of the play, the deafening roar of a jet plane is heard passing overhead. Nancy complains of the noise, and Charlie declares that someday those jets will crash into the dunes. He fails to see "what good they do" (p. 3). If the planes are accepted as the symbols of winged transcendence, Nancy and Charlie's negative responses show their dread of this next higher plane of development. At the close of this scene, which sets up their present stage in life's journey, the jet planes fly over again. Charlie and Nancy repeat the same reactions and the same words, creating a refrain such as marks a stanza's end.

When conversation resumes, a new stanza presents another phase of their lives – their past. Charlie and Nancy review their progress through the earlier developmental stages. Charlie has always been slow to move forward into a new stage. When he was a little boy, his friends had wanted to soar on wings, like Icarus, but Charlie had wanted to be a fish and live under the sea (p. 13). His delight was to submerge himself and sit on the bottom. Until he was twelve or thirteen, he had enjoyed this symbolic regression to his beginnings in the womb. Finally, at seventeen he had begun his manhood and thereafter had been satisfied on earth's firm ground. Despite Nancy's entreaties that he recapture his youth by submerging again, Charlie refuses to retrench. He insists on remaining where he is. He had, however, had a seven-month decline before moving from maturity to middle age. Nancy was thirty when Charlie had had his "thing," his "melancholia" (p. 20). Then, as now, the deeper his inertia had gone, the more alive she had felt (p. 21). Finally, however, he had come back, but life had been quieter, more full of accommodations (p. 24). Now the time has come to progress from middle age to old age with its proximity to death. But Charlie wants to rest, to remain on familiar ground, to give in to inertia again. He fears "the crags" and "the glaciers" (p. 38). And the imagery of his words reveals his feelings about the next stage. He sees the future life as jagged and rough, like steep rocks rising above the surrounding rock mass. He sees the future life as cold and bleak, like a large mass of ice, rising where snow can accumulate faster than it melts. Like the jet plane, which Charlie figures will someday crash into the sandy earth, the glacier, when it does melt, slides down the mountain into the valley below. Charlie feels unequal to such a "scary" new life. He wants the comfort of "settling in" – where he is (pp. 38–39).

The backward look at Nancy's life reveals the differing role of woman. While he has accepted the traditionally active roles of manhood – wooer, sire, breadwinner, sturdy shoulder (pp. 29–30) – she has accepted the traditionally passive roles of womanhood. She has acquiesced to her husband's needs, accepted his way and place of life, reared their children, and waited out his inertia even at the height of her own sexuality. Nancy, therefore, feels she has earned "a little life" (p. 37). She is piqued by Charlie's use of the past tense with regard to her life. She compares her feelings about his phrase "You've *had* a good life" (p. 32) to his experience of being stung by a bee. He can still remember his swollen cheek and his half-closed eye (p. 33), and she can still remember all the ill-considered and near-impossible demands upon her ingenuity and her energy. Once he had called for "Mud!" and there was none; so he had insisted, "Well, *make* some." But she had felt helpless to make mud: she lacked a recipe, the right pan (pp. 32–33). She can remember staying neat and busy, not prying, during his "seven-month decline" (p. 21), wondering if he had found another girl, realizing their "rough and tumble in the sheets" was over, and considering a divorce as an entree into a more daring life (pp. 21–23). But she had passed through this difficult period by recognizing the mutuality of loneliness – even at the climax of love, "*Le petit mort*" (p. 24). Then he had come back, and she was "halfway there, halfway to compassion" (p. 24). Now they look back on the pyramid of children they have built together. She sees it as an individual, private effort – a precarious and difficult feat of engineering — which their children will now begin. He says, "It's all one" (pp. 14–15).

Each in his own way, then, has arrived at this new plateau — retirement age. Henderson says that those who have experienced adventure and change usually seek "a settled life" at this time, while those who have adhered to a pattern seek a "liberating change."[19] And he seems to be describing the contrast between Charlie and Nancy as they pause on the brink of a new transcendence.

The moment is appropriate, therefore, for the entrance of the lizards. Earlier Nancy had sensed their presence or spotted them in the distance during her recollections of Charlie's love of submerging (p. 14). Later they reenter her vision as she makes her final plea to him to descend into the sea again – bare (pp. 27–28). These references to excursions into the underworld make the lizards' ascent into the upper world somehow less astonishing, a foreshadowing in reverse. The lizards, thus linked to Charlie's past, appear now as heralds, callers to a new adventure. Joseph Campbell says that the herald is a "representative of the repressed fecundity" within man; this description is certainly fitting to the present aridity of the man who once behaved like a fish. Campbell also describes the herald as "dark, loathly, or terrifying,"[20] and indeed the lizards do frighten Charlie. They arouse his deepest animal instincts, for he assumes a position on all fours. He also returns to his old habits and orders Nancy to get him a stick. Nancy reacts as though he had been stung by a bee again; she can see no sticks. Eventually, however, she does find him a thin, smallish one (p. 44). Perhaps this is the piece of wood symbolic of primordial origins. At any rate, she too takes to all fours as she crawls toward Charlie with the stick between her teeth (p. 44). Charlie's protective instincts are to the fore. When Leslie's throat-clearing assumes the character of a growl, "Charlie gathers Nancy to him," and he brandishes his stick in a pathetic attempt to "go down fighting" (p. 45). Nancy seems more fascinated than fearful. She is filled with wonder at the lizards' beauty (p. 45). But as Leslie threatens them by waving his own stout, four-foot stick, Charlie and Nancy remember to exchange, "I love you" (p. 46). They are prepared for crisis! Leslie and Sarah approach! Then the jet planes fly overhead again, frightening the lizards into a retreat toward the water. The refrain repeats its twofold function: symbolically it shows the creature-fear of unknown heights, and technically it marks the end of another stanza, so to speak.

The remainder of Act One gives Charlie and Nancy their moment to recover. Charlie intuitively recognizes that the lizards are the "glaciers and the crags" (p. 47). He even imagines he and Nancy are already dead – poisoned by Nancy's liver paste (p. 50). But when Leslie and Sarah approach again, Charlie and Nancy know by their fright that they are still alive. Nancy, with her feminine instinct, suggests they assume the animal posture of submission – on their backs, legs drawn up, hands curled like paws, "smiling broadly" (p. 51). Thus begins the rite of submission, the first step in answering the call, the prelude to the process of initiation.

The third stanza of Albee's poetic fairy tale is devoted to what Joseph Campbell has called the outgrowing of "old concepts and emotional patterns."[21] At this point, Leslie and Sarah, representing the unconscious selves and the evolutionary predecessors of Charlie and Nancy, provoke for their conscious, modern counterparts a new and instructive look at the familiar. Consequently, old behavior patterns give rise to new self-realizations. The submissive females turn out to be more adventuresome and less fearful than the supposedly aggressive males, for Nancy and Sarah prod their men into friendly contact. Charlie and Nancy are forced to recognize that they are members of a dangerous species who kill other living things and eat all but their own kind. Both the lizards and the human beings discover in their own responses that the different and the unknown cause fears which spur defensive hostility. Leslie brandishes his stick out of fright just as Charlie does. The lizards reveal themselves to be as bigoted against fish as men are against other races. In his own defense, Leslie asks what frightens Charlie, what makes him panic. Charlie answers the question for himself as well as Leslie: "Oh … deep space? Mortality? Nancy … not being with me? Great … green … creatures coming up from the sea." Leslie is able to sum it all up, "what we don't know" (p. 73). And his words occasion in the dramatic imagination a greater Consciousness beyond earthly comprehension.

In that spirit the lizards and the human beings consider the enormous differences that time has made between them. Man's simplest everyday customs, like shaking hands, are strange to the lizards, and Charlie and Nancy recall earlier forms of human greeting which are now strange to modern man. The lizards are puzzled by clothes, and Charlie and Nancy grope to explain them. Leslie and Sarah have never seen a woman's breasts. Nancy's willingness to show hers to both Sarah and Leslie causes Charlie to reassess his feelings of jealousy and of love for Nancy's body. The most startling revelation, however, is of the enormity of the changes wrought by evolution. Leslie and Sarah are not even mammals. Their reproductive patterns are entirely different. Sarah has laid perhaps seven thousand eggs, many of which floated away or were eaten (pp. 82–83). Bearing one child at a time and lovingly nurturing him for eighteen to twenty years take on the aspect of a wondrous gift. This insight leads to the discovery that Leslie and Sarah do not know the emotions of love and loss. To borrow Carl Jung's phrase, they have not yet "blundered into consciousness"; consequently, they "have a share" in both the "daemonically superhuman" and the "bestially subhuman."[22]

While contemplating their differences, the animals and the human beings exhibit some similarities also; these reinforce the notion that Leslie and Sarah are counterparts, in this instance more subhuman than superhuman, to Nancy and Charlie. Sarah, like Nancy, submits willingly to her mate's decisions (p. 100); like Nancy, Sarah is fascinated by new experiences (p. 103). Both males, on the other hand, feel inadequate at being unable to explain and understand, so they vent their feelings in anger at each other. Sarah is fascinated by the birds, but they activate Leslie's instinct to seek an escape route. Nancy is delighted to have been here "when Sarah saw it all" (p. 102), but Charlie, she chides, "has decided that the wonders do not occur; that what we have not known does not exist; that what we cannot fathom cannot be ... " (p. 105). As a final similarity, both couples react negatively to the recurring sound of the jet planes overhead. Leslie and Sarah rush back over the dunes, and Charlie and Nancy repeat their refrain.

The last stanza brings the grasping of the opportunity offered by the initiation rites and the final understanding. It begins in Nancy's compassion for the lizards' fear of the jets: "Oh, Charlie; they're frightened. They're so frightened!" Charlie picks up her feelings: "They are" (p. 111); and both offer the comfort of explanations. Thus, they grasp their opportunity to consolidate the results of this encounter with the representatives of the unconscious, private and collective. The experiences which follow provide intuitive enlightenment to both the lizards and the human beings, and they also offer thematic statements to the student of Albee's play.

Overall the clear message is that individual human growth is analogous to the evolution of mankind. Authoritative testimony reinforces Albee's statement. Heuscher says a study of the "best known Grimms' tales" led repeatedly to the realization that "the growth of the individual is closely interrelated with the historical fate of the human race."[23] Charlie began in his mother's watery womb, and after his birth he liked to retire to its symbolic equivalent, but eventually he moved on to adolescence and then adulthood and middle age. Now he is ready for the final step of life on this intermediate stage of earth. In the same way, mankind began in the "primordial soup." There was a "heartbreaking second" when "the sugars and the acids and the ultraviolets" all came together, and creatures began "crawling around, and swimming and carrying on" down there (p. 118). In the eons that followed, they dropped tails and changed spots – they mutated (p. 123), until one day a "slimy creature poked his head out of the muck" and decided to stay up on land (p. 124). Thus, Charlie verbalizes one level of the symbolism of Leslie and Sarah. The implication is that Charlie and Nancy are the present product of the mutations that earlier Leslies and Sarahs have undergone. And now, as human beings, they must move on to the third level of life, symbolized by air.

Within this overall pattern are meaningful individual thematic statements. The first of these is that discontent is the springboard of growth. Henderson supports Albee's intuitive accuracy. He states that a "spirit of divine discontent ... forces all free men to face some new discovery or to live their lives in a new way."[24] Charlie no longer wishes to submerge himself in the sea. He knows he could not find satisfaction now in this twelve-year-old's game: "it wasn't ... finding out" (p. 115). Leslie and Sarah have come up from the sea because they no longer felt they *belonged* there (p. 116). The fish in the "glop" became dissatisfied and "sprouted things — tails, spots, fins, feathers" (p. 121).

Second, these developmental stages are gradual but inevitable. Creatures and men come to believe they have always been as they are. Leslie says he has "*always* had a *tail*" (p. 122). Sarah says that their discomfort under the sea was "a growing thing, nothing abrupt"; it was a "sense of having changed" (p. 116). Charlie calls it "flux" (p. 124). And it is ultimately unstoppable. Before each new transition, creatures, as well as men, have the urge to turn back. Leslie and Sarah epitomize this wish to retreat at the very end of the play. Leslie states sadly that he is ready to "go back down," and Sarah concurs (p. 132). But Nancy overrules them with her insistence that they will have to come back eventually. They have no choice, she says (p. 134). Charlie agrees, "You've got to *do* it – sooner or later" (p. 135). Heuscher also concludes that individually and culturally, "growth appears as a never-ending process." He places this thought in an optimistic framework which parallels the bright future he says is always present in fairy tales. He explains that the adult person who knows the challenge of continuing development "finds himself wedded to the goddess of eternal youth."[25]

The play's third statement is the most meaningful: knowledge of one's own mortality is the key to being truly alive and human. Martin Grotjahn, in *The Voice of the Symbol*, confirms the importance of understanding finiteness. He explains that in old age man is given one last chance to understand himself and his world, and that chance "is created by the recognition that human life is terminable." Integrating the meaning of mortality and accepting it "without narcissistic delusion" accomplishes, he says, "the transition from maturation to wisdom."[26] Nancy sees this awareness as evidence of true progress in evolution; she thinks men are more interesting than animals because they "use tools, ... make art" and know death (p. 125). Charlie, whose great fear is separation from Nancy in death, intuitively forces Sarah to face this same possibility. He asks her what she would do if she knew Leslie "was never coming back" (p. 129). Once they have absorbed Charlie's question, Leslie and Sarah have learned what emotion is. They know their love for each other; they know the fear of loss. Sarah says she would cry her eyes out if she lost Leslie. Leslie almost kills Charlie for making Sarah cry (p. 131). Both lizards wish to return to the sea where, in Charlie's parlance, the brute beasts are "free from it all" (p. 128). But the whole experience has deepened the human beings' compassion and the lizards' trust. The constructive feminine spirit of man, Nancy, points out the inevitability of growth, and her other half holds out his hand in their mutual offer of help. Leslie straightens as he accepts, "All right. Begin" (p. 135).

The full meaning of "Begin" is contained in the play's central analogy. Both couples are ready now to begin the death of the old life and the birth of the new. Leslie and Sarah will die as lizards to be reborn as men; by gaining consciousness they have moved their home from the underworld of the sea to the middle ground of earth. Charlie and Nancy will die as men and be reborn to a higher plane of existence symbolized by winged flight in the upper world of air. Albee's analogy spares him the necessity of prophesying the nature of this new plane of existence, but its prelude seems to be ego-integration. On another level, "Begin" suggests the start of total reconciliation of all conflicting elements of the self – the past with the present, the subconscious with the conscious, and even the animus with the anima. Charlie and Nancy join hands with Leslie and Sarah to begin the attainment of oneness. Thus, through the language of symbols, Albee speaks his major theme — acceptance of death is transcendence.

Seascape offers a message of wisdom and comfort presented in a fanciful style that allows people to sip only as much as they thirst for. But Albee's intent is clear in his choice of form. Bettelheim has verbalized it: "If there is a central theme to the wide variety of fairy tales, it is that of rebirth to a higher plane."[27]

NOTES

1 Bruno Bettelheim, *The Uses of Enchantment*, (New York, 1976), p. 5.

2 *Ibid.*, p. 62.

3 *Ibid.*, p. 12.

4 Norman O. Brown, *Life Against Death* (Middletown, Conn., 1959), p. 108.

5 J.E. Cirlot, *A Dictionary of Symbols*, trans. Jack Sage (New York, 1962), p. 268.

6 Joseph L. Henderson, "Ancient Myths and Modern Man," in *Man and His Symbols,* edd. Carl G. Jung and M.L. von Franz (New York, 1968), p. 100.

7 *Ibid.,* p. 146.

8 *Ibid.,* p. 150.

9 *Ibid.,* p. 151.

10 *Ibid.,* p. 152.

11 *Ibid.,* p. 153.

12 *Ibid.,* p. 155.

13 *Ibid.,* p. 156.

14 Joseph Campbell, *Hero With A Thousand Faces* (Cleveland and New York, 1956), p. 51.

15 Julius Heuscher, *A Psychiatric Study of Myths and Fairy Tales* (Springfield, Ill., 1974), p. 193.

16 Carl G. Jung, *Four Archetypes,* trans. R.F.C. Hull (London, 1972), p. 95.

17 Edward Albee, *Seascape* (New York, 1975), p. 3. (Subsequent references to this play will appear in the body of the text.)

18 Cirlot, p. 303.

19 Henderson, p. 151.

20 Campbell, p. 53.

21 *Ibid.,* p. 51.

22 Jung, p. 108.

23 Heuscher, p. 189.

24 Henderson, p. 151.

25 Heuscher, p. 189.

26 Martin Grotjahn, *The Voice of the Symbol* (New York, 1973), p. 45.

27 Bettelheim, p. 179.

Part Four
Sam Shepard
1943–

Defusion of Menace in the Plays of Sam Shepard

CHARLES R. BACHMAN

For several years Sam Shepard has been acknowledged as the most talented and promising playwright to emerge from the Off-off Broadway movement. Now, more than a decade after his work was first performed, he is increasingly recognized as one of the more significant dramatists in the English-speaking world. Praised by Edward Albee and Elizabeth Hardwick,[1] he has been called "One of the three or four most gifted playwrights alive"[2] and "the most talented of his generation."[3] Catherine Hughes rightfully acknowledges that "there is no young American playwright who can match Shepard in his ability to employ language."[4] Ren Frutkin in an article in *Yale Theatre* asserts that "he has brought the word back into the theatre,"[5] and London director Kenneth Chubb believes that Shepard's "perspective on his material has a relevance and universality that earmarks great writers."[6] Granted the tendency of some reviewers to exaggerate in the enthusiasm of the moment, the body of positive opinion regarding Shepard's work is impressive. At least twenty-seven of his plays have been performed, not only in the United States and the United Kingdom,[7] but in Canada[8] and Australia[9] as well. At least twelve plays have been performed in London alone, where he has been living for the past four years.[10] Nineteen of his plays, as well as a book of poetry and prose, are in published form, and he has several screenplays to his credit.[11]

Shepard draws much of his material from popular culture sources such as B-grade westerns, sci-fi and horror films, popular folklore, country and rock music and murder-mysteries. In his best work he transforms the original stereotyped characters and situations into an imaginative, linguistically brilliant, quasi-surrealistic chemistry of text and stage presentation which is original and authentically his own. One source of the unique quality and tension of his dramas is his ambivalent attitude toward violence. The structure of his work reflects both an abhorrence for and fascination with it, and with the menace which may lead to it. This fascination is partly apparent in the "force of competitive virtuosity" noted by Frutkin in various pairs of Shepard characters, which in 1969 led that critic to observe that in Shepard's plays "the main dynamism ... is not that of union – the dynamism of love – but of displacement — the dynamism of power."[12] At least until his last three published plays, however, such competition produces very little real menace or terrifying physical violence. What Shepard's ambivalent attitude toward violence, menace and power does result in throughout his dramas is the following pattern of action: Menacing, potentially violent characters or forces are introduced, only to have the terror they create defused either by an avoidance of the threatened violence, or vitiation of its effect through audience alienation devices. In the dramas preceding *The Tooth of Crime* (1972),[13] this structure frequently involves characters who are self-indulgent, who often find their whims almost instantly gratified. Such a pattern is in contrast, for example, to that employed in Pinter's dramas, in which menace is almost never defused, but continues to build throughout the action, at times exploding into terrifying conflict.

Shepard's dramatic pattern, while never resulting in anything as sentimental as love or even union, bears some resemblance to the fictional patterns of Thomas Hardy, who, like Shepard, created in various novels all the ingredients for violent confrontation, then scrupulously avoided the potential conflict. Like Hardy's characters, those of Shepard ultimately turn out to be potential communers rather than potential conflicters.[14] Examples of this pattern throughout Shepard's work are the defusion of the threat posed by Bill Howard and the offstage plane in *Icarus's Mother* (1965), Jim in *Red Cross* (1966), Doc and Boy in *La Turista* (1966), the Exterminators in *Forensic and the Navigators* (1967), Peter in *Melodrama Play* (1967), Geez in *Shaved Splits* (1969), the Young Man, Blood, and the Desert Tactical Troops in *Operation Sidewinder* (1970), Sycamore and The Kid in *The Unseen Hand* (1970), the Chindi and Ice in *The Holy Ghostly* (1970), the Beast in *Back Bog Beast Bait* (1971), and Yahoodi's threat to Captain Kidd in *Mad Dog Blues* (1971).

In *Melodrama Play* the defusion of menace occurs most obviously in regard to Peter, a huge henchman assigned to guard a rock star and his friends. After having shot the star's girlfriend in the head (significantly, this is not taken very seriously by the others) and knocked the star unconscious with his club, Peter sits the others on the couch and says: "I'd like to ask you both what you think of me as a person. Just frankly. Don't be afraid of hurting my feelings or anything like that. Just tell me what you think."[15] In spite of further head bashings and threats, this concern of Peter's, revealed also in two lengthy monologues, and the sudden resurrection and exit of the dead girl and one of the men, prevent Peter's poised club over the brother's head at the end of the play from being anything but comic or melodramatic – a propos of the title.

Forensic and the Navigators, a more satisfying drama, follows a similar pattern of defusion. The first menace is between Emmet and Forensic, two co-conspirators, who begin grappling over how to go about capturing a fortress (prison? mental insitution?). Immediately a girl named Oolan enters, flipping a pancake, whereupon the fight ceases. The next source of terror is the two Exterminators who knock at the door. In spite of their being well-armed and *"huge men ... dressed like California Highway Patrolmen."*[16] they speak with a harmless politeness which would do credit to a roach exterminator, become confused in their roles and susceptible to Oolan's charms, and end up as frightened of their home office as Emmet and Forensic were at their knock on the door. As at the end of *Melodrama Play,* a loud banging is heard on the door. Any remaining menace is the offstage and unknown source of the gas filling the auditorium. Terror from unknown sources is in fact almost the only kind which is ever very frightening in Shepard's work, and is the only type of terror he himself has specifically mentioned.[17]

In *Mad Dog Blues* the characters are engaged in one big, comical self-gratification quest, led by Kosmo, a rock star, and his friend-envier, Yahoodi. In this work a character merely has to say he imagines Mae West or Marlene Dietrich, and she appears. A desire for buried treasure produces Captain Kidd, who has intuitive knowledge of its whereabouts. Until the fruitless interpersonal quest in the last section of the play, a character always has someone available to berate, talk or make love to, or somehow carry on with. The closest thing to menace in the drama occurs when Yahoodi threatens and shoots Captain Kidd. The latter does not remain dead, however, and the only thing denied the characters in this play is "roots," identity, fulfillment – though a short musical version of even that occurs in the linked-hand singing of "Home" at the end of the play.[18]

In *Cowboy Mouth* (1971), *The Tooth of Crime* (1972) and *Geography of a Horse Dreamer* (1974), Shepard utilizes to a much greater extent than before the methods of conventional dramatic realism such as believable characterization, psychological and emotional tension and crescendo of suspense. Concomitant with this development comes a virtual elimination of the brilliant, surrealistically grotesque monologues of his earlier work, and a more tightly-disciplined form. This affects his use of menace, which now becomes more seriously threatening than before, and approaches closer to actual physical conflict and violence.

In *Cowboy Mouth* a woman named Cavale ("mare") has kidnapped a half-resentful, half-fascinated Slim, hoping to turn him into a rock star. Like his earlier namesake in *Back Bog Beast Bait,* Slim loves to play the coyote (to Cavale's crow), but combines within himself some of the frustrations of both Kosmo and Yahoodi of *Mad Dog Blues.* Unlike the earlier Slim, however, he is young, and carries only faint traces of that perennial Shepardian character – the outlaw-hero of the American Southwest. This is, in fact, the first play since *Shaved Splits* which does not include such a figure. As in *Mad Dog Blues,* instant gratification patterns appear in the form of immediately-realized fantasies which may fuse with the concept of menace. Cavale wants red shoes, and, through the transformation technique of simply saying the word, she and Slim immediately imagine themselves downtown (or actually are downtown, depending upon one's interpretation) buying her shoes. When they want some lobster, they call the Lobster Man. Later, they want him back to play with. On both occasions, he enters looking like a giant lobster. Whatever hints of menace he carries with him onto the stage are quickly dissipated by his obvious harmlessness, reflected in his becoming the object of ridicule by Slim and Cavale. He is a comic-grotesque descendent of the Sidewinder, the Chindi in *The Holy Ghostly,* and the two-headed Beast in *Back Bog Beast Bait.* Like Cavale's stuffed crow, he is a stage version of Gerard de Nerval's pet – and just as peaceful. He plays a crucial role in the quest for a musical epiphany, which in this play is the most direct and sustained of any in Shepard's dramas. Johny Ace, the first potential rock and roll "savior," had blown his brains out with a revolver in front of his audience. Slim, or someone else, will hopefully be the new one. Several of the numerous literary allusions in the play such as "rocking [sic] toward Bethlehem to be born"[19] relate to this hoped-for savior. Finally, the Lobster Man emerges from his shell as such a figure and points a revolver at his head. It fails to fire. End of play.

On the way to this final defusion of violence and terror, the major menace occurs between Slim and Cavale as they engage in cycles of aggression and amity with each other; and, for the first time in a play by Shepard, this involves some actual confrontation and conflict. At one point Cavale threatens Slim with her revolver. When he wards her off verbally, she accuses him of "wrecking" everything. At another time he "*starts tearing the place apart*" after calling her a "fucking cunt" (100). Yet no real violence comes to either of them. Its nearest approach is when Slim says, "Coyote he howl and howl and chomp down on that crow now. Tear into the crow now!" and "*jumps on* CAVALE *and tears into her.* THEY *roll around on the floor for awhile, then stop*" (103). Since this occurs within the context of the "coyote and crow game," it is not as menacing as it otherwise might be. Yet it is more menacing and believable than such situations in Shepard's earlier plays because, unlike earlier role-playing characters, Cavale and Slim are not mainly unaware enactors in a larger role-playing game which is the drama itself, but are themselves conscious and deliberate authors of several of their own interactive games. This is integral to their being more psychologically realistic than earlier Shepard characters, and permits the playwright to allow their outbursts of aggression to build more believably than before, and to explode at appropriate moments – but never into anything as direct as someone actually getting beaten or shot, as in the preceding eight plays.[20] *Cowboy Mouth* is more believably violent and aggressive than any previous Shepard play.

In *The Tooth of Crime* (1972), probably Shepard's best play to date[21] and his personal favorite,[22] the aggressive menace intensifies as the hoped-for rock and roll savior, the "beast rocking toward Bethlehem to be born," appears onstage in the form of the rock singer Crow. The name itself is not only one which recurred throughout *Cowboy Mouth,* but of course also recalls the controlling metaphor and titular anti-hero of Ted Hughes' magnificent series of poems. Whether or not Hughes was an actual influence, the searing image of "Crow" — as has been suggested numerous times – may well be an apt metaphor for our disillusioned time. Not coincidentally, it is the kind of image suggested by Mick Jagger of the Rolling Stones, and by Keith Richard, his co-writer for the group. In *Cowboy Mouth* Cavale felt that Mick Jagger was almost the rock and roll savior. In *The Tooth of Crime* Crow, upon entering the stage in the second act to challenge the older star, Hoss, in a battle of styles, is described as looking "just like Keith Richard."

As the play opens, Hoss, the aging Elvis Presley-style star, is sitting a bit uncomfortably on his throne. Aided by his advisor Becky, his Shepardian cowboy sidekick Cheyenne, and his stargazers and other miscellaneous retinue, he tries to "suss the scene" – to discover how close he is to really being at the top, and who the chief threats to his eminence might be. Though at a literal level Hoss's chief identity is in music, Shepard creates an effective build of biting menace by using the controlling metaphor of a Mafia-type battle over "turf." As Hoss discovers that some upstart has "knocked over Vegas" – up to now part of his "turf" – and he prepares to do battle with "skivs" (knives), it almost appears that the conflict is in fact not over popularity at all, but is of a more directly violent nature. Interwoven with the criminal turf metaphor is a masterful delineation of styles – which is what the conflict eventually comes down to. In spite of reassurances by Galactic Jack (Wolfman Jack) that "you is in, Jim. In like a stone winner" (14), and "You're number one with a bullet and you ain't even got the needle in the groove" (18). Hoss's unease remains. Like the style of "Gypsies" who threaten him by playing outside the charts and going immediately for the top-level kill, Hoss's style is not only defined by his music, but involves himself almost entirely: his cars, clothes and diction, his moves and gestures. Somewhat arrogant in his self-esteem, he possesses a hip version of hubris before the fall, and embodies several of those traditional values which many of Shepard's self-indulgent, immediately gratified characters have tended thus far to reject: (1) Restraint and repression of fantasy gratification while young: he envies Crow that he "Lived out his fantasies" (71); (2) Patience, persistence, and desire for security: he tells Crow, "All my turf?! You know how long it's taken me to collect that ground? You know how many kills it's taken! I'm a fuckin' champion man [...]. All my turf! That's all I've got"

(64). After Hoss, defeated, ends his life, Cheyenne tells Crow, "He earned his style" (75).

Hoss is also troubled simply by his humanity. After his loss to Crow, the latter tells him, "Get mean. There's too much pity, man. Too much empathy" (66). Hoss yearns for a restored sense of personal identity, courage, non-vulnerability:

> HOSS Now I'm outa control. I'm pulled and pushed from one image to another. Nothin' takes a solid form. Nothin' sure and final. Where do I stand! Where the fuck do I stand!
> CROW Alone. Leathers. [...] Too much searchin'. I got no answers. Go beyond confidence. Beyond loathing ... Keep away from fantasy. Shake off the image. No pictures, just pure focus. How does it feel? [...] Get down his animal. [...] Keep him comin'. Pull him into ya'. Put on his gestures. Wear him like a suit a' clothes.
> HOSS Yeah. It *is* me. Just like I always wanted to be. (65ff.)

Crow wins the match because he has sensed and articulated Hoss's vulnerability – a vulnerability he does not share because he has tightly disciplined himself into "pure focus," pure style, knife-like, sexual and super-cool down to his marrow, with no room for anything else. His style is all he is — and thus he has seemingly solved the age-old problems of security, repression, piety, justice and personal identity with which Hoss and Shepard have been burdened. The new savior is indeed enviable and/or pitiable, depending on one's mood and psychological set. He is certainly a Yeatsian "rough beast," with a hard edge much less cosmic yet, in its way, as pitiless as Hughes' Crow itself:

> Crow laughed.
> He bit the Worm, God's only son,
> Into two writhing halves.
>
> He stuffed into man the tail half
> With the wounded end hanging out.
> ....
> Man awoke being dragged across the grass.
> Woman awoke to see him coming.
> Neither knew what had happened.
> God went on sleeping.
>
> Crow went on laughing.[23]

Hoss believes only at a conscious level that "Power. That's all there is." Crow knows it at gut-level as he *"cruises the stage with true contempt"* (41).

The only time in the three-round fight when Hoss begins to get to Crow occurs in Round Two, when he correctly shows him how little he knows – or wishes to acknowledge – of the origins of his style in Black soul music, including that of Little Brother Montgomery, King Oliver, Ma Rainey and Blind Lemon Jefferson. "You'd like a free ride on a Black Man's back," he tells Crow (59). That round, however, is called a draw, presumably because in the new order of things, a sense of historical indebtedness is irrelevant to "pure focus." Crow wins a TKO when he tells Hoss that in spite of trying to "Sound like a Dylan, sound like a Jagger," he "Can't get it together."

The Tooth of Crime utilizes to an even greater degree than *Cowboy Mouth* the traditional dramatic values of taut, disciplined structure, vivid and consistent characterization, and crescendo of suspense. In these it reflects both its major characters. Hoss may have been more self-restrained in not having lived out all his fantasies, but Crow is the more tightly disciplined of the two. The temptation arises to see the pattern of value conflict and its outcome in this drama as a fantasy of the playwright's reluctant yielding to what he feels is the necessity for a tighter discipline and control in his own work. Whether or not this is true, the tighter structure results in the almost complete disappearance of the casual movement patterns, instant gratifications and uninhibited, anti-hangup behaviors of characters in previous plays. For the first itme, Shepard has brought onstage two potentially menacing characters, and placed them in open confrontation with each other. Temperamentally, they are nearer to Shepard's many cowboy heroes of the Southwest than to rock stars in previous plays.[24] Unlike their cowboy predecessors, however, they are not rendered harmless by being stereotyped, caricatured, or by immediately revealing cowardice and vulnerability. Even Hoss, the more vulnerable of the two, plays out the match, confident of victory. With the possible exception of a rather over-theatrical cheerleading scene during Round One (55) and Becky's famous auto-seduction scene (admittedly dramatic and comic in itself), the potential and actual conflict moves forward with an inevitability that is new in Shepard. As a result, this is his most menacing play.

The music adds to the menace. Shepard's plays contain many songs, and most of them serve to reinforce the movement and tone of the work in which they occur, sometimes adding touches of comedy or pathos, as in *Mad Dog Blues*. This is hardly surprising, since Shepard is a serious musician himself. But in *The Tooth of Crime,* Shepard's fourth play to contain rock musician characters,[25] music plays a more integral part than in any of his other works. The music in this play – written, along with the lyrics, by Shepard – not only helps to define and differentiate the styles of the two contenders; it is also strong

enough, harmonically, melodically and rhythmically, to be consistent with and
to reinforce the stylistic battle of the two opposing singers, though no songs are
sung during the actual battle itself. In the hands of a strong-voiced rock singer,
Crow's three songs especially have the potential of being menacingly
chilling.[26]

The direct terror of even this confrontation, however, is eventually defused.
Brechtian-style devices such as the auto-seduction scene and the presence and
activity of cheerleaders and referee during the style battle reduce somewhat the
immediate physical menace, though the audience is never quite sure that knives
won't actually be used. The chief defusion occurs after Crow wins. Had he been
as merciless as he is portrayed to that point, he would presumably have been
less willing to teach Hoss his style. Yet their interaction after the battle is quite
amiable. Shepard's impulse toward communion once more overrides the
identifiable menace and potential violence in his drama. Hoss dies, not at the
hands of Crow, but by committing suicide onstage. His recognition of an
old-fashioned vulnerability and humanity in himself leads him to realize that
suicide is the only authentic gesture he has left to make; and he makes it cleanly
and dramatically, his back to the audience, with a revolver shot in the mouth.
The suicidal ghost of de Nerval which had haunted the imagination of Cavale in
Cowboy Mouth but was unrealized as the pistol failed to fire, has here – for the
first time in Shepard – entered the stage. Becky's immediate willingness to be
part of Crow's entourage, and Cheyenne's refusal, are both believable and do
not detract from the effect of Hoss's death. His final act forms the most
appropriate finale to the agonized/comic search for authenticity, self, and
community that has plagued Shepard's characters from the beginning. Yet
Shepard never allows it to appear as an over-sentimental gesture. Crow's "A
genius mark. I gotta hand it to ya'. It took ya long enough but you slid right
home" (74), is the closest he comes.

The menace which remains at the end of *The Tooth of Crime* is of the same
kind as ends most of Shepard's plays – the terror of the unknown that the
playwright himself has spoken of. Here it is simultaneously two unknowns: at a
superficial level, whatever unnamed singer will threaten, dethrone and destroy
Crow, as he has destroyed Hoss; at a deeper level, the more terrifying and even
vaguer menace of the exclusively stylistic value system represented by Crow
himself, as he stands alone on stage, singing to a hauntingly relentless 6/8 beat
and lament-style melody the words of "Rollin' Down":

If I'm a fool then keep me blind
I'd rather feel my way
If I'm a fool for bigger game
You better get down – you better get down and pray [...] (82).

Shepard's most recently published play, *Geography of a Horse Dreamer* (1974), is probably too derivative for its otherwise quite palpable menace to be very terrifying – in spite of the fact that the work involves perhaps Shepard's two most startling scenes of violence. Appropriately subtitled "A Mystery in Two acts," this play is Shepard's closest attempt thus far at conventional realism. It combines a Runyonesque situation and a Raymond Chandler/ Dashiell Hammett style with a touch of the one-sided western shoot-out at the end. Initially, the chief menace appears to be Fingers, whose syndicate keeps a Wyoming cowboy named Cody prisoner so that he can dream successful racehorse winners. The syndicate is displeased with Cody's slump, however. After conversation creates Fingers' menacing quality, he enters with an associate, the Doctor. Almost immediately, the terror aroused by Fingers is softened and finally shifted to the Doctor (who "looks like Sidney Greenstreet") as Fingers reveals a soft under-belly of sympathy and sensitivity. In the first of the two scenes of violence, the Doctor throws Fingers across the room and becomes steadily more menacing as he prepares to remove Cody's dreaming bone from his skull. Even this menace is defused, however, in the most violent ending Shepard has yet devised. Cody's two huge cowboy brothers enter with shotguns, cutting down Beaujo, Santee and the Doctor, but – with poetic justice – sparing Fingers.

There is no doubt that the initial impact of this scene, like that of the Doctor's violence toward Fingers, is startling. But whereas the impact of both these scenes suffers from the derivatively melodramatic quality of the play generally, the final scene is even less effective because, once the first split-second of total surprise is over, it conveys a completely deus ex machina quality – too sudden and unprepared to have been the outcome of suspense, but occurring in too serious a murder-mystery context to be defended as parodistic or deliberately comic.

The menace in this play is therefore not only defused, but also rendered clumsy. Unlike Shepard's best work – *Chicago* (1965), Forensic and the Navigators, Cowboy Mouth and *The Tooth of Crime* – the characterization, dialogue and plot in *Geography of a Horse Dreamer* fail to develop beyond the stereotypes which were their sources. Fingers is the only character who begins to assume individuality and, significantly, his characterization is tightly integrated with the steady erosion of the menace he seems to represent. Equally significant for this essay is the fact that this drama contains no actual violent conflict: Cody cringes away from all threats, Fingers yields to the Doctor, who in turn has no chance against Cody's brothers. This action follows the pattern in all Shepard's dramas. It remains to be seen whether he will again utilize a conventionally realistic structure – but one that is less derivative – to do something he has not yet done: combine a crescendo of menace with its explosion in believably terrifying violence or violent conflict. Productions of his more recent plays suggest that he has moved in other directions for the present.[27]

NOTES

1 Harold Clurman, *Nation,* 30 March 1970, 380.
2 Edith Oliver, *New Yorker,* 17 March 1973, 92.
3 Stanley Kauffmann, *New Republic,* 24 March 1973, 22.
4 Catherine Hughes, *America,* 31 March 1973, 290.
5 Ren Frutkin, "Sam Shepard: Paired Existence Meets the Monster," *Yale Theatre,* 2, No. 2 (Summer 1969), 22.
6 Kenneth Chubb, "Fruitful Difficulties of Directing Shepard," *Theatre Quarterly* (August, 1974), 17.
7 The best single source for performance statistics in the U.S. and U.K., synopses of the performed plays, and a bibliography on Shepard is C.W.E. Bigsby et al., "Theatre Checklist No. 3 Sam Shepard," *Theatre-facts* (Aug.-Oct., 1974), 3–11.
8 Chubb, p. 17.
9 *The Tooth of Crime* opened at the Nimrod Theatre, Sydney, Jan. 1974, and *The Unseen Hand* at the Stables, Sydney, July, 1975.
10 This does not include the final scene of *Rock Garden,* which was performed in London as part of *Oh! Calcutta* in 1970.
11 See *Theatrefacts* checklist.
12 Frutkin, p. 24.
13 Years in parentheses refer to dates of first performances.
14 See Charles R. Bachman, "Communion and Conflict in Hardy and Hauptmann: A Contrast in Artistic Temperaments," *Revue des Langues Vivantes,* 35.3 (Autumn 1969), 283–293.
15 *Five Plays by Sam Shepard* (Indianapolis, 1967), p. 157. Parenthetical page numbers refer to the edition of a drama cited in a footnote.
16 Sam Shepard, *The Unseen Hand and Other Plays* (Indianapolis, 1972), p. 57.
17 In discussing the experience which stimulated him to write *Icarus's Mother,* he commented, "And then you've got this emotional thing that goes a long way back, which creates a certain kind of chaos, a kind of terror, you don't know what the fuck's going on. ... There's a vague kind of terror going on, the people not really knowing what is happening [...]" "Metaphors, Mad Dogs and Old-Time Cowboys," *Theatre Quarterly* (August, 1974), 9.
18 Sam Shepard, *Mad Dog Blues and Other Plays* (New York, 1972), pp. 80–81.

19 *Mad Dog Blues and Other Plays*, p. 99.

20 These are *Melodrama Play, Cowboys #2*, Forensic and the Navigators,
The Holy Ghostly, The Unseen Hand, Operation Sidewinder, Shaved
Splits and *Mad Dog Blues*.

21 This opinion is shared by most reviews, which have been generally favorable to the script but unfavorable or mixed toward The Performance
Group and Open Space productions. Some samples include: "Establishes
him as a major theater figure" (Clurman, *New York Times*, 8 March
1973, 34); "Stunning in its sheer verbal dexterity" (Catherine Hughes,
America, 31 March 1973, 290); "As chillingly old as a tribal rite"
(T.E. Kalem, *Time* 27 Nov. 1972, 73); "Shepard's play picks up a fluid
aural tradition and converts it into a precise literary shape" (Irving
Wardle, *The Times*, 4 Sept. 1974, 9).

   The Royal Court production of June, 1974, in which much of the
dialogue and most of the lyrics were evidently drowned out by high
sound volume, received some unfavorable reviews. See *Guardian*, 6 June
and *Sunday Times*, 9 June.

22 Michael White, "Underground Landscapes," interview with Shepard,
Guardian, 20 Feb. 1974, 8.

23 Ted Hughes, "A Childish Prank," in *Crow* (New York, 1971), 7.

24 Southwestern figures include the two leads in *Cowboys #2* and *Forensic
and the Navigators*, Pop in *The Holy Ghostly*, the Morphan brothers in
The Unseen Hand, Mickey Free in *Operation Sidewinder*, Waco in *Mad
Dog Blues*, and Slim and Shadow in *Back Bog Beast Bait*.

25 The others are *Melodrama Play, Mad Dog Blues* and *Cowboy Mouth*.

26 A judgment based upon my several years of experience as a professional
musician. The actor-singers in the Performance Group production did
not present the songs in the manner they deserve. Neither, evidently, did
the Open Space or Royal Court productions. Shepard has said that he
felt Lou Reed of the Velvet Underground would be right for the role of
Crow (Chubb, p. 21).

27 See, for example, reviews of *Killer's Head* and *Action*, in *The Times*, 18
Sept. 1974, and *Nation*, 3 May 1975.

The Tooth of Crime:
Sam Shepard's Way With Music

BRUCE W. POWE

In the electronic age we are living entirely by music.
Marshall McLuhan

I sing the body electric.
Walt Whitman

In her poem about Sam Shepard, "Sam Shepard 9 Random Years [7 + 2]," rock star Patti Smith describes that playwright's use of music, and particularly rock 'n' roll, as an evocation of immediacy and energy, as an expression of the disruptive rhythms of the present, and as a kind of force that can affect both the audience and perhaps even the way certain characters speak:

the poetry of Speed:
the fast moving car
the engine
the black mustang pony
the electric guitar.

And:

Cut with a new demon ... rock n' roll. With an amplifier
for a heart he slid into Detroit,
The motor city: cars and radios.
His father was a Dixieland drummer
The roots of his theatre was music too.

And, lastly:

His theatre encompassed all those rhythm trade-offs all
those special dialogues of the heart.[1]

"Speed" is, of course, motion, tempo, hence a rhythm, and an addictive drug,
which is a mixture of cocaine and morphine. "The poetry of Speed ... " is a
statement that could reflect our own frenetic times, something, as Patti Smith
goes on to outline, plugged into current inventions and realities: "the fast
moving car ... " and "the electric guitar." Speed addicts shoot up; electric
guitars plug in; the car is turned on; and everything moves to the beat of change.
This is an image of the accelerando of affluent American society, a suggestive
illumination of a rhythmic principle inherent in Shepard's use of rock 'n' roll
and especially in *The Tooth of Crime,* of language, and finally a remark
concerning the energy, the drive, as it were, of some of Shepard's plays
themselves. And as Patti Smith – the first female "punk" star – says, "The roots
... " (the source and the tonic?) of Shepard's theatre are in music – that is, in the
sound, rhythm, and electric texture of rock 'n' roll.

To which one can add the following: Shepard's *Suicide in Bb,* one of his most
recent works, is an intriguing parable on the mysterious effects of music on
performers, on audiences (from the Latin *audire,* "to hear," derivative words
being "audibly," "audit"), on aural reception, on tuning in on what strange
forces compel people "now." Two detectives investigate the possible murder or
suicide of a renowned musician. In the process of their attempt to reconstruct
the crime, they encounter sinister unseen powers, voices, echoes, and allusions
– an enigmatic soundscape of innuendo, rumour, stories, and the possibility of
the supernatural (where spectres are heard):

LOUIS *stands suddenly, listening intently for a noise. No sound.*

LOUIS What was that?
PABLO What was what?
LOUIS That.

They both listen for a second. Again nothing.

PABLO Not only are you a dead weight but you're a lunatic.
LOUIS No, listen!
PABLO I'm not going to listen! I'm through listening.
LOUIS Like a woman screaming. A terrible screaming. Like a woman being tortured.
PABLO It's your ears, Louis! Your ears are telling you stories![2]

This is another aspect of what I intend to call Shepard's "tuning in"; he uses
music not only for its instantaneous and affective qualities, and to invoke in his

work an aura of energy ("the poetry of Speed ... "), but also to structure and evoke the actual speech patterns of particular types of characters involved in special situations. In performance, rock music is an immediate invisible power that "ravishes" its listeners in a circumambient onslaught of sounds and rhythms and melody and suggestiveness; but, as we shall find, particularly in *The Tooth of Crime,* Shepard often employs language as a musical instrument too, the heavily cadenced words surging as sound, to "tell stories to the ears," to act as intense oral communication. Shepard's ear for the "motion of words," as Ezra Pound called the use of pure sound in language, is frequently manipulated for great effect.

These are among the major elements of some of Shepard's most interesting plays. He is, I believe, a writer conscious of – or, perhaps, more accurately, thoroughly imbued with – the tempo and tones and talk of his time; in short, like most important artists, he expresses his age. So Louis, one of the detectives in *Suicide in Bb,* describes the relationship between the artist and his *Zeitgeist,* his environments, even his own body and mind, and the need to penetrate into, and to vivisect vividly and present these factors:

A boy hears sound. He hears sound before he has a name. He hears gurgling, pounding under water. He hears an ocean of blood swimming around him. Through his veins. Through his mother. He breaks into the light of day. He's shocked that he has a voice. He finds his voice and screams. He hears ... Atoms. Nuclear rushes of wind through his nose holes. ... Books falling on pianos. Electricity humming even when the lights are off. Internal combustion engines. Turbo jets. Then one day he hears what they call music. He hears what they call "music" in the same way he hears what they call "noise." In the same stream. Music as an extension of sound. An organization. Another way of putting it. He's disappointed. He's disappointed and exhilerated (sic) at the same time. Exhilerated (sic) because he sees an opening. An adventure. A way inside.[3]

Shepard is, then, acutely conscious of the impact that live music can have as an integral part of his metaphorical exposition of present fears and myths. As critics have commented a number of times, Shepard's plays strive for primarily emotional effects ("For Shepard's strength is his ability to pick the exact image and the exact word that strikes a chord in the imagination, that communicates as music does, emotionally, not literally," writes Kenneth Chubb[4]); and *electric music* – being, in a way, uncannily erotic – is one element of this strategy. Thus, *The Tooth of Crime, Cowboy Mouth, Operation Sidewinder, Mad Dog Blues, Melodrama Play,* and *Suicide in Bb* are simultaneously mosaics of speech habits, manners, styles, and feelings of America today, set in forms that are mythic, parodic, hallucinatory, and apocalyptic, and arranged to include an actual repertoire of songs. These works generally reveal concerns with rock 'n' roll, drugs, dreams, film, TV, radio, and show the effects of such things on everyone from cowboys, political revolutionaries, music stars, shamans and ghosts, to detectives, freaks, farmers, and teenagers.

The language itself of the plays, under the pressures of Shepard's own consciousness of what he hears, sees, and feels, of what he picks up on the air-waves, as it were, becomes alternately colloquial and poetic, slangy and austere, profane and lyrical, inarticulate and as precise as a textbook and riddled with jargon, puns, and clichés. His song lyrics, especially in *The Tooth of Crime, Operation Sidewinder,* and *Cowboy Mouth,* demonstrate all the candid, colloquial simplicities and compressed ironies of the rock lyric. But more than just being a mere recorder, a kind of dramatic journalist (a Tom Wolfe writing for the stage), Shepard uses all these qualities to explore causes, to depict mystery, to create images of emotional conditions, to investigate vanishing values, and sometimes to explode in ritualistic violence. Electric music frequently becomes a correlative for these concerns – "another way of putting it." His plays, because of this, are rarely static, they *move*; they are charged with the insistent force of primitive communication.

However, Shepard does on occasion use music purely as a counterpoint to the spoken word, especially in what I would call the rock 'n' roll plays, *Cowboy Mouth, Melodrama Play, The Tooth of Crime,* and in the pop sonic blitz, *Operation Sidewinder.* Used in this fashion, the music becomes a device for providing a commentary on the progression of the work, a way of briefly stepping outside the unfolding drama. In these works music is employed also, as I have said, as a correlative for expression, to suggest the multiplicity and depth of individual feeling, to create a more immediate and sensational effect on the audience.

Shepard is an extraordinarily prolific writer; so, to do his work justice in short space, I must concentrate on a handful of plays. *The Tooth of Crime* is, at present, his ultimate rock 'n' roll play: "A Play with Music ... " that articulates a vision of stars, styles and death. It is his *Star Wars*: a brilliant combination of western movie clichés, gangland rituals, organized sports, science fiction – in the future there will be no war, but there will be rock 'n' roll – and the star system in the pop world. (Interestingly, the whole last act of *The Tooth of Crime* is curiously reminiscent of an obscure western of the early seventies called *A Gunfight,* with Kirk Douglas and Johnny Cash. In that film, two gunfighters are convinced to give one last fight before a paying audience. Whether consciously or not, the film's producers created a striking image of the battle for public notice between film stars and pop musicians: who will be the new hero? the ultimate gunslinger by whom all aspiring "cowboys" must judge themselves?) In this play, Shepard creates a texture of language and music that echoes these distinctly American traditions and concerns by using songs, slang, profanity, quotations from rock hits, and words themselves as music. The form is surreal, yet anchored in a realistic frame, the rock music scene.

Like *Angel City, Mad Dog Blues, 4-H Club, Killer's Head*, and *Cowboys #2*, The Tooth of Crime begins with a stage that is bare, except for one evil-looking black chair. Also, very characteristically, this play starts with music, low strains from a hidden band. Shepard's plays frequently open with off-stage music playing: *Seduced* starts with Randy Newman's plaintive "Sail Away"[5]; *Suicide in B♭*, with a jazz piano sounding[6]; *Angel City*, with a portentous tympani.[7] Here the music is specifically employed to establish an ominous mood; it is a warm-up, an overture. Then Hoss enters. He is an Elvis Presley type; but like Elvis in his later years, he is past his prime. He has become isolated and protected: a star, unreal and manufactured.

Hoss starts the production with a song, "The Way Things Are."[8] The song illuminates the underlying theme of the play, which is, as it turns out, one of Shepard's major concerns:

You may think every picture you see is a true history
of the way things used to be or the way things are
While you're ridin' in your radio or walkin' through the late late show ain't it a drag to
know you just don't know
you just don't know

So here's another illusion to add to your confusion
Of the way things are

Illusions, "to add to your confusion": illusions are deceptions, mocking images, often fantastic, as if in a dream. Is that the way things are? Confused, and phantasmagoric, and potentially dangerous:

So here's another sleep-walkin' dream
A livin' talkin' show of the way things seem

"the way things seem": a reference, perhaps, to the theatrical experience itself: the apprehension of a reality that is, paradoxically, artificial. It is, as Hoss sings, both a "sleep-walkin' dream" and "a livin' talkin' show."

I used to believe in rhythm and blues
Always wore my blue suede shoes
Now everything I do goes down in doubt.

Allusions to rhythm and blues and old Elvis hits – "Blue Suede Shoes" – establish both a mythical and a contemporary reference; the present has its live traditions. Elvis and the fifties, early rock 'n' roll, blue suede shoes: how many suggestions of clothing and hair styles are embedded in those lines!

Thus, the song is a prelude. Shepard is informing us from the beginning that *The Tooth of Crime* is going to be set in a dream structure. It will not be logical or realistic; it will have the surrealism of a dream, the violence of surprise, the playfulness of one adept with illusion. The lyrics are also an admonition to the audience to watch out, to catch what happens when what "seems to be" is pushed to extremes.

But why a song to say this? Music communicates, emotionally and sensually, before it is rationally understood. It does not mediate; it is not reflective; it expresses and absorbs instantaneously. (Schopenhauer, in a famous comment on music in *The World as Will and Idea*, says: "This is why the effect of music is more powerful and penetrating than the other arts, for they speak only of shadows, while it speaks of the thing itself."[9]) Shepard himself speaks of this effect in a *Theatre Quarterly* interview: "I think music's really important, especially in plays and theatre – it adds a whole different kind of perspective, it immediately brings the audience to terms with an emotional reality. Because nothing communicates emotions better than music, not even the greatest play in the world."[10] This statement makes one realize that unlike many modern writers, Shepard is committed to expressing deep feelings. What occurs in the theatre, then, is the instant establishment of "a common note" ("an emotional reality") shared by the performer, the play, and the audience.

Shepard continues: "What I think is that music, no matter what its structure, has a very powerful emotional influence, it can't help but have that – it's in the nature of music, it's when you can play a note and there's a response immediately – you don't have to build up to it through seven scenes."[10] But he also says: "I wanted the music in *The Tooth of Crime* so that you could step out of the play for a minute, every time a song comes, and be brought to an emotional comment on what's been taking place in the play."[12] As in Brecht's plays ("He's my favorite playwright ...," Shepard says[13]), the songs can serve as a counterpoint to the dialogue and the break-up of the narrative flow, providing interludes. Unlike Brecht's intentions, though, Shepard's are visceral rather than intellectual, moody rather than political. The loud volume and tempo affect listeners – whether they want to be touched or not. The raw energy of rock can engender excitement: it literally *resounds*.

The use of music in Shepard's plays, then, has several primary functions. First, it communicates the emotional perspective of either a character or situation, or the thematic centre of a work; it establishes mood and tone. Second, it initiates a kind of communion, a community of involved listeners; and, since rock 'n' roll is *rape*, seduction through the release of energy and rhythm, it increases tension in a volatile scene. Third, through their lyrics, the songs provide another comment on some action or situation in the work and hence yet another link with the audience.

In *The Tooth of Crime*, the songs function in all these ways. Hoss begins the show with a tune that initiates us into the play's aims and themes – it is a "sleep-walkin' dream" – and illuminates something about himself. Hoss is an old rocker; he is becoming passé; but he is equally a part of the fantasy, a superstar. At the end of Act One, Crow, Hoss's nemesis, sings "Poison":

Ever since I was good
I wanted to be – evil
Ever since I went bad
I wanted to be – badder

Ever since I was dead
I wanted to be – born like a maniac
And now that I got all that I wished
I don't see me ever goin' back

At the moment the angel grew in me
I started to strangle her oh so tenderly[14]

This is like a Rolling Stones put-on; and, not surprisingly, in Act Two we are told that Crow resembles the Stones' Keith Richard. The song suggests the pseudo-satanic image of the punk, a raunchy, playful rock "evil" based on a street-tough aesthetic ("Have sympathy for the devil," as the Stones used to sing). "Poison" communicates who and what Crow is, and his threat to Hoss. And because rock 'n' roll is played loud and fast, on gleaming electric instruments under intense spotlights, emphasizing physical intensity and stressing – in the music – a repeated beat that can practically mesmerize an audience, elements of a visual spectacle and aural force are also introduced. This is purely a stage effect and impossible to perceive in the text. However, the rock 'n' roll sound and light show is a "sensational" part of the live impact.

This effect is achieved even more elaborately in the earlier *Operation Sidewinder,* where Shepard's employment of rock 'n' roll, as a bridge between scenes, as a commentary on the action, as an explosive method of establishing feelings, brings out other ironic and comic dimensions of a scene. The music was performed in the first production by an authentic country rock band, The Holy Modal Rounders (who, incidentally, did some of the music for the film *Easy Rider).* Though some of the songs were not written by Shepard, he assimilates all of them into the play's structure. At the end of Scene One, for example, after Honey has been caught by the rattlesnake-computer, and it wraps around her in a frankly sexual embrace – the snake itself, of course, being a sexual image – this song is heard:

DO IT GIRL
Everytime I see you wanna do it girl
Right out in the street I wanna do it girl
In front of everybody wanna do it girl
I'm losing my control I feel it in my soul

I wanna do it I wanna do it
I wanna do it, do it, do it, do it,
do it, do it, do it, do it, do it[15]

This is obviously an absurd and hilarious comment on the snake's embrace. The use of rock clichés and orgasmic repetition (as in an old Presley number) – "do it, do it" – reinforces the comical effect.

At the end of *Operation Sidewinder,* in the *Close Encounters of the Third Kind* sequence, Shepard combines Hopi Indian chants, the electronic rhythms of the snake and the unseen flying saucer, and the staccato chatter of machine guns, in a fantastic display that integrates science fiction, the music of the spheres, and ritual transformation. All of this is whirled together in a light show reminiscent of the acid rock concerts at Bill Graham's Fillmore in the sixties. The impact of music, voices and light is of a non-verbal apocalypse. ("Everywhere that language ceases, I meet with the musical," Kierkegaard writes in his chapter on Mozart in *Either/Or.*[16]) Here the effect is also of a large-scale assemblage of elements and allusions culled from a variety of sources, combined to create a simultaneity of events.

Against this effect may be set *Cowboy Mouth* (or "Who's Afraid of Janis Joplin?"), which uses music as a deliberately frenetic and inarticulate counterpoint to the profane, slangy clichés and monosyllables that Cavale and Slim speak with nearly random abandon. "Have No Fear" is played "*loud … with a lot of feedback*"; it is "mean, shitkickin' rock-and-roll"[17]:

Have no fear
The worst is here
The worst has come
So don't run
Let it come
Let it go
Let it rock and roll
The worst has come.

"Have No Fear" is as debased and violent as Cavale and Slim have become. The numbing volume, the dumb lyrics, the screeching feedback (feedback is reverberation) are expressions of aggression, hostility, and fear. It is the music in *Cowboy Mouth* – which is about the myth of a super-rock-star-saviour — which underlies the anger and the absurdity of such a situation. The play depicts two characters in a surreal nightmare, and the music enhances the frantic mood and helps as well to accelerate the crude accents of tension that build to the outbreak of violence at the play's end. The image of the Lobster-Man turned rock saviour playing Russian roulette is an ominous image of the American star system as suicide, which prefigures the threats of annihilation in *The Tooth of Crime* and *Suicide in Bb*. Roulette is nihilism – the trivialization of life to the point of a game, the testing of individual endurance through murderous chance – and the fast-talking blues played over this gesture reinforces the energy and near despair, "the close to the edge" feelings, that the principals feel.

In its original off-off-Broadway production, *Cowboy Mouth* featured one genuine rock star – Patti Smith. Her music is up-tempo, hard rock 'n' roll, very theatrical; the intensity of her live performance, the extremity it achieves in execution, is part of her musical strategy. The more apparently spontaneous it is, the more "electric" the effect. And Shepard's collaboration with her in *Cowboy Mouth* looks forward to the duel in *The Tooth of Crime*, in the battle of the two stars, the rock *Götterdämmerung*. Shepard appears to have learned a great deal from rock 'n' roll stars, in fact, about how to stage an "event" – which differs from a "happening" in that the former is planned for specific effects, whereas the latter is unstructured and cannot be repeated. Most rock acts try to achieve both; the spontaneity of, say, The Who – one of the best live bands – is always achieved within the organized limits of a definite production, with planned songs, laser shows, routines of physical gestures. The unexpected is encouraged; but it has to fit. This rock "event," which is, in every way, a creation or manipulation of the performer's *presence,* relates to Shepard's thematic concern with the effect of heroism, the mythic dimensions of a bold character, the potential within a tumultuous individual. As he writes of Bob Dylan in the *Rolling Thunder Logbook*:

This is Dylan's true magic. Leave aside his lyrical genius for a second and just watch this transformation of energy which he carries. Only a few minutes ago the place was deadly thick with tension and embarrassment, and now he's blown the top right off it. He's infused the room with a high feeling of life-giving excitement. It's not the kind of energy that drives people off the deep end but the kind that brings courage and hope and above all brings life pounding into the foreground. If he can do it here ... then it's no wonder he can rock the nation.[18]

Obviously, this is precisely the flip side of the destructiveness in *Cowboy Mouth,* but it accurately illuminates the dynamic situations in *The Tooth of Crime*. The notion of a performer offering "life-giving excitement" is central to

Shepard's theatricality. Thus, his use of electric music – the songs are always amplified – as a formal device is highly involving (communal), immediate and sensual. The rock beat itself often becomes analogous to the electrified sensibilities of Cavale and Slim, and of Hoss and Crow in *The Tooth of Crime*. But, importantly, as Shepard surely knows, at a rock concert there are no passive audiences: the listeners *feed back,* clap, yell, yelp, and dance, adding to the charge of the occasion. The whole atmosphere can become, potentially, one of "joining together."

We should also note that rock 'n' roll is the music of the spoken word, of idiomatic speech; rock 'n' roll comes closer to the way we speak than any other form of music. Listen to Bob Dylan's "Desolation Row" or the Rolling Stones' "Sympathy for the Devil," and hear how a vigorously colloquial speech is employed in the singing. As such, then, the dynamic range of the vocals are severely limited. But this again is an attempt to locate the music in an intimate, identifiable realm between audience and performer, the instantly understandable communication of that which is *commonly* apprehended. So, for example, in Round I in *The Tooth of Crime,* in the duel itself, Shepard invests the language with musical qualities – that is, the diction, allusions, colloquialisms, and rhythms are attuned to sound, to the rock beat – making it, in a sense, unaccompanied rock talk:

CROW Pants down. The moon show. Ass out the window. Belt lash. Whip lash. Slide lash to the kid with a lisp. The dumb kid. The loser. The runt. The mutt. The shame kid. Kid on his belly. Belly to the blacktop. Slide on the rooftop. Slide through the parkin' lot. Slide kid. Shame kid. Slide. Slide.[19]

The repetition of words and sounds, of perfect and imperfect rhymes, makes the passage formulaic, like a song. Traditional motifs of the rock loser, "The runt," "The shame kid," are intoned; variations on sounds, in "Ass," "lash," "runt," "mutt," "top," "lot," are stressed. The syntax – though there are no full sentences here – is expressive; the diction is orally associative; the rushing rhythm, the accelerando, is accented at the end by the alliterative "Slide kid. Shame kid. Slide. Slide."

One observes, too, the use of colloquialisms and jargon – hard, cutting words that exist in the characters' mouths like savage, affective things. Characters hurtle the words as if they were notes from a sax or a guitar; they project them, perform them. Employed in this way, words are *dangerous*. They have power precisely because they are alive as sound. Thus, the complex relationship between music and the spoken word, rhythm and pacing, performing and acting and being, is explored in this exchange.

Obviously, all this is quite different from the integration of songs into the play's structure. As Shepard's stage direction before the duel tells us:

They [Hoss and Crow] *begin their assaults just talking the words in rhythmic patterns, sometimes going with the music, sometimes counterpointing it. As the round progresses, the music builds with drums and piano coming in, maybe a rhythm guitar, too. Their voices build so that sometimes they sing the words or shout. The words remain as intelligible as possible, like a sort of talking opera.*[20]

Shepard is conscious, then, of how words can be arranged dynamically, orchestrated to form both a pounding, alliterative tension and a discordant duet.

Hoss responds to Crow's greaseball chatter by quoting what are in fact the origins of rock 'n' roll, the Carl ("Blue Suede Shoes") Perkins type of rockabilly:

Never catch me with beer in my hand. Never caught me with my pecker out. Never get caught. Never once. Never, never. Fast on the hoof. Fast on the roof.[21]

Again the repetition enforces tempo, the short staccato sentences augment the rhythmic thrust; the unadorned diction recalls old country song lyrics; the images conjure bars, teenagers, and the American Midwest.

Later in Round I, we find an even more graphic example of language as music:

CROW Coughin' in the corner. Dyin' from pneumonia. Can't play after dinner. Lonely in a bedroom. Dyin' for attention. Starts to hit the small time. Knockin' over pay phones. Rollin' over Beethoven. Rockin' pneumonia. Beboppin' to the Fat Man. Drivin' to the small talk. Gotta make his big mark. Take a crack at the teacher. Find him in the can can. There he's doin' time time. Losin' like a wino. Got losin' on his mind. Got losin' all the time.[22]

In a collage of song titles, from Chuck Berry – "Roll over Beethoven" – to Little Richard, in a string of adolescent clichés – "Lonely in a bedroom. Dyin' for attention" – repeated words, as in a chorus – "Got losin' on his mind" – and images evoking *Rebel Without a Cause,* these lines fall naturally into the specifically measured fragments of a melody:

Rollin' over Beethoven/Rockin' pneumonia/Beboppin' to the Fat Man/Drivin' to the small talk/

This is composed virtually in 4/4 time (all rock 'n' roll is counted in common time, with the second and fourth beats accented), up-tempo, rushing, in that "poetry of Speed." Also, it is highly compact speech, held together by the tension of the character's delivery. Behind these lines is the articulation and the associative verbal drive of a personality who has discovered his rhythm, his beat, his idiom, what Crow refers to as "the walk." These "walk" references that surface throughout Act Two are significant because they suggest a visual counterpoint for the beat. Crow imitates Hoss's walk, his "gait," his beat, which is representative of style, direction, motion, force. He talks of finding a new pattern of walking as a mode of being: "Now try out yer walk"; "Start movin' to a different drummer man."[23] Crow looks for the dominant cadence, the key to a form of personal expression (a different "walk" of life). His speech is cast in the evocative strain of rock talk; his whole physical movement is integral to what he says and how his words move. "The walk" is, then, suggestive of the use of language as an instrument, as a reflection of being.

This emphasis on vocal stylistics, on the motion of words, on delivery (performance), enhances the understanding that language for Shepard is, when manipulated orally, resonant, near musical, a definite force.

In the *Rolling Thunder Logbook,* a chronicle of his fascination with music and musicians, Shepard describes music's connotative powers: "One thing that gets me about Dylan's songs is how they conjure up images, whole scenes that are being played out in full color as you listen."[24] And earlier: "One thing for sure is that you never doubt it [a Dylan song] when it hits you. You recognize something going on in your chest cavity that wasn't going on before."[25] Shepard's use of music, then, is centred primarily in this application of it as expression, as an affective agent to incite and inspire, as another means of theatrical presentation – that is, to intensify the proceedings with sound – and as a lyrical counterpoint. But it is worth remembering that his use of music is only one part of the total form that he creates, that the presence of music is a part of the unfolding of his often ritualistic examinations of myths and images. A revealing comment can be found in Kenneth Chubb's article, in which Shepard is quoted as saying: "I'm interested in exploring the writing of plays through attitudes derived from other forms such as music, painting, sculpture, film, etc., all the time keeping in mind that I'm writing for the theatre."[26]

The attitudes derived from "music, painting, sculpture, film, ..." in the three-dimensional arrangement of the stage, combine with cowboys and gangsters, rock and rock stars, science fiction, realism, hopped-up hipsters, artists, and families, in a pop art pastiche. And because there is a non-intellectualized, intuitive, and subjective aspect to this pattern – one must be "inside" the work, feeling it, following it, willing to let it go in whatever direction it chooses – a sense of enthralling possibility, of audience involvement, seems to be constantly breaking out. Music is integral to this; music is always "now," "here," direct, touching. So Shepard relies heavily on music in those plays which deal explicitly with energy and expression to create mood, propel the story, design a sensational sound and light show, and not only to reflect a response to the electronic present, but to articulate its dynamic reality. As he writes in *Suicide in Bb:*

NILES Did you listen or just watch?
PETRONE What do you mean?
NILES Did you listen to the music?
PETRONE Yeah. Sure.
NILES What did it say?
PETRONE What?
NILES What did the music say? Did you hear it?
PETRONE Yes. It wasn't words. I mean it wasn't words like we're talking now.[27]

To see and hear Shepard's plays in all their dazzling theatricality is to recognize a young playwright shaping his language and form and music to express contemporary images and voices. And learning to see and hear Shepard's work is like learning to see and hear "now."

NOTES

1 Patti Smith, "Sam Shepard 9 Random Years [7+2]," in Sam Shepard, *Angel City, Curse of the Starving Class and Other Plays* (New York 1967), p. 244.
2 Sam Shepard, *Suicide in B♭*, in *Buried Child & Seduced & Suicide in B♭* (Vancouver, 1979), pp. 124–125.
3 *Ibid.*, p. 122.
4 Kenneth Chubb, "Fruitful Difficulties of Directing Shepard," *Theatre Quarterly*, IV (Aug.-Oct. 1974), 24.
5 Sam Shepard, *Seduced*, in *Buried Child & Seduced & Suicide in B♭*, p. 75.
6 *Suicide in B♭*, p. 119.
7 Sam Shepard, *Angel City*, in *Angel City, Curse of the Starving Class and Other Plays*, p. 7.
8 Sam Shepard, *The Tooth of Crime*, in *The Tooth of Crime and Geography of a Horse Dreamer* (New York, 1974), p. 4.
9 Arthur Schopenhauer, *The World as Will and Idea*, trans. R.B. Haldane and J. Kemp, I (New York, 1888), 133.
10 Sam Shepard, "Metaphors, Mad Dogs and Old Time Cowboys: Interview with the Editors and Kenneth Chubb," *Theatre Quarterly*, IV (Aug.-Oct. 1974), 12.
11 Ibid.
12 Ibid.
13 Ibid.
14 *The Tooth of Crime*, p. 39.
15 Sam Shepard, *Operation Sidewinder* (New York 1970), p. 7.
16 Soren Kierkegaard, *Either/or*, trans. David F. Swenson and L.M. Swenson (Princeton, 1944), p. 56.
17 Sam Shepard, *Cowboy Mouth*, in *Angel City, ...*, p. 203.
18 Sam Shepard, *Rolling Thunder Logbook* (New York, 1978), pp. 31–32.

19 *The Tooth of Crime*, p. 53.

20 *Ibid.*, pp. 52–53.

21 *Ibid.*, p. 53.

22 *Ibid.*, pp. 54–55.

23 *Ibid.*, p. 67.

24 *Rolling Thunder Logbook*, p. 53.

25 *Ibid.*, p. 52.

26 Sam Shepard, quoted in Chubb, "Fruitful Difficulties of Directing Shepard," 20.

27 *Suicide in Bb, p. 152.*

Mythic Levels in Shepard's *True West*

TUCKER ORBISON

Yes! I remember that! I remember thinking this is the West! This is really The West! Then we got to that town where Buffalo Bill lived. ... Oh what a town! ... And at night. At night it was magical. Like praying. I'd never heard such a silence as that. Nowhere on the earth. So vast and lonely. Just the brisk cold night blowing in through the hotel window. And outside, the blue peaks of the Big Horn mountains. The moon shining on their snowy caps. The prairie stretching out and out like a great ocean. I felt that God was in me then. The earth held me in its arms.

Fingers in *Geography of a Horse Dreamer*[1]

Sam Shepard is gradually becoming recognized as one of America's foremost playwrights.[2] An indication of his dramatic power is his continuing ability to create mythic meanings on several simultaneous levels. Analysis of the mythic levels in *True West,* for example, demonstrates that even though, as most critics realize, Shepard has moved from a relatively mysterious, mythic, surreal theatre to a more realistic and conventional one, he continues to draw on the resources of myth. Moreover, this investigation may put to rest the canard that, compared to the early, the later Shepard is flatter, less complex, less exciting. Ruby Cohn has rightly pointed to the recent tendency to oversimplify Shepard's plays by reducing them to themes.[3] Reviews of *True West,* for example, tend to focus on themes of sibling rivalry or role reversal to the exclusion of other possibilities. To be sure, Shepard said in a 1974 interview, "I'd like to try a whole different way of writing now, which is very stark and not so flashy and not full of a lot of mythic figures and everything, and try to scrape it down to the bone as much as possible."[4] We should not conclude, however, that mythic elements have dropped out of his recent plays. Though perhaps less obvious in *True West* than in his earlier work, the myths are there, sometimes helping to create conscious thematic material on what might be called the sociohistorical and artistic levels, always working on a third, a psychological level.

I

True West takes place in a small suburban home in the outskirts of Los Angeles. Lee, the elder of the two brothers whom we meet in the opening scene, characterizes the atmosphere of the neighborhood as "a sweet kinda' suburban silence. ... Like a paradise. ... Warm yellow lights. Mexican tile all around. Copper pots hangin' over the stove. Ya' know like they got in the magazines. Blonde people movin' in and outa' the rooms, talkin' to each other. (*pause*) Kinda' place you wish you sorta' grew up in, ya' know."[5] Austin, the younger brother, treats the theme ironically in scene 7 and thereby reveals his awareness that this Eden is deceptive:

... I'm lookin' forward to the smell of the night. The bushes. Orange blossoms. Dust in the driveways. Rain bird sprinklers. Lights in people's houses. You're right about the lights, Lee. Everybody else is livin' the life. Indoors. Safe. This is a Paradise down here. You know that? We're livin' in a Paradise. We've forgotten about that. (p. 39)

To "live the life" in this context is to conform to a commercialized, childlike existence in which one is warm and safe. Lee always understands what Austin, at the beginning, does not – that this is, says Lee, the "Kinda' place that sorta' kills ya' inside" (p. 12). The death that enters this Paradise is not physical but spiritual. Shepard once wrote an introduction to *The Unseen Hand,* a play that takes place in a town named Azusa. It explains his feelings about the Los Angeles suburb where he grew up:

AZUSA is a real place. A real town. About forty miles outside Los Angeles just off the San Bernardino Freeway. Its real slogan is "Everything from A to Z in the USA" and it's just like that. A collection of junk. Mostly people. It's the neighboring town of Duarte where I grew up, more less [*sic*]. These towns are obsessions of mine because of their accidentalness. ... They grew out of nothing and nowhere. Originally the valley was covered with citrus groves. ... Eventually Los Angeles had a population kick back. People who couldn't make it in the big city just drove away from it. They got so far and just quit the road. ... Lots of them lived in trailer camps. ... It was a temporary society that became permanent. Everybody still had the itch to get on to something better for themselves but found themselves stuck. It was a car culture for the young. For the old it was just a dead end. ... [T]hese Southern California towns have stuck with me not so much as a fond memory but as a jumping off place. They hold a kind of junk magic.[6]

The young need cars to escape the trap of a dead end in a temporary nonculture devoid of meaning or significance – magically nostalgic, perhaps, but junk all the same. Once upon a time there were orange blossoms and citrus groves, but, as Lee says, the whole aspect of the area has changed. "This country's real different." When Austin answers, "Well, it's been built up," Lee sneers, "Built up? Wiped out is more like it" (p. 11). In short, whereas the setting of *The Unseen Hand* is a collection of actual garbage and junk, in *True West* Shepard complicates his vision by presenting, at the outset, the suburban home as an apparent paradise; only in scene 9, when "*the stage is ravaged*" (p. 50), does it become a literal image of chaos. The setting of the play, then, is superficially edenic; in reality it is a void.

The condition of spiritual death finds its dramatic expression in Austin and Saul. The first scene sees Austin as the successful, serious writer, a member of the cultural elite. Yet like contemporary, suburban Los Angeles, he is hollow. When a child, he used to pretend to be Geronimo. He "enjoyed [his] imagination" (p. 12). Now, however, he writes scripts according to formula for Saul, a Hollywood producer. Lee immediately sees that his brother is just "[h]angin' around bein' a parasite offa' other fools" (p. 22). Austin's persona has so fully taken over his life that he is devoid of human feelings: he has not seen his brother Lee for five years; he has rejected his father; he lets his "business" take him away from his family (whom he never talks about); and even though he has worked on his script with Saul for months, he says he does not really know him. Saul, too, is concerned only with succeeding in a materialistic society, with manipulating people like bags of money. Discussing Austin's script, he tells Austin: "I am absolutely convinced we can get this thing off the ground. I mean we'll have to make a sale to television and that means getting a major star. Somebody bankable" (p. 15). He is troubled so little by people's feelings that he does not bother to consult with Austin before dropping the script that Austin has been working on for so long. He even has the crassness to offer Austin the job of writing the script that Lee has developed in his head: "Three hundred thousand, Austin. Just for a first draft. Now you've never been offered that kind of money before" (p. 34). Austin's sense of betrayal not only forbids him to write the script, but also begins his reordering of the values represented by his vocation, his style, his life.

The new, modern West, then, is a superficially civilized "collection of junk." This is the real West – the West of temporary living, full freeways, and empty hearts. It is the West limned by Joan Didion in her pictures of Los Angeles and the San Bernardino Valley in *Slouching Towards Bethlehem*, where because the present and future are everything, the past means nothing. But this new West is a false, demonic West: it has crushed imagination and feelings, and substituted material success. The talent and self-discipline Austin possesses are prostituted to Saul, who owns his soul. Saul is the ideal denizen of Shepard's new West, and Austin is his victim.

If the Los Angeles suburbs stand in a general way for the new West, the desert is their opposite. When, in scene 2, Lee and Austin are comparing the merits of life in the desert and in the suburbs, Lee argues that, whereas the heat around Los Angeles "was drivin' [him] crazy," the Mojave heat is tolerable because it is "clean" (p. 11). Similarly, the desert coyotes can be themselves (they can "howl"), but the natures of those around Los Angeles are subverted (they just "yap") (p. 10). For Shepard, as for Henry David Thoreau, there are a real West and an ideal West, and Shepard would agree with Thoreau's conception of the ideal West:

The *great west* and *north west* stretching on infinitely far and grand and wild, qualifying all our thoughts. That is the only America I know. I prize this western reserve chiefly for its intellectual value. That is the road to new life and freedom. ... That great northwest where several of our shrubs, fruitless here, retain and mature their fruits properly.[7]

Just as Thoreau's West was not so much a place as a country of the mind, the desert, for Shepard, is a condition of the soul, a life-giving place where God can take up residence, as Fingers says in *Geography of a Horse Dreamer*: "the prairie stretching out and out like a great ocean." A man like Lee can live there untrammeled by the perverted values of Los Angeles. The desert is Lee's mental home (it naturally is the setting for his scenario).

Lee does not represent in some simple way, however, the noble frontiersman whom James Fenimore Cooper imagined in Deerslayer. Rather, he more closely resembles the aged Natty Bumppo in *The Pioneers,* as described by Walter Allen:

Natty is a surly, quarrelsome, pathetic old man, almost an outcast, who lives in a squalid shack on the outskirts of town, a derelict who poaches deer out of season, is in constant trouble with the authorities, and is unable to cope with the encroachments of the civilisation that has destroyed his way of life. He is a displaced person. ...[8]

Lee is clearly not pathetic, but he is often sullen and ill-tempered, he is a derelict who steals TVs, and he is "displaced" in Los Angeles. In fact, Lee is a con man and a bully. He even carries in him some of that quality described by D.H. Lawrence as belonging to "the essential American soul ... hard, isolate, stoic, and a killer."[9] At the same time he continually insists on his freedom and prides himself on his independence, perhaps the quintessential value of the archetypal Western hero, whether Jesse James in *Mad Dog Blues* or Mickey Free in *Operation Sidewinder*. He ridicules the idea that he need fear Saul and his kind: "They can't touch me anyway. They can't put a finger on me. I'm gone. I can come in through the window and go out through the door. They never knew what hit 'em" (p. 31). Whereas Lee can escape the dead end of

Saul's permanently temporary society, Austin, like the people of Azusa and Duarte, is to be pitied: "You, yer stuck," says Lee. "Yer the one that's stuck" (p. 31). Lee cannot even abide the thought of being "invaded by Idaho," as he uncovers its picture on his dinner plate (p. 10). He refuses Austin's offers of help. He will not allow Austin to serve him breakfast. Life in the desert is elemental, crude, and rough (Lee has been making his living by dogfighting), but it is also clean, sane, and free. What remains of True West is to be found here. With all its shortcomings, it is the West that America has lost with its adoption of materialism and a parasitical lifestyle. Austin points out that the values of the Old West of American myth are extinct, at least in suburban Southern California, as he shouts at Saul: "There's no such thing as the West anymore! It's a dead issue! It's dried up, Saul, and so are you" (p. 35).[10]

True West, then, opposes two places, two characters, two ways of life. America's golden age has departed. In its place is an iron age of stolen toasters, TV sets, smashed typewriters, ripped-out telephones, and empty beer cans – the collection of junk that piles up during the course of the play – the detritus of a materialist society. Shepard's stage direction at the beginning of the last scene reads: "*All the debris from previous scene is now starkly visible in intense yellow light, the effect should be like a desert junkyard at high noon ...* " (p. 50). True West, like true North, is not a magnetic point on the compass; it is the geographical center on a mythic map – the West of Geronimo, one of the most courageous and fiercely independent of the last Apache chieftains, betrayed and then forced to surrender in the Southwestern desert to the forces of the United States Government in 1886. As trite and simple as Lee's scenario is, his plot does attempt to capture a similar kind of elemental conflict in his story of betrayal and revenge.

II

A second level of myth points to one of Shepard's concerns in *True West*: the mystery of the artist. In one of his essays, he wrote: "I feel a lot of reluctance in attempting to describe any part of a process [of dramatic creation] which, by its truest nature, holds an unending mystery."[11] For him this mystery lies at the heart of myth. Indeed, it defines myth: "By myth I mean a sense of mystery and not necessarily a traditional formula" (p. 217). How is a mythic drama created? Shepard explains the process as he experiences it:

... A search for "new forms" doesn't seem to be exactly where it's at.

There comes a point where the exterior gyrations are no longer the most interesting aspects of what you're practicing, and brand-new exploration starts to take root. For example: In the writing of a particular character where does the character take shape? In my experience the character is visualized, he appears out of nowhere in three dimensions and speaks. (p. 214)

The artistic process is intuitive – not imposed from without:

The picture is moving in the mind and being allowed to move more and more freely as you follow it. The following of it is the writing part. In other words, I'm taking notes in as much detail as possible on an event that's happening somewhere inside me. ... If I find myself pushing the character in a certain direction, it's almost always a sure sign that I've fallen back on technique and lost the real thread of the thing. (p. 215)

Shepard creates his mystery, then, in accordance with, as he says, "an open-ended structure where anything could happen as opposed to a carefully planned and regurgitated event" (p. 214). This creative process, whose end is a sense of mystery, can arise only from mythic awareness. To create a work of art by means of formula and technique is an impossibility, for the material must arise from the unconscious, from "nowhere."

These two opposed methods of creation are easily seen in Austin and Lee. Although Austin tells Lee that he used to enjoy his "imagination" (p. 12), the play contains no suggestion that he has become an artist, that he can create a mystery. The way he talks about the artistic process declares him a hack writer. He calls what he does "a project," "just a little research" (pp. 13, 6). He describes his script pedantically as "a period piece" (p. 13). When Austin complains, "I wish I didn't have to be doing business down here," Lee replies, "I though it was 'Art' you were doin'" (p. 14). No, Austin does not do Art. Saul's expectation that scripts will follow cut and dried formulas becomes clear when, after Lee asks, "What kinda' stuff do ya' go in for?" Saul answers, "Oh, the usual. You know. Good love interest. Lots of action. (*chuckles at* AUSTIN)" (p. 18). In later describing his script as "a simple love story" (p. 31), Austin stands self-condemned. He admits that his real business is "trying to work out a deal" with Saul (p. 14).

By contrast, Shepard shows Lee in the process of creating myth. When Austin objects that Lee's scenario is "not enough like real life," that men "don't end up chasing each other across the Panhandle," Lee rejects the criticism : "They do in this movie!" (p. 21). Lee holds to his belief that his story, which he calls a "Contemporary Western" (p. 18), will be justified if it arises not from some superficial verisimilitude but from a firmly held sense of the undercurrents in life, much as, presumably, the stories in the magazine *True West* arise. Austin also complains that Lee's characters are only "illusions of characters. ... fantasies of a long lost boyhood" (p. 40). For Shepard, of course, it is illusion, dream, and fantasy that form the nature of character, not some external verisimilitude. As he has written, his subject matter arises from past experience that has been stored away in an "inner library":

... How is this inner visualization different from ordinary daydreaming or ordinary nightdreaming? The difference seems to lie in the idea of a "watcher" being engaged while writing, whereas ordinarily this watcher is absent. ... It must be true that we're continuously taking in images of experience from the outside world through our senses, even when we're not aware of it. How else could whole scenes from our past which we thought we'd long forgotten suddenly spring up in living technicolor? These tastes from our life must then be stored away somewhere in some kind of inner library. ... From this point of view, I'm diving back into the actual experience of having been there and writing from it as though it's happening now.[12]

Even Saul, perhaps out of his long experience with Westerns, can still respond to the vigorousness in Lee's story: "It has the ring of truth, ... Something about the real West. ... Something about the land. Your brother is speaking from experience," he tells Austin (p. 35). The mythic True West can never be revealed in the way Austin experiences it: "I drive on the freeway every day. I swallow the smog. I watch the news in color. I shop in the Safeway. I'm the one who's in touch! Not [Lee]!" (p. 35). Because Austin's sense of reality is imprisoned by the quotidian, he cannot write a true Western. Rather, "the first authentic Western to come along in a decade" (p. 30), as Saul describes Lee's scenario, will arise from the artist's inner library, it will reflect a deep sense of the values inherent in the True West, and it will present an archetypal situation in which ancient conflicts are fraught with the terrors of nightdreaming: anxiety, violence, fear, the way lost, and no certain end:

So they take off after each other straight into an endless black prairie. The sun is just comin' down and they can feel the night on their backs. What they don't know is that each one of 'em is afraid, see. Each one separately thinks that he's the only one that's afraid. And they keep ridin' like that straight into the night. Not knowing. And the one who's chasin' doesn't know where the other one is taking him. And the one who's being chased doesn't know where he's going.
(*lights to black, typing stops in the dark, crickets fade*) (p. 27)

The myth of True West, then, is not simply embodied in a place, a type of character, and a country of the mind; it is as well a type of narrative, a type that Shepard's own play dramatizes, for on an elemental level *True West* concerns one of the most ancient of all conflicts – what Jung calls "the archetype of the hostile brothers."[13] The war between them will take Austin, and the audience, into unknown pathways shadowed by menace and apparently without end.

III

In a recent interview with Susan Sontag, the editors of *Performing Arts Journal* made the statement, "Consciousness is the principal subject of modern art," and Shepard, in the same issue, expressed his agreement: "The only thing which still remains [from the sixties] and still persists as the single most important idea is the idea of consciousness."[14] He specified more precisely what he meant when, in a letter to Patrick Fennell, he explained, "I'm interested in states of mind, in mystery, in psychotic behavior, in possession, in trance states, in magic."[15] Shepard would agree with D.H. Lawrence that "the inscrutable well-heads whence the living self bubbles up ... must ever remain a mystery."[16] Still, *True West* does shed some light on this mystery. One may speculate, for example, that just as Natty Bumppo in *The Pioneers* could be seen by Lawrence as Cooper's true inner self, Austin and Lee are alternate selves of Shepard.[17] A more useful approach for our purposes, perhaps, will be to notice that Shepard's characters "appear out of nowhere" in such a way as to bear a close psychic resemblance to each other. It can be argued, in fact, that Lee and Austin together form dual, opposed elements in a single self.

The first impressions of Lee and Austin, as made for example in New York's Cherry Lane production in 1982–1984,[18] create a sense of such dissimilarity that the two hardly seem brothers at all. Thus, Austin is neat and clean, Lee messy and dirty; Austin's hair is combed, Lee's is tousled; Austin wears a white shirt with collar, Lee an old T-shirt; Austin is cleanshaven, Lee has a day's growth of beard. Austin's speech is proper, clear, and restrained; Lee's is foul, drunkenly slurred, and from time to time furiously uncontrolled. All the more puzzling for an audience, then, when Shepard gradually reveals that they are in some ways identical. Indeed, at the beginning of scene 7 the two switch roles.

This *coup de théâtre* is, however, carefully prepared for. When in scene 4, Austin agrees to help Lee write a screenplay, Lee becomes sarcastic: "I'll just turn myself right inside out. I could be just like you then, huh? Sittin' around dreamin' stuff up. Gettin' paid to dream" (p. 25). Before the scene ends, both brothers explain how they used to daydream about what it would be like to be the other:

LEE ... I always wondered what'd be like to be you.

AUSTIN You did?

LEE Yeah, sure. I used to picture you walkin' around some campus with yer arms fulla' books. Blondes chasin' after ya'.

AUSTIN Blondes? That's funny.

LEE What's funny about it?

AUSTIN Because I always used to picture you somewhere. ... And I used to say to myself, "Lee's got the right idea. He's out there in the world and here I am. What am I doing?" (p. 26)

Two different impressions are made here. Shepard introduces the idea of internal similarity under the external differences and reveals the yearning of each to be like the other. Lee and Austin are psychically related, it appears, in the same way C.F. Keppler describes the relation between a self and a second self:

But what then *is* the second self? The answer is given us by what has just been said about the two main spurious second selves that are so often taken for it: the fact that what each of them lacks is exactly what the other possesses. The objective second self possesses external reality, clearly independent of the first self. ... The subjective second self does share a basic psychical identity with the first self. ... It is [the] quality of paradox that makes the second self so difficult a figure to talk about. ... He is always "there," a self in his own right, never translatable into a product of mental aberration; yet he is always "here" as well, his psyche intergrown by untraceable shared tendrils with that of his counterpart. ... [19]

In short, the second self is subjectively identified with the first and at the same time is objectively an opposite.

Is it Austin, or is it Lee, who is the second self? Keppler points out that "the second self always *suggests* some aspect of the first self that has been suppressed or unrealized," he always "intrude[s] into the life of the first," and he is "responsible for the dynamic tension that always exists between them. He is the self that has been left behind, or overlooked, or unrealized, or otherwise excluded from the first self's self-conception; he is the self that must be come to terms with."[20] Clearly, then, Lee is Austin's second self, Austin the first self or ego. Separately, they form the archetypal pattern of the hostile brothers, the elder violent and often unrestrained, the younger self-possessed and controlled. Together, they comprise opposite sides of one psychic entity.

Shepard structures his play in such a way that during the first six scenes the audience is centrally conscious of the duality of the two brothers. Between scenes 6 and 7, after Saul has told Austin that he has dropped Austin's script for Lee's scenario, the role reversal occurs. The opening of scene 7 sees Lee sitting at Austin's table typing a script, while Austin is sprawled drunkenly on the floor – spectacles and sweater gone, shirt out, bottle in hand. Lee has taken on Austin's role as screenwriter; Austin has become the shiftless ne'er-do-well. More precisely, Lee has taken on an external role (he is still the same old Lee), but in Austin's case the submerged "Lee" in him has risen to the surface. The audience is not surprised to hear Austin mumble, "He [Saul] things [*sic*] we're the same person. ... He does! ... Thinks we're one and the same" (pp. 36–37). Lee is Austin's shadow self.

One becomes vulnerable to the inroads of the collective unconscious when one finds it difficult to adapt to problems in the outside world. When a state of anxiety induces inner tensions that create a divided self, the ego must make fresh attempts to achieve an internal harmony, succeeding only after coming to terms with the negative side of the personality, which makes its appearance like an intruder in the night. In scene 1, Austin seems perfectly content. As the opening scenes unfold, however, the audience can sense his repressed anxiety: can he bring off his "deal" with Saul, a job he has been working on for several months? In his relationship with the studio, Austin has been on the edge for some time. Past failures are clearly implied when Saul tells Austin, referring to the latter's script, "You've really managed to capture something this time" (p. 15). Austin points out the cutthroat nature of the movie business when he later taunts Lee, who is by then trying to write his own script: "The pressure's on, boy. This is it. You gotta' come up with it now. You don't come up with a winner on your first time out they just cut your head off. They don't give you a second chance ya' know" (p. 40).[21] Austin's ability to hold his job, his self-respect, and even his whole style of life are on the line.

It is at this point in Austin's life that his shadow side makes his appearance. Gary Sinese's staging of the play's first scene at the Cherry Lane established the possibility of this reading. When the theatre lights went down, the stage was completely dark. The audience's attention was first drawn to the lighting of a candle. Austin was seen working alone, at night. Only as the lights came up did we see Lee leaning against the kitchen counter, appearing, it would seem, from nowhere. The effect was startling. Lee came out of the shadow, so to say, and into Austin's life.

From his first words, Lee acts precisely like a shadow figure. Jung characterizes the shadow as emotional, autonomous, and possessive.[22] In John Malkovich's impersonation, Lee interrupted Austin's typing, interfered with his train of thought, and after the first few minutes, became domineering and even explosive. He represented a continual threat to Austin's composure in such lines as, "Don't worry about me. I'm not the one to worry about" (p. 6). "... Somewhere," writes Jung, "we have a sinister and frightful brother, our own flesh-and-blood counterpart, who holds and maliciously hoards everything that we would so willingly hide under the table."[23] As the play develops, Lee forces Austin to face the problematic side of his own nature in such a way that Austin must question his vocation, his values, and even his identity. About such a problem Shepard has written: "I feel that language is a veil hiding demons and angels which the characters are always out of touch with. Their quest in the play is the same as ours in life – to find those forces, to meet them face to face and end the mystery."[24] This confrontation between the conscious ego (Austin) and the hidden psychic forces (Lee) forms the initial action of the play.

The battle between Lee and Austin begins in a subdued fashion. Lee first attacks Austin by questioning his "Art," by rejecting the offer of breakfast, by accusing him of "hustling" Saul, and even by physically attacking him. Lee points out to Austin the bitter truth of his parasitism, his condescension, and his cultural imprisonment. He finally destroys Austin's occupation. Lee is relentless; Austin knows what he is in for, because at the end of scene 1, when he asks Lee if he wants to go to bed, Lee replies, "I don't sleep" (p. 9). The messages from the unconscious are continuous. Will Austin listen?

Austin does listen. He takes the first step toward individuation by understanding that he has led a patterned, inauthentic existence. Toward the end of the play, he is able to realize that imitating the style and values of Saul Kimmer leads only down wrong paths and to eventual disorientation:

There's nothin' down here for me. There never was. When we were kids here it was different. There was a life here then. But now – I keep comin' down here thinkin' it's the fifties or somethin'. I keep finding myself getting off the freeway at familiar landmarks that turn out to be unfamiliar. On the way to appointments. Wandering down streets I thought I recognized that turn out to be replicas of streets I remember. Streets I misremember. Streets I can't tell if I lived on or saw in a postcard. Fields that don't even exist anymore. (p. 49)[25]

Because Austin has been able to grasp this truth, he can reject the Hollywood world and ask Lee, "What if I come with you out to the desert?" (p. 48). To live in the desert, with all that implies, requires, however, more than a new vision. It demands an integrated self.

In attempting to achieve this new self – the play's second dramatic action – Austin adopts only Lee's negative nature, not his fierce self-sufficiency. In scene 1 Lee is self-centered, materialistic, crass, childish, and thoughtless – the hidden Austin. After Saul accepts Lee's script idea and turns down Austin's script, Austin gets drunk, refuses to help Lee, even taunts Lee for his lack of writing ability. He childishly accepts Lee's dare that he cannot steal a toaster. As Stanley Crouch wrote in his review of the play, Austin becomes "progressively brutish, childish, and self-pitying."[26] If Austin's individuation is to become successful, he must not *become* his shadow; he must integrate his negative qualities into an adult, independent self. Lee questions his ability to do this: "You wouldn't last a day out there [in the desert] pal" (p. 48). Austin pathetically responds: "I could make it, Lee. I'm not that helpless. I can cook. ... I can make fires. I know how to get fresh water from condensation." But Lee retorts, "It's not somethin' you learn out of a Boy Scout handbook!" He sees that Austin has not the basic self-reliance and courage required: "Yer worse than a dog" (p. 49). Austin would be eaten alive by the desert's untamed coyotes.

To dramatize Austin's lack of "desert" qualities, Shepard provides a test: the entrance of Mom. Austin's every action when he sees his mother demonstrates his inability to command himself. Unlike Lee, he abjectly offers to clean up the "mess," he throws Lee's shirt to him so that he can look more presentable, and he allows Lee to take responsibility for the dead plants that were in his own charge. He cannot even acknowledge the truth about the toasters: they are the result "of a contest," he tells his mother, rather than theft (p. 54). Although he had agreed in scene 8 that Austin could accompany him to the desert if Austin continued to work with him on his scenario, Lee finally decides that Austin is not "cut out for the desert" (p. 55); Austin belongs in Mom's home, where he was in scene 1 – still a child. Austin just makes matters worse by complaining: "It's gone past postponing! I'm doing everything you said. I'm writing down exactly what you tell me" (p. 56). His dependency shows he is not yet ready for the desert.

Is it desperate courage or a childish tantrum (one of the play's many ambiguities) that then makes Austin lunge at Lee and begin to strangle him? At all events, he is driven to the very "act of violence" that he said in scene 4 he would never commit (p. 24). He cannot, however, kill Lee, for to kill Lee would be to kill part of himself. Yet he cannot let Lee go, either. He tries a foolish compromise: *he* will leave, Lee will stay. But as Joseph L. Henderson points out, "Ego and shadow, ... although separate, are inextricably linked together."[27] Austin cannot leave. Shepard ends the play when he began it – at night. As soon as Austin starts for the door, Lee (who never sleeps) springs up ready to do battle. The last tableau shows the brothers squaring off against each other, the light fades to moonlight, and the action moves surrealistically from the kitchen to the desert: "*the figures of the brothers now appear to be caught in a vast desert-like landscape*" (p. 60). Austin cannot achieve a total psychic integration, for, as Jung writes: "The serious problems in life ... are never fully solved. If ever they would appear to be so it is a sure sign that something has been lost. The meaning and purpose of a problem seem to lie not in its solution but in our working at it incessantly."[28] Shepard agrees. About *True West* he has said:

I wanted to write a play about double nature, one that wouldn't be symbolic or metaphorical or any of that stuff. I just wanted to give a taste of what it feels like to be two-sided. It's a real thing, double nature. I think we're split in a much more devastating way than psychology can ever reveal. It's not so cute. Not some little thing we can get over. It's something we've got to live with.[29]

So, like the characters in Lee's scenario, Austin and Lee continue their night journey on "an endless black prairie" (p. 27).

True West is one of Shepard's more realistic plays. As analysis demonstrates, however, Shepard's realism does not exclude mythic levels. Mythic structures form underlying patterns, one of which Shepard himself has shown a general interest in. "The idea of dying and being reborn," he said in the Chubb interview, "is really an interesting one, you know. It's always there at the back of my head" (p. 207). Austin's battle with his other self suggests another side of myth – its function as an agent of renewal. Shepard uses mythic elements in his plays because, as he has said, myth "short-circuits the intellect and hooks you up with feeling."[30] Even more important to Shepard than mythic themes is the transforming nature of theatre. Austin's confrontation with Lee creates in the audience anxieties and tensions which it cannot easily rid itself of, for Shepard has deliberately avoided a catharsis. The action of the play ends, but the audience, with Austin, must continue to confront its shadow self in an unending, mysterious conflict. Shepard's last stage direction reads, in part: *"lights go slowly to black as the after-image of the brothers pulses in the dark"* (p. 60) – the dark of the theatre and the dark of our minds.

NOTES

1 Sam Shepard, *Geography of a Horse Dreamer,* in *Four Two-Act Plays* (New York, 1980), pp. 142–144.

2 In his review of *Fool for Love,* Robert Brustein, for example, wrote that Shepard "may be ... America's leading playwright" (*New Republic,* 27 June 1983, p. 25).

3 Ruby Cohn, *New American Dramatists: 1960-1980* (New York, 1982), p. 185.

4 Kenneth Chubb and the Editors of *Theatre Quarterly,* "Metaphors, Mad Dogs and Old Time Cowboys: Interview with Sam Shepard," in *American Dreams: The Imagination of Sam Shepard,* ed. Bonnie Marranca (New York, 1981), p. 208 (hereafter referred to as the Chubb interview).

5 Sam Shepard, *True West,* in *Seven Plays,* intro. Richard Gilman (New York, 1981), p. 12. All quotations from *True West* are taken from this edition and will appear in parentheses in the text.

6 Sam Shepard, "AZUSA is a real place: Sam Shepard writes a special preface to 'The Unseen Hand,'" *Plays and Players,* 20 (May 1973), I (centerfold).

7 From a Thoreau letter to Thomas Cholmondeley, quoted in Edwin Fussell, *Frontier: American Literature and the American West* (Princeton, 1965), p. 189.

8 Walter Allen, *The Urgent West: The American Dream and Modern Man* (New York, 1969), p. 112.

9 D.H. Lawrence, *Studies in Classic American Literature* (New York, 1923), p. 92.

10 Shepard's view of the changing values of the West finds corroboration in Paul Hendrickson, "At Heart, a Cowboy: William Albert Allard's Tender Images of the West," Washington *Post,* 29 November 1982, p. C3: "No other American myth ... can touch the man who went westering a century ago. Westering was always the grandest American dream. But sometimes the dream got sad as Palm Sunday. ... The West vanished, all right, but it keeps coming back in new skins and masks. It haunts us 'with a mythology of disappearance,' says author Tom McGuane. ... "

11 Sam Shepard, "Language, Visualization and the Inner Library," in *American Dreams,* p. 214. Subsequent references will be given in parentheses in the text.

12 *Ibid.*, p. 215.
13 C.G. Jung, *Psychology and Religion: West and East,* trans. R.F.C. Hull, 2nd ed. (Princeton, 1969), p. 173, n. 19. Jung writes: "To take but one example: Yahweh had one good son and one who was a failure. Cain and Abel, Jacob and Esau, correspond to this prototype, and so, in all ages and in all parts of the world, does the motif of the hostile brothers ... " (p. 400).
14 "On Art and Consciousness," *Performing Arts Journal,* 2 (Fall 1977), 29; Special Section [Sam Shepard et al.], "American Experimental Theatre: Then and Now," *Performing Arts Journal,* 2 (Fall 1977), 14.
15 Patrick J. Fennell, "Sam Shepard: The Flesh and Blood of Theatre," Unpubl. diss., Univ. of California, Santa Barbara, 1977, p. 18.
16 D.H. Lawrence, *The Symbolic Meaning: The uncollected versions of "Studies in Classic American Literature,"* ed. Armin Arnold (London, 1962), p. 74. Shepard has, in fact, written: "A character for me is a composite of different mysteries. He's an unknown quantity" ("Language, Visualization and the Inner Library," p. 217).
17 William Kleb, "Worse Than Being Homeless: *True West* and the Divided Self," in *American Dreams,* p. 124, has developed this idea in some detail.
18 The Cherry Lane production was *True West*'s second New York run. As is widely known, the play's first New York run was unsuccessful, largely because Joseph Papp's interference caused Robert Woodruff, who had directed the successful première in San Francisco, to resign. As a result, Shepard himself disowned the production.
19 C.F. Keppler, *The Literature of the Second Self* (Tucson, Ariz., 1972), pp. 9–10.
20 *Ibid.*, pp. 9, 11.
21 Shepard is not alone is sensing the strain of life in and around Los Angeles. Compare Charles Marowitz: "The stresses of life in California – the struggle to maintain status ... , the desire to prove one's worth in the face of fierce competition, the need to ... complete deals and fulfil expectations while, at the same time, losing heart, coping with treachery and being forced to drop out – all of these stresses are unbearable" ("To know Los Angeles, turn to its small ads," *The Listener* [21 October 1982], p. 18).
22 C.G. Jung, *Aion: Researches into the Phenomenology of the Self,* trans. R.F.C. Hull, 2nd ed. (Princeton, 1968), p. 8.
23 C.G. Jung, "The Psychology of the Unconscious," in *Two Essays on Analytical Psychology,* trans. R.F.C. Hull, 2nd ed. (Princeton, 1966), p. 38.
24 Quoted by Kenneth Chubb, "Fruitful Difficulties of Directing Shepard," *Theatre Quarterly,* 4 (August–October 1974), 24.
25 Marowitz, p. 18, describes "the average Los Angelian" as "socially disorientated ... spiritually lost. ... "
26 Stanley Crouch, "American Perfection," *Village Voice,* 2 November 1982, p. 85.

27 Joseph L. Henderson, "Ancient Myths and Modern Man," in *Man and his Symbols*, eds. C.G. Jung, M.-L. von Franz, and John Freeman (New York, 1964), p. 118.

28 C.G. Jung, "The Stages of Life," in *The Structure and Dynamics of the Psyche*, trans. R.F.C. Hull, 2nd ed. (Princeton, 1969), p. 394.

29 Quoted by Robert Coe in "Saga of Sam Shepard," *New York Times Magazine*, 23 November 1980, p. 122.

30 Quoted by Ruby Cohn in "Sam Shepard: Today's Passionate Shepard and His Loves," *Essays on Contemporary American Drama*, edd. Hedwig Bock and Albert Wertheim (Munich, 1981), p. 161.

Sam Shepard's *Buried Child*: The Ironic Use of Folklore

THOMAS NASH

Although Sam Shepard's *Buried Child* won the 1979 Pulitzer Prize for drama, this eerie and provocative story continues to baffle critics and audiences alike – at least those who have not done their homework in folklore and anthropology. *Buried Child*, like the famous Shirley Jackson short story "The Lottery," borrows heavily from the images and motifs found in Sir James Frazer's *The Golden Bough*. Those who do not see the hand of the anthropologist in Shepard's play – and there are surprisingly many who write review columns – have called *Buried Child* "an American gothic comedy" or "a poor impression of a play by Pinter or Albee." Directors are also not immune from confusion, sometimes interpreting as comedy several scenes of the play which are clearly intended as ritual. In fact, *Buried Child* is a serious statement that pulls at the very bone and marrow, its plot a modern version of the central theme of Western mythology, the death and rebirth of the Corn King.

What bothers and even mortifies so many viewers is Shepard's style. Like Jackson, who angered thousands of readers when "The Lottery" first appeared in a 1948 edition of *The New Yorker*, Shepard begins his story in the manner of realism. His realistically drawn characters bicker, argue, and insult one another, establishing the recognizable beacons of a domestic conflict. However, in the course of plot development, the influence of folklore and mythology becomes more forceful, so that the realism of the early scenes fades like twilight; in the final scenes, Shepard's characters, like Jackson's, move in the dusky light of ritual. Both authors employ what Northrop Frye calls the *ironic mode,* a style that "begins in realism and dispassionate observation. But as it does so, it moves steadily towards myth, and dim outlines of sacrificial rituals and dying gods begin to reappear in it."[1] Both authors, Jackson and Shepard, conclude their works with the revelation of murders that are tied to the growth of corn. In "The Lottery," Old Man Warner obliquely justifies the approaching ritual sacrifice of a community member when he recites the ancient proverb "Lottery in June, corn be heavy soon." In *Buried Child,* the dramatist ties the regeneration of the long fallow cornfields to the resurrection of the young boy who was buried between the rows some forty years ago, having been murdered by Dodge, the family patriarch. Jackson's story ends with the festive stoning of Tessie Hutchinson as homeopathic insurance of fertile fields; Shepard's play concludes with the ritual return of the buried child, come to life to claim his inheritance and to preside benignly over the scene of his murderer's death.

The initial curtain of *Buried Child* reveals an old man watching television in a decrepit farmhouse in Middle America. Dodge, a man in his seventies, sits like Eliot's Gerontion, awaiting death as a release from the boredom of a hollow life. Occasionally he swigs at a bottle of whiskey hidden in the lumpy folds of his couch. As Halie, his wife, nags and pontificates from the top of the stairs, we discover that an incessant rain has been falling in the untilled fields. A significant rain, it washes the marrow from the bones of the buried child, fertilizing the long neglected cornfields, preparing the land for a miraculous rebirth.

Dodge has fathered three sons. Tilden, the eldest, once an all-American football player, is now a half-wit, reduced by the Fall of this House of Oedipus to the mentality of a child. As the play begins, he is plodding through the fields, picking the suddenly emergent corn. Bradley, the second son, has designs on his father's property; but he also has been reduced to a grotesque, having lost a leg in a chain-saw accident some years earlier. The youngest son, Ansel, is dead, killed in his motel room on the night of his honeymoon, after having married unwisely into a family with connections to the Mob. The youngest son, as we are constantly reminded by Halie, "was a hero," and he "would've stopped him!"[2] In folklore, it is a recognized rule of narrative that the third son is the heroic one.[3] Therefore, as the folkloric roots of the drama become more evident, it is clear that a kind of "heroic vacuum" paralyzes the family, a void that will soon be filled, however.

Like the House of Oedipus, the family of Dodge and Halie is cursed by the combined acts of *overrating* and *underrating* blood relations, to use Claude Lévi-Strauss's terms.[4] Dodge explains the origins of the curse to the one character who has the least right to know – Shelly, a stranger:

Halie had this kid. This baby boy. She had it. I let her have it on her own. All the other boys I had had the best doctors, best nurses, everything. This one I let her have by herself. This one hurt real bad. Almost killed her, but she had it anyway. It lived, see. It lived. It wanted to grow up in this family. It wanted to be just like us. It wanted to be a part of us. It wanted to pretend that I was its father. She wanted me to believe in it. Even when everyone around us knew. Everyone. All our boys knew. Tilden knew. ... Tilden was the one who knew. Better than any of us. He'd walk for miles with that kid in his arms. Halie let him take it. All night sometimes. He'd walk all night out there in the pasture with it. Talkin' to it. Singin' to it. Used to hear him singing to it. He'd make up stories. He'd tell that kid all kinds a' stories. Even when he knew it couldn't understand him. ... We couldn't let a thing like that continue. We couldn't allow that to grow up right in the middle of our lives. It made everything we'd accomplished look like it was nothin'. Everything was cancelled out by this one mistake. This one weakness. (p. 65)

In this initial scene of conflict, the family's dark secret reveals an *overrating* of blood relations: Tilden's incest and the subsequent birth of the unwanted child. The secret also reveals the *underrating* of blood ties: the infanticide that Dodge later confesses. As Lévi-Strauss says in "The Structural Study of Myth," this polarization can be resolved only by the introduction of a third element that subsumes the antithetical properties of the first two.[5] Vince, the grandson of Dodge and Halie, is the mediating element; he is also a character whose entry into the drama marks the beginning of the mythic theme.

The first of the three acts of *Buried Child* establishes the naturalistic setting that Vince will invade in the second act. In the early moments of the play, Dodge awaits death in a costume of khaki clothes, his body draped in colors that symbolically represent the withering of his body and soul. He and Halie recall their domestic troubles, their losses, their tragedies; Tilden then enters with arms full of corn and is accused of stealing from the neighbors' fields; Bradley, thumping in on his wooden leg, arrives to give his father a vicious haircut. Throughout, the gloom of impending death casts a long shadow; a destructive emptiness pervades the scene.

When Vince, the grandson, finally arrives, the drama assumes a different character, a remoteness and communality that accompany the ritual of the killing of the Corn Spirit – the Old Man of the European Harvest, as Frazer describes him. At first, Dodge and the other family members do not recognize Vince; he is an intruder into a home where no one has the will to throw him out. And yet, Tilden offers some clue to the boy's identity. He says, "I thought I recognized him. I thought I recognized something about him. ... I thought I saw a face inside his face" (p. 44). The face, of course, is his son's. Yet Vince remains unrecognized because he is the reincarnation of the buried child, now returned to claim his patrimony, a return signaled by the sudden and startling growth of corn in the fields. However, Vince is also the lost brother Ansel and, in fact, the spirit of all the children born to Dodge's ancestry. And Vince himself recognizes his multifarious identities. In Act III, after having tried to escape the madness of the farmhouse scene by getting drunk and driving west, he returns to explain a vision that visited him on his journey:

... last night. ... I could see myself in the windshield. My face. My eyes. I studied my face. Studied everything about it. As though I was looking at another man. As though I could see his whole race behind him. Like a mummy's face. I saw him dead and alive at the same time. In the same breath. In the windshield, I watched him breathe as though he was frozen in time. And every breath marked him. Marked him forever without him knowing. And then his face changed. His face became his father's face. Same bones, Same eyes. Same nose. Same breath. And his father's face changed to his Grandfather's face. And it went on like that. Changing. Clear on back to faces I'd never seen before but still recognized. Still recognized the bones underneath. The eyes. The breath. The mouth. I followed my family clear into Iowa. Every last one. Straight into the Corn Belt and further. Straight back as far as they'd take me. (pp. 70–71)

Gradually, as Act III unfolds, the play reveals its ritual quality and its roots in folk drama. For instance, when Vince returns from his drunken travels into the night, he enters the house – drunk and boisterous – by cutting his way through a locked screen door. Now he is recognized by all. Clearly Shepard has used his dramatic moment as a *symbolic rebirth,* calculated to correspond to the exact moment when Tilden, alone in the rain, must be pulling the decayed corpse of the buried child from the mud of the cornfields. Ironically, in the next moment Dodge, who has previously ignored the boy, announces that his house and property will be given to Vince.

The ritual atmosphere of this rebirth scene is reinforced in several ways. First, Dodge's testament and Vince's reawakening are presided over by the ineffectual figure of Father Dewis, slightly drunk, who has returned from town with Halie. Second, when Halie stumbles into the assembly, she carries a single rose, which she drops between the legs of Dodge, who is lying on the floor. The moment is given more meaning when we recall early events in the play. In Act I, while Dodge sleeps on the couch, he is visited by his sons Tilden and Bradley. Tilden, after shucking an entire basket of corn, spreads the husks gravely over the body of his father, suggesting Dodge's symbolic role as the Corn King in the winter of his life. Bradley, as though to emphasize the impotence of the dying patriarch, sneaks up on Dodge and gives him a vicious haircut, leaving bloody scars and lacerations across the old man's scalp. Halie's rose apparently signifies the figurative castration and imminent death of the old man, coming especially as it does during the moment of Vince's rebirth. Finally, having allowed Vince to fill the "heroic vacuum" in the family, Dodge announces his own impending death and asks for a burial suitable for the dying Corn King:

The house goes to my Grandson, Vincent. All the furnishings, accoutrements and paraphernalia therein. Everything tacked to the walls or otherwise resting under this roof. My tools – namely my band saw, my skill saw, my drill press, my chain saw, my lathe, my electric sander, all go to my eldest son, Tilden. That is, if he ever shows up again. My shed and gasoline powered equipment, namely my tractor, my dozer, my hand tiller plus all the attachments and riggings for the above mentioned machinery, namely my spring tooth harrow, my deep plows, my disk plows, my automatic fertilizing equipment, my reaper, my swather, my seeder, my John Deere Harvester, my post hole digger, my jackhammer, my lathe. ... Did I mention my lathe? I already mentioned my lathe – my Bennie Goodman records, my harnesses, my bits, my halters, my brace, my rough rasp, my forge, my welding equipment, my shoeing nails, my levels and bevels, my milking stool – no, not my milking stool – my hammers and chisels, my hinges, my cattle gates, my barbed wire, self-tapping augers, my horse hair ropes and all related materials are to be pushed into a gigantic heap and set ablaze in the very center of my fields. When the blaze is at its highest, preferably on a cold, windless night, my body is to be pitched into the middle of it and burned til nothing remains but ash. (pp. 69–70)

In *The Golden Bough,* Frazer explains the special reasons why agrarian dwellers use fire to consume the body of any figure who represents the spirit of vegetation: "light and heat are necessary for vegetable growth; and, on the principle of sympathetic magic, by subjecting the personal representative of vegetation to their influence, you secure a supply of these necessaries for trees and crops. In other words, by burning the spirit of vegetation in a fire which represents the sun, you make sure that, for the time being at least, vegetation shall have plenty of sun."[6] Dodge, after his symbolic burial under a blanket of cornhusks, and after his symbolic castration under the attack of Bradley's clippers, now seeks the proper end for a Corn King too enfeebled by age and impotent to continue his rule: the ceremonial pyre.

As if by an act of will, Dodge dies, his head dropping to his chest. Few of the family members notice, however, for the house's lights have dimmed, revealing the hulking figure of Tilden, who appears framed in the smoky light of a distant doorway. Very slowly he comes forward, bearing a small burden through the dark halls. Dramatically, as Tilden reaches the center of the stage, the harsher light from Halie's upstairs room illuminates him. Raised to eye level, Tilden's burden is the tattered corpse of a small child, its bones wrapped in muddy, rotten cloth. As Tilden climbs the lighted stairs, Halie's voice intrudes from above. Ironically, she addresses Dodge, now lying dead, in terms rich with ambiguity:

Good hard rain. Takes everything straight down deep to the roots. The rest takes care of itself. You can't force a thing to grow. You can't interfere with it. It's all hidden. It's all unseen. You just gotta wait til it pops up out of the ground. Tiny little shoot. Tiny little white shoot. All hairy and fragile. Strong though. Strong enough to break the earth even. It's a miracle, Dodge. I've never seen a crop like this in my whole life. Maybe it's the sun. Maybe that's it. Maybe it's the sun. (p. 72)

The play has come full circle. *Buried Child* achieves what Lévi-Strauss describes happening in the course of the relation of a myth: binary opposites are reconciled by a third, mediating element. In fact, the polar opposites of Shepard's play — the overrating and underrating of blood relations – are the same ones used by Lévi-Strauss to describe the structure of the Oedipus myth. The blood ties of family were overrated in Tilden's incest with Halie; they were underrated in the infanticide that became the family secret. In the end, Vince's rebirth reconciles these antitheses. The Corn Spirit has died, ending his tenure in the symbolic lick of the flames, but he lives again in the person of the new king.

As in "The Lottery," the debts to tradition and to folklore are not apparent until the final scene of epiphany, even though a symbolic level of meaning has been emerging since the first act. *Buried Child,* like the Jackson story of similar tone, moves from realism to ritual in a manner that can clearly be called "ironic," for here, behind the seemingly trivial squabbles and musings of a typical Midwestern family, are the shadows of sacrificial rites and the shades of dying gods.

NOTES

1 Northrop Frye, *Anatomy of Criticism* (New York, 1967), p. 42.
2 Quotations from Shepard are from *Buried Child and Other Plays* (New York, 1979), pp. 20 and 65. All subsequent references to Shepard's work will be cited parenthetically in the text.
3 Some explanation for the significance and importance of the third member of a group is provided by Axel Olrik, "Epic Laws of Folk Narrative," in *The Study of Folklore,* ed. Alan Dundes (Englewood Cliffs, N.J., 1965), pp. 129–141, especially the *law of the three* (p. 133) and the *importance of initial and final position* (pp. 136–137). Olrik's article originally appeared as "Epische Gesetze der Volksdichtung," *Zeitschrift für Deutsches Altertum,* 51 (1909), 1–12.
4 Lévi-Strauss, in "The Structural Study of Myth," says that myths may be characterized as having "bundles" of relations, usually involving groups of units that are polarized. For example, the Oedipus myth is, among other things, the story of overrating blood relations (Oedipus marries his mother) and underrating blood relations (Oedipus kills his father Laius). Lévi-Strauss points out also that such bundles of binary opposites must be mediated by an event or character that combines and alters the nature of the original pair. "The Structural Study of Myth," originally published in the *Journal of American Folklore,* 68 (1955), is reprinted in *Myth: A Symposium,* ed. Thomas A. Sebeok (Bloomington, Ind., 1958), pp. 81–106.

5 Lévi-Strauss states in *Myth: A Symposium,* p. 99: " ... two opposite terms
   with no intermediary always tend to be replaced by two equivalent
   terms which allows a third one as a mediator."
6 Sir James G. Frazer, *The Golden Bough,* abridged ed. (New York, 1951),
   I, 755.

Chronology

1911 Born 26 March in Columbia, Mississippi, to Cornelius Coffin and Edwina Dakin Williams.

1918 Family moved to St. Louis, Missouri.

1929 Entered University of Missouri at Columbia.

1931 At father's instigation, left university for the International Shoe Company.

1935 *Cairo! Shanghai! Bombay!* produced in Memphis, Tennessee.

1936 Enrolled in Washington University, St. Louis, Missouri. Two short plays, *The Magic Tower* and *Headlines,* produced.

1937 *Candles to the Sun* produced in St. Louis. Left Washington for the University of Iowa, Iowa City, Iowa. Sister, Rose Williams, underwent prefrontal lobotomy. *The Fugitive Kind* produced in St. Louis.

1938 Graduated from University of Iowa. Submitted short plays comprising *American Blues* (*Moony's Kid Don't Cry, The Dark Room,* and *Case of the Crushed Petunias*) to play contest sponsored by Group Theatre, New York City.

1939 Awarded $100 for short plays. *Not About Nightingales* produced in St. Louis. Short story, 'The Field of Blue Children,' published in *Story* magazine, his first work to appear under name Tennessee Williams. Awarded Rockefeller grant of $1,000 and moved to New York City. From this year through 1944 lived for short periods in many different parts of the United States, including New York City, Provincetown, New Orleans, Taos and Georgia.

1940 *The Long Goodbye* produced in New York City. *Battle of Angels* produced in Boston.

1942 *This Property is Condemned* produced in New York.

1943 Six-month contract with Metro-Goldwin-Mayer resulted in screenplay, *The Gentleman Caller*, the precursor of *The Glass Menagerie*. Co-author with Donald Windham, *You Touched Me*.

1944 *The Purification* produced in Pasadena, California. *The Glass Menagerie* opened in Chicago.

1945 *Stairs to the Roof* produced in Pasadena. *The Glass Menagerie* opened in New York City to critical acclaim, won New York Drama Critics' Circle Award, Donaldson, and Sidney Howard Awards. *You Touched Me* opened in New York.

1947 *A Streetcar Named Desire* opened in New York.

1948 *One Arm* published.

1950 *The Roman Spring of Mrs. Stone* published. Film of *Menagerie* released.

1951 *The Rose Tattoo* opened in New York, to win Tony Award. Film of *Streetcar* released.

1952 *Streetcar* film won New York Film Critics' Circle Award. *Summer and Smoke* opened in New York.

1953 *In the Winter of Cities* published. *Camino Real* opened in New York.

1954 *Hard Candy* published.

1955 *Cat on a Hot Tin Roof* opened in New York, won Pulitzer Prize, Drama Critics' Circle, Donaldson Awards. Film of *The Rose Tattoo* released.

1956 *Baby Doll* film composed in part of *Twenty Seven Wagons Full of Cotton*, and *The Long Stay Cut Short* released.

1957 *Orpheus Descending* opened in New York.

1958 *Garden District* opened in New York. Film of *Cat* released.

1959 *Sweet Bird of Youth* opened in New York. *I Rise in Flame, Cried the Phoenix* produced in New York. Film of *Suddenly Last Summer* released.

1960 *Period of Adjustment* opened in New York. *Fugitive Kind* (film of *Orpheus Descending*) released.

1961 Films of *Summer and Smoke* and *The Roman Spring of Mrs. Stone* released.

1962 *Night of the Iguana* won New York Critics' Circle Drama Award. *The Milk Train Doesn't Stop Here Anymore* premiered at the Spoleto Festival, Italy. Films of *Sweet Bird* and *Period of Adjustment* released.

1964 Film of *Iguana* released.

1965 *Iguana* produced in England, and won London Critics' Award for *Best Foreign Play*.

1966 *The Knightly Quest* published. *Slapstick Tragedy* opened in New York. Film of *This Property is Condemned* released.

1967 *The Two Character Play* premiered in London.

1968   27 March, *Kingdom of Earth,* opened in New York.
1969   Baptised into the Roman Catholic Church. *In the Bar of a Tokyo Hotel* opened in New York. Committed for three months to the Renard Psychiatric Division of Barnes Hospital in St. Louis. *Last of the Mobile Hot Shots* (film version of *Kingdom of Earth,* retitled *Blood Kin* in Europe) released. Awarded Doctor of Humanities degree of University of Missouri and Gold Medal for Drama by American Academy of Arts and Letters.
1971   *Confessional* produced in Bar Harbor, Maine. *Out Cry,* the rewritten *Two Character Play,* opened in Chicago.
1972   *Small Craft Warnings* opened in New York. Won National Theatre Conference Annual Award, and given Doctor of Humanities degree by University of Hartford.
1974   *Eight Mortal Ladies Possessed* published. Received Entertainment Hall of Fame Award, and Medal of Honor for Literature from National Arts Club.
1975   *Moise and the World of Reason* and *Memoirs* published.
1977   *Demolition Downtown* produced in London, *Vieux Carré* in New York, and *Red Devil* in London. Tennessee Williams Fine Arts Center dedicated at the Florida Keys Community College, Key West, Florida.
1978   *Crève Coeur* given its American premiere at the Spoleto Festival in North Carolina. *Tiger Tail,* stage version of film screenplay *Baby Doll,* produced in Atlanta.
1979   10 January, *Crève Coeur* given New York premiere.
1980   January: *Will Mr. Merriwether Return from Memphis?* presented in a limited run at the Tennessee Williams Performing Arts Center. *Clothes for a Summer Hotel* opened in Chicago. November: *Some Problems for the Moose Lodge* (workshop version of *A House Not Meant to Stand*) presented in Chicago.
1981   *Something Cloudy, Something Clear* produced in New York.
1982   *A House Not Meant to Stand* produced in Chicago. *It Happened the Day the Sun Rose* and *The Bag People* published.
1983   24 February – died in New York City.

ARTHUR MILLER

1915   Born 17 October in New York City to Isidore and Augusta Barrett Miller.
1932   Graduated from Abraham Lincoln High School.
1934   Entered University of Michigan.
1936   Won Hopwood Award for *Honors at Dawn.*

1937 Won Hopwood Award for *No Villain*.
1938 A.B. from University of Michigan. Won Theatre Guild Award for *They Too Arise*.
1940 Married Mary Grace Slattery.
1944 Published *Situation Normal*, a wartime journal; *The Man Who Had All the Luck* opened and immediately closed on Broadway.
1945 Wrote *Focus*, a novel.
1947 *All My Sons* won N.Y. Drama Critics' Circle Award.
1949 *Death of a Salesman* won Pulitzer Prize, Drama Critics' Circle Award.
1950 Adapted Ibsen's *An Enemy of the People* for Broadway.
1953 *The Crucible* won Antoinette Perry (Tony) Award.
1955 Two one-act plays: *A Memory of Two Mondays* and *A View from the Bridge* produced and won Drama Critics' Circle Award. Divorced Mary Jane Slattery.
1956 Received Honorary Doctorate of Letters, University of Michigan. Married Marilyn Monroe. Called before House Committee on Un-American Activities.
1957 Tried for Contempt of Congress and found guilty.
1958 Miller's conviction overturned by U.S. Court of Appeals.
1959 Received National Institute of Arts and Letters Gold Medal for Drama.
1960 Wrote screenplay *The Misfits*.
1961 Miller and Monroe divorced.
1962 Married Ingeborg Morath.
1964 Wrote *After the Fall* and *Incident at Vichy*.
1965 Became President of P.E.N.
1968 *The Price* written.
1969 Received Brandeis University Creative Arts Medal.
1972 *The Creation of the World and Other Business* written.
1977 *The Archbishop's Ceiling* written.
1980 *The American Clock*, adapted from Studs Terkel's *Hard Times*; T.V. screenplay, *Playing for Time*.
1982 *Elegy for a Lady* and *Some Kind of Love Story* written. Presented under omnibus title of *2 by A.M.*.
1984 Published *Salesman in Beijing*, a journal of the dramatic progress of a production of *Death of a Salesman* in China.

EDWARD ALBEE

1928 Born in Washington 12 March. Adopted when he was two weeks old by millionaire theatre-owner, Reed Albee and wife Frances.

46–47 Started Trinity College, Hartford, Connecticut, where he stayed for a year and a half. Wrote continuity material for music programmes on radio.

1949 Six months at Columbia University.

48–58 Worked at various odd jobs. Served in U.S. Army.

1958 *The Zoo Story* produced in Berlin.

1959 Won Berlin Festival Award for *The Zoo Story*. Wrote *The American Dream, The Death of Bessie Smith,* and *The Sandbox.*

1960 Won Vernon Rice Memorial Award and an Obie Award for *The Zoo Story; The Death of Bessie Smith* and *The American Dream* chosen as best plays for the 1960–61 season by Foreign Press Association.

1961 Wrote *Who's Afraid of Virginia Woolf?* Won Berlin Festival Award for *The Death of Bessie Smith* and Lola D'Annunzio Award for *The American Dream.*

1963 Won New York Drama Critics' Circle Award, Foreign Press Association Award, American National Theatre and Academy (ANTA) Award, two Tony awards and one Outer Circle Award for *Who's Afraid of Virginia Woolf? The Ballad of the Sad Cafe* produced.

1964 Wrote *Tiny Alice.*

65–66 Wrote *A Delicate Balance.* Elected to the National Institute of Arts and Letters. *Malcolm* produced.

1967 Awarded Pulitzer Prize for *A Delicate Balance.* Received D. Litt., Emerson College, Boston, Mass. *Everything in the Garden* produced.

1968 *Box and Quotations from Mao Tse-Tung* produced.

1971 *All Over* produced.

1974 Received D. Litt. from Trinity College, Hartford, Connecticut.

1975 *Seascape* produced. Received Pulitzer Prize.

1977 Two Chamber plays, *Listening* and *Counting the Ways,* written and produced.

1980 *Lady from Dubuque* produced. Awarded Gold Medal for Drama, The Academy and Institute of Arts and Letters.

1984 *Lolita*: a play, adapted from a novel by Vladimir Nabokov.

SAM SHEPARD

1943 Born 5 November at Fort Sheridan, Illinois, to Samuel Shepard Rogers and Jane Schook Rogers.

43–55 Family moved from army base to army base, including a stay at Guam.

1955 Family settled in California, eventually residing in Duarte.

1962 Shepard joined Bishop's Company Repertory Players and toured the United States.

1963 Shepard arrived in New York and moved into the East Village.

1964 First plays produced: *Cowboys* and *The Rock Garden*.

1965 *Up to Thursday, Dog and Rocking Chair, Chicago, Icarus's Mother, 4-H Club* produced.

1966 *Fourteen Hundred Thousand, Red Cross* produced.

1967 *La Turista* produced. *Melodrama Play* awarded Obie for distinguished play. *Cowboys #2* produced. *Forensic and the Navigators* awarded Obie for distinguished play. Received Rockefeller Foundation grant.

1968 Co-author, screenplay for *Me and My Brother*. Received Guggenheim Foundation grant.

1969 *The Holy Ghostly* and *The Unseen Hand* produced. Married O-Lan Johnson.

1970 *Operation Sidewinder* and *Shaved Splits* produced. Co-author, with Michelangelo Antonioni and others. *Zabriskie Point,* directed by Michelangelo Antonioni. Appeared in the film *Brand X*. Son Jesse born.

1971 Wrote *The Mad Dog Blues*. *Cowboy Mouth*, co-written with Patti Smith (acted in the cast). *Back Bog Beast Bait* produced. Screenplay for *Ringeleevio*. Shepard, wife O'Lan, and son Jesse moved to England.

1972 *The Tooth of Crime* awarded Obie for distinguished play. *Blue Bitch* (BBC) produced. *Hawk Moon* published (collection of stories, poems, and monologues).

1973 *Nightwalk* contributor, along with Jean-Claude Itallie and Megan Terry.

1974 Wrote and directed *The Geography of a Horse Dreamer*. *Little Ocean* produced. Wrote and directed *Action* which received Obie award. Shepard and family returned to the United States and settled in California.

1975 *Killer's Head* produced. Travelled with Bob Dylan's Rolling Thunder Revue.

1976 *Angel City* written and directed. Wrote *Suicide in B flat* and *The Sad Lament of Pecos Bill on the Eve of Killing His Wife*. Received Brandeis University Creative Arts Medal.

1977 Wrote *Inacoma. Curse of the Starving Class* awarded Obie for best new play and *Rolling Thunder Logbook* published (account of his travels with the Rolling Thunder Revue).

1978 Wrote *Seduced. Buried Child* awarded Obie for distinguished play. *Tongues* co-authored with Joseph Chaikin. Acted in film *Days of Heaven*.

1979 *Savage/Love* co-authored with Joseph Chaikin. Awarded Pulitzer Prize for *Buried Child*.

1980 Wrote *True West*. Received Obie Award for "sustained achievement" of his career as playwright. Acted in film *Resurrection*.

1981 Acted in film *Raggedy Man*.

1982 *Motel Chronicles* published (collection of autobiographical prose pieces and poems). Acted in film *Frances*.

1983 Wrote and directed *Fool for Love* which won four Obie Awards, including best play and best director. Acted in film *The Right Stuff*, nominated for Academy Award for best actor in a supporting role.

1984 Wrote screenplay for *Paris, Texas*.

1985 Acted in film *Country*, directed by Jessica Lange. Wrote screenplay and acted main role in film version of *Fool for Love*.

1986 *A Lie of the Mind* produced.

Bibliographical Note

The articles reprinted in this book were originally published in the following issues of the journal *Modern Drama*.

Bachman, Charles R., "Defusion of Menace in the Plays of Sam Shepard," *Modern Drama* 19 (1976), 405–15

Bennett, Robert B., "Tragic Vision in *The Zoo Story*," *Modern Drama* 20 (1977), 55–65

Bigsby, C.W.E., "The Fall and After: Arthur Miller's Confession," *Modern Drama* 10 (1967–8), 137–43

Bigsby, C.W.E., "Curiouser and Curiouser: A Study of Edward Albee's *Tiny Alice*," *Modern Drama* 10 (1967–8), 258–66

Corrigan, Mary Ann, "Realism and Theatricalism in *A Streetcar Named Desire*," *Modern Drama* 19)1976), 385–96

Glasch, Joy, "Games People Play in *Who's Afraid of Virginia Woolf?*," *Modern Drama* 10 (1967–8), 280–8

Gabbard, Lucina P., "Albee's *Seascape*: An Adult Fairy Tale," *Modern Drama* 21 (1978), 307–16

Gross, Barry, "*All My Sons* and the Larger Context," *Modern Drama* 18 (1975), 15–27

Lowenthal, Lawrence D., "Arthur Miller's *Incident at Vichy*: A Sartrean Interpretation," *Modern Drama* 18 (1975), 29–41

Martin, Robert A., "Arthur Miller's *The Crucible*: Background and Sources," *Modern Drama* 20 (1977), 279–92

Moses, Robbie Odom, "Death as a Mirror of Life: Edward Albee's *All Over*," *Modern Drama* 19 (1976), 67–77

Nash, Thomas, "Sam Shepard's *Buried Child*: The Ironic Use of Folklore," *Modern Drama* 26 (1983), 486–91

Orbison, Tucker, "Mythic Levels in Shepard's *True West*," *Modern Drama* 27 (1984), 506–19

Parker, Brian, "The Composition of *The Glass Menagerie*: An Argument for Complexity," *Modern Drama* 25 (1982), 409–22

Powe, Bruce W., "*The Tooth of Crime*: Sam Shepard's Way with Music," *Modern Drama* 24 (1981), 13–25

Starnes, Leland, "The Grotesque Children of *The Rose Tattoo*," *Modern Drama* 12 (1968–9), 357–69

Traubitz, Nancy B., "Myth as a Basis of Dramatic Structure in *Orpheus Descending*," *Modern Drama* 19 (1976), 57–66